Dialogue in Focus Groups

Studies in Language and Communication
Series Editors: Srikant Sarangi & Christopher N Candlin

Language and Communication Studies is now a well-established field of interdisciplinary inquiry. The main aim of this innovative series is to consolidate and extend its major themes and issues in accessible ways. The challenge for the series is to reflect new areas of theoretical, ethical and methodological significance while attempting to maintain the practical relevance of the field.

Advisory Board:
Malcolm Coulthard (University of Birmingham)
Yrjö Engeström (University of Helsinki)
Janet Holmes (Victoria University of Wellington)
Per Linell (Linköping University)
Celia Roberts (King's College, London)
John Swales (University of Michigan)
Theo van Leeuwen (Cardiff University)

Published in the series:

Writing the Economy: Activity, genre and technology in the world of banking
Graham Smart

Dialogue in Focus Groups

Exploring Socially Shared Knowledge

Ivana Marková, Per Linell, Michèle Grossen and
Anne Salazar Orvig

LONDON   OAKVILLE

Published by
UK: Equinox Publishing Ltd., Unit 6, The Village, 101 Amies St.,
London SW11 2JW
USA: DBBC, 28 Main Street, Oakville, CT 06779
www.equinoxpub.com

First published 2007
Reprinted 2007

British Library Cataloguing-in-Publication Data
A catalogue record for this book is available from the British Library.

ISBN-13   978 1 84553 049 5   (hardback)
           978 1 84553 050 1   (paperback)

Library of Congress Cataloging-in-Publication Data

Dialogue in focus groups : exploring socially shared knowledge / Ivana
Marková ... [et al.].
    p. cm. -- (Studies in language and communication)
Includes bibliographical references and index.
ISBN-13: 978-1-84553-049-5 (hb)
ISBN-13: 978-1-84553-050-1 (pb)
1. Sociolinguistics. 2. Dialogue analysis. 3. Communication in small
groups. 4. Social interaction. I. Marková, Ivana.
P40.5.D53D53 2007
306.44--dc22

                        2007002416

Typeset by Catchline, Milton Keynes (www.catchline.com)
Printed and bound in Great Britain and the USA

Contents

Preface   1

1   Dialogism: interaction, social knowledge and dialogue   7

1.1   Introduction   7
1.2   What kind of dialogism?   8
1.3   Interaction   9
1.4   Socially shared knowledge   14
1.5   Dialogue   24

2   Focus groups through the lens of dialogism   31

2.1   Introduction   31
2.2   What are focus groups?   32
2.3   Focus groups: where is the group?   35
2.4   A step back to research into small group dynamics   38
2.5   Focus groups and dialogism   45
2.6   The use of analytical tools in the study of focus group: four main assumptions   48

3   Dialogical analyses of focus groups: data and analytical approaches   51

3.1   Introduction   51
3.2   Presentation of the focus-group data   52
3.3   Dialogical analytical assumptions at work: a first overview   55
3.4   Conclusion   66

4   Focus groups as communicative activity types   69

4.1   Introduction: communicative activity types   69
4.2   Framings and activity roles in communicative activity types   71
4.3   Focus groups as communicative activity types   74
4.4   Communicative activity type analysis of two kinds of focus group   79
4.5   Hybridities of framing   88
4.6   Focus groups as informal conversations   90
4.7   Summary and discussion   101

5   Who is speaking in focus groups? The dialogical
     display of heterogeneity   103
5.1 Introduction   103
5.2 Positioning in dialogical dynamics   105
5.3 The heterogeneity of the speaker   108
5.4 From where is one speaking?   110
5.5 The play of identification through wording: coding
     and slippages   115
5.6 Relations between discourses   119
5.7 Other voices   122
5.8 Self-dialogism   126
5.9 Conclusion   128

6   Dialogue and the circulation of ideas   131
6.1 Introduction   131
6.2 The dialogue of ideas   132
6.3 Topic analysis: from the flow of discourse to topics
     and themes   135
6.4 Trying out arguments and understandings: analogies
     and distinctions   139
6.5 Analogy-distinction cycles and topical trajectories   146
6.6 Arguments: stories in the service of arguing a point   151
6.7 Metaphors, metonymies, prototypical examples and
     other discursive figures   154
6.8 Quotes and hypothetical quotes   157
6.9 From themes to global patterns and underlying
     assumptions   159
6.10 Conclusion   164

7   Themata in dialogue: taking social knowledge
     as shared   167
7.1 Introduction   167
7.2 From relational categories to concepts with 'more
     complex content'   168
7.3 Themata underlying social representations of AIDS   176
7.4 From trust/distrust (proto-thema, thema) to medical
     confidentiality (topic)   178
7.5 Conclusion   192

8   Focus groups as a dialogical method   195

8.1   Introduction   195
8.2   What is a good method?   196
8.3   The method by proof and the method by invention   197
8.4   Towards a dialogical analysis of content   202
8.5   Conclusion   206

References   208

**Appendix 1 Basic bibliography on tool kits and
          methodological guidelines**   222

Appendix 2 Focus group data corpuses   224

**Appendix 3 The 'moral dilemma' focus groups:
          excerpts in original language**   227

Index   241

This volume is the result of a research project conducted under the International Programme for Advanced Studies (www.piea-ipas.msh-paris.fr), run by the Maison des Sciences de l'Homme Paris, in collaboration with the Columbia University Institute for Scholars at Reid Hall, Paris (www.columbia.edu/cu/reidhall) and by the European Laboratory of Social Psychology (LEPS) of the Maison des Sciences de l'Homme (www//leps.msh-paris.fr).

Preface

Focus group has become one of the widely used methods of exploration in the human and social sciences and in marketing. For some, a focus group promises an easy access to public opinions, whether they concern opinions about the National Health Service, or consumers' preferences for certain kinds of product. For others, focus groups can address, better than other research methods, specific theoretical and methodological issues about communication and social knowledge. Whatever the expected promise of focus-group research, it has led to the publication, during the last two decades, of a number of methodological kits, manuals and guide of how to use focus groups. These publications enable researchers to devise and organise focus groups, collect and transcribe data, as well as to make them aware of the ethical problems involved.

This book is different. It is an introduction to understanding focus groups as an analytical means for exploring socially shared knowledge, for example social representations, beliefs, lay explanations etc. of AIDS, medical confidentiality and biotechnology, and other specific social phenomena. In this book we are adopting a dialogical perspective. The adjective 'dialogical' does not refer here only to the noun 'dialogue' as a kind of interaction but above all, to a theoretical approach that is called dialogism. This theoretical approach emphasises that humans live in the world of others and that their existence, thought and language are thoroughly interdependent with the existence, thought and language of others. Our point of departure therefore is not the individual but the self-others interdependence. Theoretically, these ideas are related, in various ways, to dialogism of Mikhail Bakhtin and they also have some affinities to certain kinds of contemporary discourse analyses. In view of the dialogical perspective that we adopt, the main emphasis of this book is to examine how to analyse interactions, forms of socially shared knowledge and their relations as they are expressed in focus groups. The book considers different kinds of dynamic interdependencies among participants who hold the diverse and heterogeneous positions. It explores contents of ideas and their circulation; it is concerned with language in real social interactions and with sense-making, which are embedded in history and culture. It poses questions about the ways people draw upon and transform socially shared knowledge, as well as assume that they share certain kinds of knowledge when they talk and think together in dialogue. It also focuses on the ways people generate heterogeneous meanings in the group dynamics. Meanings and content of the participants' communicative interactions derive their significance both from the situations in which these interactions take place and from relatively stabilised forms of socially shared knowledge and interactions. Through analyses of these phenomena, focus groups can provide researchers with insights into the formation and change of social representations, beliefs, knowledge and ideologies that circulate in societies. Language and interactions are not transparent and they can reveal as well as hide the participants' thoughts, beliefs, emotions, and otherwise. It is a challenge as well as an opportunity that focus groups present in researchers' attempt to deepen understanding of these phenomena.

This book is co-authored, not edited, by four researchers. We come from different academic backgrounds (psychology, linguistics, communication studies, philosophy), different language traditions (French, Swedish, Czech) and English is for us the second or the third language. Our commitment to a dialogical approach is partly shaped by these circumstances as well as by our professional and personal backgrounds. We consider a dialogical approach particularly important in studying focus groups; focus groups are situated communication activities in which we can examine language, thinking and knowledge in action and so they provide manifold research opportunities for taking a dynamic research perspective. Despite our commitment to a dialogical approach, as the four authors, we differ in our theoretical perspectives and terminological preferences, which we have tried to minimise. Although we have discussed, read and re-read each others' draft chapters, each of us takes main responsibility for individual chapters. Marková is responsible for Chapters 1, 7 and 8. Grossen is responsible for Chapters 2 and 3. Linell is responsible for Chapters 4 and 6. Salazar Orvig has written Chapter 5.

Chapters 1 and 2 set the scene by defining a theoretical framework in terms of dialogism and to that extent by stating some basic presuppositions on which the empirical chapters (4–7) are built. Chapter 2 discusses specifically what it means to treat a focus group as a group and it draws attention to implications of group dynamics for dialogical analysis. With these theoretical grounds, Chapter 3 portrays a range of interactional and discursive phenomena that our dialogical analysis attempts to capture in focus groups. Presenting them in their wholeness as pointers that are being developed in detail later in the book, Chapter 3 reminds that while researchers must keep in mind complex dialogical relations, they cannot study them all simultaneously in their entirety. This chapter shows that carrying out successfully research with focus groups requires more than collecting and analysing data. Equally important are questions that the researcher should ask even before embarking on methodological issues. What analytical and theoretical questions should the researcher consider? For example, what kinds of dynamic interdependencies co-exist among the participants and their ideas? What are the participants' motives or incentives to discuss issues in question? What possible 'dialogues' may the researcher encounter? What is it that underlies socially shared knowledge: is it language as the individual's achievement of a system of signs or is it dialogue as a social achievement; or is it both language and dialogue?

Chapters 4–7 each pose specific kinds of questions and issues although we cannot say that these exhaust everything that a dialogical analysis might examine. First, we treat dialogue as an interaction between and within speakers in the situated encounter. Rather than being conceived as a series of juxtaposed individual contributions by autonomous speakers, we shall view interaction as an intricate web of sense-making and sense-creating in which, in principle, each contribution is interdependent with previous and possible next contributions. Secondly, we consider dialogue as an interaction between thoughts, ideas and arguments in the discursive or textual web that is generated by participants. In other words, we are interested in how ideas are being formed and how they develop; in thematisation or silencing of topics; and in the negotiation of conflicts and opposing perspectives. This can be studied irrespective of who exactly, in the focus groups, produces the particular constituents of the joint dialogical contribution. This point also concerns the external and internal framing of the situation. For example, this can refer to how the task of the focus group is being interpreted, taken up and possibly reformulated by the participants. Thirdly, we consider dialogue in terms of implicitly shared themata embedded in language and thinking and of being brought to public awareness. Thematised by individuals, groups and institutions etc., they contribute to the transformation of social representations in question.

Dialogue as an interaction of speaking and sense-making subjects in a situated encounter cannot be properly treated without considering cultural assumptions and contents of messages. However, since one cannot treat all phenomena simultaneously, some chapters place more emphasis on one form of dialogical interaction rather than on the other. Thus the empirical part of the book focuses first on the interaction between and within speakers, then on the interaction of thoughts and ideas (e.g. topic, theme, arguments, analogies, metaphors, global patterns) and then on culturally embedded themata. But we must stress once again that these different perspectives are strongly interdependent. The main goal of the book is to demonstrate that focus groups can provide researchers with insights into the formation and change of social representations, beliefs, knowledge and ideologies that circulate in societies (Chapter 8).

The possibility of writing this book was due to two main sources of support. First, the ideas that we present in this book have been developing over some years in the study group on 'Language and Social Representations' that was part of the programme of the European Laboratory of Social Psychology (LEPS) in the Maison des Sciences de l'Homme in Paris, directed by Serge Moscovici. Therefore we owe a great deal to Serge Moscovici as well as to our colleagues who took part in this group, in particular to Rob Farr, Christian Hudelot, Sandra Jovchelovitch, Nikos Kalampalikis, Jenny Kitzinger, Li Lui, Birgitta Orfali and Victoria Wibeck. The work of this study group was published in May/June 2004 as a special issue of the Bulletin de Psychologie in French, entitled *Les groupes centrés*.

We wish to express our thanks to the Administrator of the Maison des Sciences de l'Homme, Professor Maurice Aymard who, over the years provided most generous help to support our work. Ivana Marková thanks for generous support the Carnegie Trust for the Universities in Scotland; Michèle Grossen wishes to thank the University of Lausanne which provided her support during this project; Anne Salazar Orvig is grateful for support of the Laboratoire d'Etudes sur l'Acquisition et la Pathologie du Langage chez l'Enfant (Paris V – CNRS); and Per Linell thanks the Bank of Sweden Tercentenary Foundation (Grant no. RJ 1005–5123) and the Swedish Research Council (421–2004–1087).

The second significant source of support is due to our participation (together with Li Liu of Beijing Normal University in China) in the International Programme of Advanced Studies (IPAS) of the Maison des Sciences de l'Homme in co-operation with the Columbia University, of which we were fellows. The possibility of us working together during September – December 2003 on the project broadly entitled 'Representations and discourses of trust and democracy: a social psychological approach', gave us a unique opportunity to develop our ideas on discourses and focus groups and to discuss the draft chapters of this book. We are particularly grateful to Jean-Luc Racine, the scientific organiser of the IPAS, to Mme

Danielle Haase-Dubosc, the Director of the Institute of Scholars at Reid Hall, Columbia University in Paris, Dr. Mihaela Bacou, research co-ordinator and Dr. Charles Walton, scientific co-ordinator. They have made our work at Reid Hall very pleasant and we felt welcome. Equally, we are grateful to Jean-Luc Lory, the Director of the Maison Suger and the staff of the Maison Suger for providing not only a place to stay, but also a congenial environment to organise our meetings and conferences.

1 Dialogism: interaction, social knowledge and dialogue

1.1 Introduction

If the title of this book announces that it is about a dialogue in focus groups, you may wonder: what is the news? What else would focus groups do if not talk – or be in dialogue? In fact, it seems that everybody is in dialogue. Governments view it as a diplomatic tool calming conflicts; dialogues proffer to solve marital discord; political and economic problems require dialogues; dialogues form the basis of psychotherapies; different cultures and religions are in dialogue; and so on.

Dialogue has also become the central concept of certain theoretical perspectives in human and social sciences, and these are sometimes referred to as dialogism. Their point of departure is not the individual and his/her mind or behaviour but the interdependence between the self and others. And so the decline of emphasis, at least in some circles, on individual consciousness and individual rationality, and the shift towards interest in dialogue, talk and language in use, have given rise to several forms of dialogism, and 'dialogistic' and 'dialogical' turns. Although all of them emphasise dialogue and communication, they originate from different theoretical traditions. For example, some of them stem from the ancient philosophy of Platonic dialogues, others from more recent forms of phenomenology; some see themselves as followers of Martin Buber's (1923/1962) 'I-Thou', others refer to George Herbert Mead's (1934) 'conversation of gestures'; some are inspired by Habermas's (1991) communicative action, and others start from the tradition of Mikhail Bakhtin.

Adopting a particular tradition implies accepting these or those presuppositions as to what dialogue is, how it is constructed and maintained. In other words, to be in dialogue can indicate different things; it does not necessarily mean adopting dialogism as a theoretical approach.

1.2   What kind of dialogism?

The kind of dialogism that we are developing in this book relies partly on ideas inherent in Mikhail Bakhtin's work and in his circle, partly on specific social psychological insights and to some extent on certain contemporary linguistic trends in dialogical and discourse analyses.

Our point of departure is the perspective that humans live in the world of others' words (Bakhtin, 1979/1986, p. 167). The limits of the self are not within the I, but within the relationship with the other, 'I and thou'. Every individual makes his/her world in terms of others by dialogically constructing and re-constructing the social world as a set of multifaceted and multivoiced realities situated in culture. Systems of symbols, texts, artistic products and historical interpretations, all have dialogical properties. They are expressions of socially shared dialogical cognitions and communicative actions. These are not engaged in a peaceful contemplation but are in tension, they clash, judge and evaluate one another. Bakhtin (1981a, p. 314) foregrounds dialogue as a strife of divergent perspectives: 'one point of view is opposed to another, one evaluation opposed to another … this dialogic tension … permits authorial intentions to be realised in a heterogeneity of languages and of ideas'. Understanding, precisely because it is active, is always evaluative.

It is dialogism so conceived that defines the trajectory of this book and gives meanings to the four main concepts on which this strategy is built: interaction, socially shared knowledge, dialogue and focus group. But why do we need to emphasise that we give meanings to these four concepts when, in fact, they are commonly used in current social sciences? We find that necessary because these concepts are already loaded with contents given to them by specific approaches within which they are used. These contents, however, are not always compatible with the dialogical approach that we are developing in this book. It is not that we wish to get involved in theoretical controversies with other approaches. Instead, in adopting dialogism as our analytic strategy, these concepts acquire meanings of dialogism. We are partly building on some established traditions within which these concepts are used in the manner that is convergent with our approach. However, it is not the convergence of their individual meanings that makes our perspective dialogical, but the meanings that these concepts acquire with respect to one another in the totality of the dialogical perspective, of which they become part. This is why in Chapters 1 and 2 we discuss these four concepts in some detail in order to clarify the perspective of dialogism. Chapter 1 is concerned with interaction, socially shared knowledge and dialogue and Chapter 2 discusses the concept of focus group.

1.3   Interaction

1.3.1   Internal and external interaction

The term 'interaction' is so commonly used in social sciences that we must specify its meaning within the dialogical perspective. Our point of departure will be, what we shall call, an internal interaction and we shall differentiate it from an external interaction that is based on non-dialogical relations between individuals (Rommetveit, 1974; Marková, 1997; 2003a).

Let us start with the latter, i.e. with an external interaction. Consider the following example from the *Handbook of Social Psychology* (Rosenberg, 1968, p. 209). This example of external relations refers to a mathematical model applied to elementary forms of two-person interaction in the laboratory:

> The two subjects are isolated so that they can neither see nor talk to each other. The interactive aspect of the situation arises from the fact that the discriminative or reinforcing stimuli (of both) for each subject depend,
> at least in part, on the behaviour of the other subject in the form of coded lights, dials …

Similar presuppositions apply to the study of interaction in which gestures between two persons have been explored in an empty little room with plain walls and without furniture, so that experimental subjects can fully concentrate on tasks given to them by the researcher. These studies assume that under such 'uncontaminated' conditions the camera can capture eye-contact and non-verbal gestures in their purity. Subsequently, gestures and eye-contacts so obtained can be submitted to quantification and statistical analysis.

The model of external interaction presupposes that two or more independent entities, e.g. individuals, groups, etc. or variables, enter into some kind of a contact. For example, they exchange messages by each taking a turn; and indeed, notions like 'exchange' or 'turn-taking' are part of the relevant terminology. The term 'turn-taking' within a joint activity, e.g. a social game implies that two (or more) individuals each make a contribution to the dialogue which is solely his or her responsibility. Likewise, 'exchange' evokes an image of two or more 'turns', in which each participant is responsible for either 'give' or 'take'.

In contrast to external interaction that is based on the idea that two or more independent entities come together and start interacting, the point of departure of internal interaction is not independent entities but a constellation of interdependent constituents, like a dyad or a focus group. Elements that constitute that particular constellation (or the whole) enter into their specific constellation together, one defining the other, like a figure-ground set up. For example, a brother and a sister in family define one another as a sibling; a father and a son define one another as a father-son constellation. Outside their relationship as siblings or as a father-son unit, these individuals can of course be in some other kinds of relations. But with respect to one another they form a constellation in which they are mutually interdependent in and through internal interaction. In other words, the constellation defines its elements; and vice versa, the elements define the unit in question. But in contrast to a figure-ground that may be considered as a static configuration, for example, in Gestalt psychology, the dialogically defined dyad is a dynamic one. The participants are in a complementary dialogical engagement in communication (e.g. Ego-Alter, I-group) and an essential feature of internal interaction is that in and through communication they both undergo simultaneous and sequential changes.

Internal interaction defines the communicative interdependence of the Ego-Alter in terms of their mutual engagement. This concept begins from the presupposition that the human species has the dialogical nature. The Ego-Alter transform one another through communicatively and symbolically shared intentions and actions that are characterised by tension and by multifaceted and heterogeneous relationships. We are using here 'Ego-Alter' as a generic term that, in a concrete dialogical form, can stand for specific dialogical relations like I-you, minority-majority, I-group, group-another group, I-culture, I-generalised other, and so on. Some of these dyads may be in highly asymmetric relationships, e.g. the I-the government of my country. However, dialogism is a theoretical perspective. Therefore, it is not invalidated by even the most extreme asymmetric cases of 'dialogues', in which one participant speaks loudly and the other is more or less silent.

1.3.2   Dialogical interaction

Over many decades, some approaches in the philosophy of language, developmental, and social psychology, have provided theoretical and empirical grounds for the presupposition of the Ego-Alter interdependence. At a theoretical level, since the nineteenth century a number of scholars have elaborated the idea that the sense and the knowledge of the self and others grow together. The idea of the Ego-Alter interdependence can be found in the work of various social and human scholars. We shall illustrate it by referring to some examples.

According to the perspective of the German sociologist Georg Simmel (1858–1918), the Ego-Alter interaction plays an essential role in the process of socialisation, communication and thinking. He also argues that trust is 'one of the most important synthetic forces within society' (Simmel, 1950, p. 318), central to psychosocial feelings and to the formation of social knowledge. Simmel conceives of interaction as the orientation of one human towards another one, as a-priori trust. Trust is a feeling that is immediately apprehended and therefore, it is not always conscious. Simmel views trust both as situated within – as well as outside – the boundaries of knowledge that individuals can form of one another. Without trust, society could hardly become established, and instead, it would run a considerable risk of falling into pieces. At the same time, Simmel (1955) conceives of conflict as a driving force of social movement, which draws individuals and members of social groups together. For him, although conflict involves negative relations, it also leads to innovation and dynamics.

If we turn to social developmental psychology of the early twentieth century, we find numerous ideas that corroborate those of Georg Simmel. In social developmental psychology of the early twentieth century, using terms like the 'dialectic of social growth', 'conversation of gestures' and 'inter- and intra-psychological processes', James Mark Baldwin (1861–1934), George Herbert Mead (1863–1931) and Lev Vygotsky (1896–1934), respectively, have proposed theories of self-consciousness built on the mutual development of the Ego-Alter. Baldwin viewed the concept of the 'dialectic of personal growth' as a process of the mutual interdependence between the Ego-Alter through give-and-take relationships in which 'the self meets self, so to speak' (Baldwin, 1895, p. 342). Baldwin postulated a theory according to which the self is originally crude, unreflective and largely organic, and it is through interpersonal interaction that it becomes 'purified and clarified'. He expressed this perspective, for example, in his studies of imitation, which were part of his theory of the self: 'My sense of myself grows by imitation of you, and my sense of yourself grows in terms of my sense of myself' (Baldwin, 1897, p. 15). Imitation for Baldwin, however, was not a passive process, but it always involved the creation and an idiosyncratic interpretation of the other person. George Herbert Mead's analysis of the development of self-consciousness and reflection was based on his presupposition that the self has an ability to call out in oneself a set of definite responses that it acquires from others (Mead, 1934, p. 277). As the self develops this ability, it becomes an object to itself: it regards itself through the eyes of others. In his essay on 'The objective reality of perspectives', Mead (1927) develops this idea to include all environmental conditions around the self. Environmental conditions, he insists, exist only for concrete human agents who use them in their own idiosyncratic ways. Human agents, on their part, are never imprisoned in their own little cages but are orientated towards others and their perspectives. Vygotsky's (1979, p. 29) analysis of self-consciousness, again, is based on the mutuality of the Ego-Alter. For him, '[t]he mechanism of knowing oneself (self-awareness) and the mechanism for knowing others are one and the same'. Consciousness of speaking and of social experience both emerge simultaneously with one another. According to Vygotsky, there is no difference between the fact that one can repeat one's own word and that of the other person. This capacity grows for self- and other-communication simultaneously. Moreover, words also express the social and historical nature of human self and other-awareness.

More recently, developmental psychologists like Newson (1979), Trevarthen (e.g. 1979; 1992) and Stern (1985), among others, have argued and provided empirical evidence that the child is born with a predisposition for intersubjectivity. In getting actively engaged with the environment, the child selects his/her own milieu. Parents, on their part, by providing a stimulating environment and indeed, by presupposing that young children already comprehend quite complex messages, further contribute to the intricate interplay between biological and cultural influences. Thus, by presupposing intersubjectivity they actually shorten the path to its achievement (Rommetveit, 1974). Trevarthen (1992, p. 102) maintains that understanding intersubjectivity can provide an explanation 'of how human social and cultural knowledge is created, how language serves a culture and how its transmission from generation to generation is secured'.

Kurt Lewin (1939/1951; 1946/1951; 1947/1951) tried to understand the fundamental dynamic relations between the individual and his/her social environment. He often characterised the concept of internal relations in his field theory and in his ecological approach by the notion of 'interdependence'. Originally, Lewin developed the field theory as a dynamic approach examining interdependencies between the individual's behaviour and his/her life space or psychological environment. Later, however, he studied the factors determining the actions of individuals in a group dynamic. Importantly, for him:

> It is not similarity or dissimilarity that decides whether two individuals belong to the same or different groups, but *social interaction or other types of interdependence*. A group is best defined as a *dynamic whole based on interdependence rather than on similarity*. (Lewin, 1948, p. 184)

This quotation is important because it places emphasis on the criterion of belonging, i.e. 'interdependence of fate' (ibid. p. 184) rather than on similarities and dissimilarities of categories, whether racial, national, religious or cultural. Kurt Lewin, just like relativity physicists, e.g. Einstein or Heisenberg, draws attention to the difference between static concepts (similarity or dissimilarity in the above quotation) and dynamic concepts based on interdependencies. This explains why concepts like tension, the level of aspiration, motivation and conflict played such an important role in Lewin's group dynamic.

The idea of the Ego-Alter or I-Others is fundamental to Moscovici's (1976b) theory of the interdependence between minority and majority and to his genetic model of social change. Dialogically, minorities are defined in terms of majorities and a group could be the majority only with respect to the specific minority. They are in an interdependent relation not because of some specific similarities or differences, e.g. gender, age or nationality. Like in Lewin's case, minorities and majorities are defined dialogically in terms of their fate. Therefore, one cannot define such characteristics as being a priori important or significant. Instead, they define a particular majority/minority relation and it might be totally irrelevant with respect to another kind of majority/minority. As long as it becomes essential in their relationships, any characteristic could define majority/minority interdependence. Minorities and majorities exert mutual effect on one another. For example, a majority may try to impose its norms and rules on a minority. However, at the same time, the majority is under the pressure from that minority which tries to make itself understood, establish its visibility and attempts to create its own rules and norms and make them accepted by the majority. Such effects are simultaneous although they can be latent and not immediately visible. As research has shown, tension between minorities and majorities is ever present but may not be immediately visible. It can reveal itself only when the invisible tension has completed its work and becomes a visible communicative outcome (Moscovici, 1976b; 1979).

In conclusion, we have brought to attention some examples of internal interaction as conceived in certain classic and current approaches in developmental and social psychology. Their point of departure is the Ego-Alter interdependence and this is why they are all relevant to our dialogical perspective. Dialogism, however, also has other features, for example, heterogeneity, multifaceted nature of interactions, intersubjectivity, hidden and internal dialogues, tension and equilibrium, asymmetries and symmetries. Since the above examples of interactions differ with respect as to whether and how they treat these features of dialogism, we can say that some are more dialogical than others and to that extent, more or less relevant to our analytical strategy.

1.4   Socially shared knowledge

1.4.1   The rationalist perspective of the individual and social knowledge

Throughout its history, European scholarship has faced a dilemma. On the one hand, it has assumed that rational thought of the individual, pure facts and 'neutral' language unbiased by emotions and imprecise meanings are suited for science, including social science (e.g. Gellner, 1992; 1998). But if this is so, a social scientist faces 'a problem': individuals live in societies, talk to one another, share experiences and are being influenced by socially shared and collective forms of knowledge – if indeed, one can call these forms 'knowledge'. And therefore a social scientist often assumes that these forms, prejudiced by culture and by everyday language, are conducive to irrational and vague ways of thought. From this perspective, if socially shared knowledge is studied at all, it is usually suspect of having a tinge of inferior features like naivety, the hypnotising power of masses, and even signs of pathological irrationality, among other characteristics. Communitarian knowledge, it follows, is antithetical to science.

This ambition 'to be scientific' has its deep historical and philosophical roots both in rationalism and empiricism. The dilemma concerning, on the one hand, a philosophical 'kind of marble temple shining on a hill' and on the other hand, the world of 'concrete personal experiences to which the street belongs … multitudinous beyond imagination, tangled, muddy, painful and perplex', is not new. William James (1975, pp. 17–18) discussed these two separate worlds as a dilemma in philosophy at the beginning of the twentieth century. Yet the dilemma has not disappeared. Instead, the simple and classic sanctuary has become a model of social sciences. For example, just like general psychology, the mainstream experimental social psychology aspires to be scientific. It assumes that it can achieve scientific purity by categorising and imposing abstract forms that render their analysis coherent. It presupposes that the study of processes, essential to acquisition of knowledge like social cognition, language and thought, must be deprived of the contaminating and biasing influence of content and context. Only variables deprived of context and of content can be scientifically controlled and submitted to experimental treatments. This is why reasoning, for example, has usually been studied by means of content-less and artificially constructed tasks like syllogisms and anagrams in order to capture pure logical thought of the individual.

Despite the rationalist arguments, the idea that knowledge is socially shared and rooted in people's everyday worlds, and therefore that it should be studied on its own terms, does have its protagonists. The nature and forms of socially shared knowledge and communication have been studied by scholars belonging to different social sciences and different traditions, ranging from Durkheim, Malinowski, Weber and Simmel to Schütz, Berger and Luckmann, among many others. Despite variations in their conceptions of socially shared knowledge, these scholars insist on the importance of groups into which people are socialised, e.g. families, peer associations and communities, for individuals' cognition. Reasoning capacities of individuals, these scholars argue, are generated in and through interdependencies with 'others', whether with respect to maintaining and changing social realities, facilitating the formation of relationships or communicating and talking about the world.

Whether for mere survival or for improving and enriching their life, people are relying upon rich spectra of socially shared knowledge that are formed, maintained and changed in and through concrete situations. Socially shared knowledge underlies most habitual activities that organise daily life in their diversities, as well as heterogeneities of speaking and thinking. For example, various forms of interpersonal interaction like politeness, know-how skills, child-rearing practices and eating habits, are all based on social beliefs and lay explanations, many of which are transmitted from parents to children, through peer relations and institutions. What prominently figures in these transmissions are not only customary public and individual needs and desires, but also intimate ways of knowing other people, and feelings like pride and appreciation, guilt and shame, embarrassment, among others.

Just like knowledge underlying habitual activities, so do other types of collective knowing, like scientific knowledge and ideologies, circulate through public discourse and transform themselves into new forms. One form of socially shared knowledge is easily substituted by another one if it no longer fulfils current needs and if it becomes irrelevant to desires of the public or to the accomplishment of certain social activities. For example, Andrew Jahoda (1995) shows the changing kinds of socially shared knowledge throughout European history in relation to learning disabilities. He refers to two major conceptions of Judeo-Christian beliefs, one based on treating those with learning disabilities as 'innocent children of god' and the other based on the belief in the 'original sin'. He also indicates how these beliefs have influenced political, moral and educational reasoning and practices. Consequently, they have also had a profound influence on the quality of life of people with learning disabilities.

More recently, these beliefs have intermingled with various scientific models, for example, with medical, biological, psychological and social ones. Such crossbred conceptions of learning disabilities have affected not only policies and ideologies of treatment but also social representations (Moscovici, 1961) of disabilities held by the general public.

From these considerations and examples we can easily see that there are profound differences between, on the one hand, the idea that knowledge is based on individual rationality, pure 'facts' and an abstract and formal language and, on the other hand, on the idea that knowledge is socially shared. The difference between them becomes contentious with respect to the assumption that the former is suitable for science and that the latter is not.

Concerning knowledge based on individual rationality, true, for better or worse, it is an elegant and a reflected-upon system that is constructed from selected and logically organised elements. This is why the individual's capacity for so conceived rational thought is assumed to warrant progress and science-making activities. Above all, individual rationality is supposed, in this kind of epistemology, to be universalistic:

> The cognitive style is more or less correctly codified by the rationalists, requiring all concepts to observe the same rules in relation to evidence, and subject to its evidence, which in turn is not controlled by culture but in large measure free of it. (Gellner, 1992, p. 53)

Rationalists do not claim that social forms of thinking do not exist. What they claim, however, is that these forms are secondary to individual reasoning and thinking and that they develop due to two kinds circumstance in relation to the individual and society.

The first kind of circumstance, it is claimed, is due to the society's imposition of various kinds of rules and norms, like those of the moral and logical order. And so the individual (Ego), the rationalist, must cope with prohibition, restriction and a straitjacket that the Alter (society) imposes. In other words, this kind of explanation of socially shared knowledge presupposes that the rationality of the individual is restrained by the rules and norms of the collective. Referring to Durkheim, Gellner points out that for him, rationality is a socially imposed and internalised compulsion. It 'can be equated with the submission to socially shared, communally distinctive, and compulsively internalized concepts. In the beginning there was the prohibition' (Gellner, 1992, p. 176).[1]

The second kind of circumstance is the rationalist point of view arguing that socially shared knowledge is a 'team game' (Gellner, 1998). This means that when the individual explores and interprets the world, he/she employs 'concepts which are carried by an entire cultural/linguistic community'. Unable to understand the rules of operation on his/her own, the individual cannot use self-created tools but instead, the community works 'through him' because the wisdom of others 'is greater than his own' (Gellner, 1998, p. 6).

We can conclude that both these rationalist perspectives assume the primacy of the individual's cognition. The first claims that individual rationality is primary and that socially shared thinking is a societal constraint. The second assumes that since the individual lacks the capacity to use self-created intellectual tools, he/she has to rely on a 'team game' in order to cope with everyday living and with complex concepts.

In contrast, the starting point of a dialogical perspective of socially shared knowledge is neither the individual rationality of the Ego, nor the collective 'team game' of the Alter. Instead, we are starting from the presupposition that socially shared knowledge of the human species has a dialogical nature. This means that each individual generates his or her knowledge in terms of the Alter, as multifaceted and multivoiced realities situated in culture.

1.4.2   A dialogical approach to socially shared knowledge

If we say that socially shared knowledge has a dialogical nature, it implies that it is formed and maintained in and through dialogical thinking and communication. This does not mean to deny that individuals as individuals have the capacity of individual reasoning and thinking. It means, however, that the Ego and Alter jointly co-constitute and transform forms of conceptual knowledge. Thinking can serve different purposes and may take place in diverse ways, like scientific, common sense, religious, metaphorical and so on. It takes detours, considers heterogeneity of circumstances and makes nuances in meaning (Moscovici, 1961; 1976a). It judges and evaluates, makes inferences and hypotheses, it flatters and manipulates. It guides us in conversations, structures our daily routines and organises social encounters.

Socially shared knowledge in its different forms is usually immersed in daily activities which people habitually perform without consciously engaging their minds. As they may not have reasons to reflect upon implicitly shared forms of knowledge and habitual activities, people would see no purpose in analysing them explicitly (Moscovici, 2000, pp. 147–148). In contrast to formalised and decontextualised forms of individual rationality discussed above, rationality of socially shared knowledge is contextualised and is warranted in communication through which it is transformed into new forms. This further entails that words and symbols do not function as parts of normative mechanisms in which information signs have a-priori specified and strictly codified semantic contents. Nevertheless, history and culture make demands on dialogical forms of thinking and communicating and constrain them in specific ways; there are different kinds of constraint of the past and the present; of the social and the individual; and of tradition and novelty.

1.4.3 Dialogical forms of socially shared knowledge

In daily life we use different forms of knowledge that are socially generated, maintained and changed. Some of them are based on contents of particular social phenomena like religious beliefs, social representations (e.g. of genetically produced food or of health issues), and so on. Other forms of socially shared knowledge are of interpersonal and inter-group nature, like rules of politeness or social norms. Certain forms of knowledge are linked with social activities like routines and habits, others with the use of artefacts, for example, in work situations (Engeström and Middleton, 1996). Some forms of knowledge may be implicitly shared but hardly ever spelled out. Other forms, on the other hand, are explicitly acquired in training and underlie highly specialised performances (ballet; piloting an aircraft). Forms of knowledge may range from temporary ones, e.g. knowing which supermarket makes best 'special offers' or who is the present minister of interior affairs, to more permanent ones like knowing the history of one's country. One could endlessly continue with such enumerations of ranges, kinds and qualities of forms of socially shared knowledge. This tremendous heterogeneity is also reflected in research terminology. Researchers may use a variety of terms emphasising specific aspects of their foci, like 'mutual knowledge', 'social representations', 'community knowledge', 'common-sense knowledge', 'naïve psychology', 'customs', 'habits', 'a team game', 'activity types', 'speech genres', among many others.

In addition to the forms of social knowledge that may be actually shared by participants in dialogue, we also need to remind that participants may think that they share knowledge when, in fact, that may not be. Indeed the latter case is very common because the extent to which individuals share knowledge, thoughts and understanding in communication is always partial, leaving a loop-hole for continuing the dialogical process. The philosopher Arne Naess (1953) discusses cases of partial understanding in his conception of the depth of intention. For instance, participants in communication may share knowledge (or understanding) at a superficial level, e.g. they may both agree that democracy means the freedom of speech. However, when probing further, they may find that they disagree about the meaning of 'freedom of speech'. Alternatively, they may assume that they disagree about the meaning of democracy, each defining democracy in a different way. For example, one may define democracy in terms of decisions of the majority while for the other it may mean the freedom in terms of market economy and privatisation. However, their subsequent conversation may reveal that despite superficial differences in their definitions of democracy they agree with one another in terms of values attached to their definitions of democracy. One would expect that the study of dialogue in focus groups could enable the social scientist to discover, at least partly, the extent to which social knowledge is actually shared or only taken-as-shared.

Linguistic communication is not the only means through which forms of socially shared knowledge are generated and transmitted. Socially shared knowledge can be generated in joint activities (e.g. putting up a tent, cooking or dancing) and/or it can be transmitted by observation and by imitation. However, since our interest in this book is the dialogue in focus groups, we shall restrict our discussion accordingly.

The forms of socially shared knowledge that are being explored in focus groups are usually topics of public concern, e.g. opinions, beliefs and social representations. Such concerns necessarily bring into attention two issues. First are contents of what is being spoken about, whether and how contents are explicitly thematised, or implicitly taken-for-granted and, therefore, not thematised. The second issue concerns the manners by which contents are framed (e.g. communicative activity types, identifications, taking positions) and orientated (e.g. whether talk and its contents are directed at the interlocutor, at absent participants, at possible audiences, and so on) in their heterogeneous and multifaceted displays. While these two issues could be studied in relation to different forms of socially shared knowledge, contents of daily conversations owe a great deal to common-sense knowledge and social representations. Since we are exploring the assumption that focus groups have many similarities with daily conversations and involve largely common-sense knowledge and social representations, the remainder of this section discusses these two forms of socially shared knowledge, i.e. common-sense knowledge and social representations.

'Common-sense knowledge' is a generic term. It usually refers to knowledge of social realities, objects, relationships, anticipated experiences that make our daily living relatively orderly because it is habitual, routinised, normative and prescriptive. It is knowledge that we take more or less for granted and accept without questioning in everyday activities and talk. As Moscovici (2000, p. 149) says, common-sense knowledge is 'the kernel of our consensual universe' and we recognise in it 'a historical, cultural and rhetorical character'. Should such recognition fail, such knowledge would be 'reduced to impoverished traits, to schemas and stereotypes without meaning'.

Common-sense knowledge can emerge in different ways. First, it manifests itself as first-hand knowledge, 'as a corpus of knowledge, based on tradition and consensus, spontaneously produced by the members of a group' (Moscovici and Hewstone, 1983, p. 105). In the past, this kind of common-sense knowledge gave birth to, and nurtured the development of science. Then, there is second-hand common-sense knowledge, that actually 'spreads and steadily builds a new consensus around recent discoveries and theories' (ibid.). In addition one can identify other sources of common-sense knowledge, e.g. those appearing through changes in child socialisation, ethics, moralities, political socialisation, and so on.

It should be apparent from this brief account that common-sense knowledge is rich and highly diversified. It is filled with dialogical tension and different perspectives: one and the 'same' thing can be now positive and then negative, desirable and undesirable, depending on circumstances, reasoning and communicative intentions of speakers. These features can be found in folk sayings and proverbs, which we use in one form or other depending on the recipient, situation, intention and appropriateness in the here-and-now.

Being dialogical, common sense knowledge is 'anchored in communication; a communication implies creativity similar to that of language, à la Humboldt, or transformation, the development of one level of knowledge to another one' (Moscovici and Marková, 2000, p. 272). For example, proverbs that we find in many languages excellently demonstrate this point. If we consider proverbs as single and separate sentences without contexts of which they are part, one proverb may appear to contradict another one. However, contradiction disappears when they are viewed as embedded in the concrete situations for which they have been created. For instance, some proverbs emphasise the value of change (e.g. 'Change your dwelling place often, for the sweetness of life consists in variety'; 'Change of pasture makes fat calves') while others advise against change (e.g. 'A tree often transplanted, bears not much fruit'; 'Three removals are as bad as a fire').

Equally, in daily life, various phenomena could be judged as positive or negative, depending on the context and perspective of the argument. For instance, in the focus groups on biotechnology that are discussed later in this book (Chapter 6), participants holding the view that nature is good, evaluate natural products as being good and preferable to genetically engineered ones. However, we can in other contexts find ideas of 'fighting the nature' and 'cursing the nature', whether it concerns earthquakes, floods or hurricanes, or even – the 'human' nature.

Different social scientists, however, emphasise different characteristics of common-sense knowledge. While the dialogical perspective foregrounds diversities and heterogeneities in common-sense knowledge, Alfred Schütz (1962, p. 312), emphasises the reciprocity of perspectives. According to him, 'the world of everyday life is from the outset an intersubjective one'. It is the world in which people are immersed and in which they share 'the stock of knowledge at hand'. We transcend the world of others by sharing and by being aware of sharing perspectives of the daily life. For example, we know that the 'same' object can have different meanings for others (Schütz, ibid. p. 11f). This is to be expected because people have different biographies, experiences, and knowledge, and these differences amount to distances among people. But we overcome these differences in perspectives because we are also aware that others (Alter) assume similar things as we do. This is so, Schütz argues, because we construct others partly in the same manner that we construct ourselves. In other words, we are aware of others as an 'alter ego'.[2]

And so we see that these two conceptions of common-sense knowledge emphasise different aspects of the Ego-Alter interdependence. The first one brings out the dialogical tension between and within the Ego-Alter, argumentation and contradictions within and between different positions and individuals. Whether something is considered to be common sense is evaluated in the backdrop of these diversities. The second perspective foregrounds the aspect of common-sense knowledge that is based on the reciprocity of perspectives of the Ego and Alter. It is not that Schütz would ignore the difference between the Ego and the Alter or that he would deny that individuals change. Rather, he focused on the reciprocity of perspectives and attached to them a priority in his theorising.

Although common-sense knowledge and social representations are inter-related, they are not the same phenomena. Common-sense knowledge, we have already pointed out, is knowledge of our habitual thinking, activities, interactions, communication and life in general. Social representations are forms of socially shared knowledge of specific social phenomena circulating in public discourse, like those of madness, democracy, citizenship, terrorism, AIDS and so on. Social scientists uncover social representations by the theoretical analysis from common-sense knowledge and from other forms of socially shared knowledge in which they could be partially or completely concealed, like habits of thought, rules, norms, laws, and so on.

Since social representations are phenomena of contemporary social concern, they may be disturbing, fear-provoking, desirable or otherwise important. They are negotiated and disputed: they always communicate something about something, referring to phenomena of relevance in public discourse. In other words, they are always directed at others: through pointing to someone they speak and through expressing something, they communicate (Moscovici, 1976a,

p. 26; Marková, 2003a, p. 120). Communication involves tension between the Ego and Alter, the fact that is not captured by what is known as 'the epidemiology of representations' (Sperber, 1985). According to Sperber (ibid. p. 73), cultural phenomena can be viewed in terms of spreading epidemics. He maintains that representations are either mental or collective, and in both cases they spread: 'Just as an epidemiology of diseases has to be rooted in individual pathology, an epidemiology of representations has to be rooted in cognitive psychology'. Some forms of communication, like rumours or information provided by the media, may seem to encourage the metaphor of the spread by contagion. However, if one adopts the dialogical perspective, then the image of epidemics of representations, spreading effortlessly and unintentionally, does not fit. Something, whether a rumour or information can become a message only in specific Ego-Alter circumstances: it must have some relevance for the individuals and groups in question and must involve communicative tension and intention.

Since social representations are always representations of something, they can be dialogically expressed by the triangular relation Ego-Alter-Object. This means that the social representation of an Object (e.g. democracy, citizenship, dictatorship or any specific event or situation) is conceived as being jointly generated through symbolic communicative relations between the Ego-Alter. Since the term 'Ego-Alter' is a generic one, we need to assume that the formation of a representation involves symbolic communicative relations between different kinds of Ego-Alter with respect to the object in question, e.g. a group-another group, minority-majority, I-you, and so on. For example, social representations of democracy are likely to involve different kinds of the Ego and Alter in the struggle for social recognition, in trust and distrust, evaluation of morality and immorality, and so on.

Such relations of antinomy usually have deep historical roots in social evolution and in culture, and they have been called themata (Moscovici and Vignaux, 1994; Marková, 2003a), e.g. trust/distrust (Chapter 7). Although such cultural themata may be implicit in language and social thinking for many generations, when particular conditions obtain, they may be brought to the public awareness and they turn into a source of tension and conflict in contemporary conditions. Thematised by individuals, groups, institutions etc., they involve different Ego-Alter interactions, all contributing to the transformation of the representation in question. They manifest themselves in and through concrete dialogical encounters displaying tension, search for intersubjectivity, mutual understanding, and so on. Consequently, the researcher may pose questions about the different forms that these relations can take, the ways of thinking and feeling in which they are expressed, communication genres or communicative activity types, continuities and discontinuities with the past.

The concept of the interdependence between Ego-Alter-Object makes the theory of social representations not only a theory of communication, but most importantly, a dialogical theory of communication. And it is the dialogical nature of the Ego-Alter-Object that conceptually separates the theory of social representations, say, from the theory of social perception à la Heider (1958). Moscovici (2005a) makes this point, insisting that it is not because we perceive objects differently from people that we judge and form different explanations with respect to these two categories. The hypothesis that attributes judgement, reasoning and explanation to perception, focuses on the nature of the perceived entity, i.e. either a person or an object, rather than on the relation or interaction between the perceiver and object (or a person). Moscovici argues that it is misleading to focus on duality of the self and the other, rather than on their interaction. In the former case, it is presupposed that it is the other, who determines the self's perception (external causality) or, alternatively, the self, who interprets the action of the other (internal causality). In the latter case the theoretical concern is the interaction between the Ego-Alter rather than external or internal causality between them (Moscovici, 2005b). The way in which the Ego selects the aspects of the situation is partly determined by his/her social experience, by expectations, by purposes he/she comprehends in that situation, and so on. In dialogical thinking, the interaction comes first; it combines and uses individuals' intellectual capacities in multiple manners and they can express their ideas in different ways using specific words, gestures and symbols. Social representations are 'discoursified' forms of thinking and cultural symbolic phenomena shaping language and communication; and that they are at the same time being shaped by language and communication (Moscovici, 2001).

Mikhail Bakhtin (1984, p. 384f), too, characterises a dialogical relationship through the orientation towards a referential object. A referential object relationship must become discourse, i.e. it must have an author and be orientated towards someone else's speech (it could be an orientation towards one's own speech).

1.5   Dialogue

1.5.1   What is dialogue?

In recent years, dialogue has become one of the key terms in discussions of human interaction and relations, and some scholars have proposed that we can witness a 'dialogical turn' in the human sciences and in society at large. Be that as it may, but the term dialogue is hardly precise. We need to distinguish between several senses of the word.

When it is said that there is a need for 'dialogue' in society, in politics, in media, in workplace and marriages etc., a normative sense of the word is usually implied. What it means is that there is need for 'a good dialogue' or 'real communication', something like open and reasonably symmetrical exchanges of ideas, opinions, understandings or relations of mutual empathy on equal terms between people. While these ideals are worthwhile orientations in everyday life among people, nations and cultures, we need more specific terms in scientific endeavours if we want to describe and explain the divergent patterns of communicative interaction that can actually be observed in the world. We shall therefore talk about 'dialogue' in four other senses.

The first of these more specific senses is concrete and empirical in its reference: a 'dialogue' is a symbolic interaction between two or several individuals who are mutually co-present (Luckmann, 1990; Marková and Foppa, 1990; Linell, 1998a). The core reference is here to face-to-face interaction between people by means of spoken language and/or bodily communication. There are obvious extensions to various artefact-borne forms, for example, by means of written messages, pictures, computer-supported communication, particularly if these are interactive in nature (rather than unidirectional) or take place in real time. Moreover, individuals and groups carry internal dialogues with themselves and with absent individuals (Moscovici, 2005b; Marková, 2006).

Second, although dialogue in focus groups takes place at specific times and locations, we shall assume that dialogue is historically and culturally situated. A single dialogue is no more than a slice taken out of this historical and cultural habitation and it makes sense only if considered within that habitation. At these levels, people engage in dialogue with less concrete others, and over longer stretches of time.

Third, in a more figurative sense we can talk about a dialogue among ideas rather than between people. Here again, this sense has its parallel in the theory of social knowledge. Thus in *The Rules of Sociological Method* (Durkheim,

1938, p. li) writes that it is necessary to investigate the ways in which social representations 'adhere to and repel one another, how they fuse or separate from one another' – in other ways, how they circulate in society.

Finally, a dialogue can also be considered in an even more abstract – or one could even say a metaphoric – manner, like, for example, a dialogue between different cultural traditions or ways of thinking in the sense of Mikhail Bakhtin (1979/1986) or Yuri Lotman (1990).

These different meanings of dialogue indicate that one might view a dialogical analysis of a discourse – or part of it – in terms of different kinds of interaction.

In a social-scientific account of communication and thinking, all four senses of 'dialogue' will be of importance in this book. In our own exploration of focus-group discourse, we will have plenty of opportunities to look at the power of the dialogue dynamics, referring then to 'dialogue' in all these senses.

1.5.2   Dialogical heterogeneity: the researcher's dilemma

Human dialogue involves tension (and communicatively shared intention) and under no circumstances can it be reduced to sheer transmission of information. Dialogues maintain existing social realities and involve thinking about, imagining and creating new social realities. There is no word or symbol in dialogue that could function as a 'neutral' display of signs, speaking to everybody in the same way. While being the historically and culturally established social products, words and symbols reflect intentions, judgements, contexts, contrasts and conflicts, all inhabiting the concrete Ego-Alter interdependencies. For a social scientist studying social knowledge and communication in focus groups, the dialogical diversity and heterogeneity presents numerous challenges throughout the analytical approach. Let us consider some of these challenges.

While scientific knowing places emphasis on the explicit expression of thoughts and language, other forms of socially shared knowledge, e.g. common sense knowing, social representations, social thinking and dialogue, thrive on implicitness. The more knowledge we share, the less we need to communicate (Rommetveit, 1974; Linell, 1998a). The range of implicitness in socially shared knowledge, thinking and dialogue could be a challenge for everybody, whether for interacting individuals and groups. Rommetveit (1974) brought this issue to attention in *On Message Structure*, where he has shown that dealing with implicitly shared knowledge is an important social skill. In daily life we rarely spell out everything we mean as do pedantic headmasters, Rommetveit argues, but instead, we must deal with implicitness without questions. Very often, 'we are supposed to know' and our quest for explicitness could be an offence.

Equally, the less aware we are of social representations, the greater their effect on our thinking, communication and other activities (Moscovici, 1984).

Secondly, dialogue is characterised by an open and heterogeneous interplay of multiple meanings and voices in continuous tension. Even if participants in dialogue establish intersubjective and close relations and even if they share a great deal of knowledge, different kinds of tension keep their dialogue going. There is tension between antinomic but mutually interdependent tendencies in talk; there is tension between the positions of the self and other, between relatively established knowledge and new knowledge, and so on. Moreover, socially shared knowledge may disguise as well as reveal itself in silences or ambiguities, reflective arguments, disagreements, negotiations and so on.

In studying socially shared knowledge in dialogue the researcher has to cope with emotional and relational problems which the participants express through a variety of symbolic means. They may have a fear of losing face or other kinds of socially induced fears, they may express antagonism against others, and so on. Not only do participants in dialogue actively attempt to understand their social world, but they also employ a variety of cunning skills to mislead others and to express certain fake intentions, which they want the others to believe to be true. They can also employ indirect communicative strategies hiding aggression against or disagreement with others. For example, Bakhtin coined the term 'hidden polemic' to refer to a specific manner, through which the individual may express an indirect attack on the other person and convey his/her critical evaluation of the other. While open polemics is directed at the interlocutor, hidden polemics is indirect, focusing, for example, on the object of discourse. Just like the speaker might express critical comments on the referential object in any discourse, he/she may do it in such a way that the negative referential meaning attacks at the same time the other person's claim about that object. As Bakhtin (1984, p. 195) puts it: 'a word, directed toward its referential object clashes with another's word within the very object itself'. So alongside the referential meaning, it is the word of the other participant that is treated adversely. What we find here is an additional and superimposed meaning that clashes with the referential meaning and that is intentionally orientated towards the words of the other participant. Since these words are the other participant's words rather than one's own words, we can talk here about double-dialogism (see Chapter 5). Bakhtin described such hidden polemic as 'double-voiced'.

Since participants in a dialogue (or focus group) may belong to various communities to which they are interactionally and intellectually committed, they may be involved not only in external dialogues with others but also in what Bakhtin called 'internal dialogism'. This means that while the participants talk to one another here-and-now, they may simultaneously carry out dialogues internally with themselves or others. This internal dialogue may be orientated to ideas held on or disputed by other individuals or groups. While being in internal dialogue with these absent others, participants may not externally express anything (whether verbally or non-verbally) or they may give off only indirect signs.

Moreover, even single utterances are loaded with other 'voices' and positions. Such dialogues could be embedded in one another as well as they could cross-breed one another. Participants in focus groups are members of many other groups, which not only cross-fertilise but also obliterate and misconstrue one another. As early as in the 1920s Voloshinov (1929/1973) raised the question about the role of such unheard voices in internal dialogues. He believed that in most instances the second voice is that of a typical representative of the social group to which the individual belongs, or to use the term of George Herbert Mead, it is the voice of 'the generalised other'. It was again Bakhtin, whose analysis of the conflict between the two different positions, the self's own norm and the self's confrontation of that norm, has become classic.

It is in *Problems of Dostoyevsky's Poetics* where he shows the antinomy between two intense positions. Before taking decisions, Dostoyevsky's Raskolnikov dialogises his internal dialogue. In this internal dialogue all words are double-voiced, and in each of them a conflict of different positions takes place. This conflict is characterised by re-creating words of the other position and filling them with intonation, indignation, evaluating and irony. This conflict between different positions has for Bakhtin (1984, pp. 212–213) a special meaning. It is a way of coping with inadequate social recognition that one receives from another person.

Dialogue consists of sense-making and sense-creating activities in the socio-cultural space, which take place in various kinds of temporal relations. For example, there is chronometric and experienced time, as well as researchers' and participants' time. While discourse researchers often base their analyses on chronometric time as something 'objective', it could be the experienced time that contributes emotional, topical and interactional significance of communication. Dialogue contains not only interactionally relevant meanings (e.g. phatic communication, asymmetries, hierarchies between interlocutors), but equally important, messages with contents (e.g. the joint construction of knowledge in interactional settings). Contents of socially shared knowledge have individual, interactional and socio-cultural significance and some of them may touch in some fundamental ways upon lives of the individuals involved.

Contents involve emotions, fears and hopes, and all these are part of socially relevant knowledge.

Dialogue involves a multitude of forms and activities in which humans communicate and think about their socially shared knowledge and imagine their social realities. These forms and activities differ according to specific local situations, institutional rules, group norms and cultural traditions. Some of them are more or less culturally or institutionally fixed, e.g. legal procedures, education discourses or doctor-patient consultations; others are more informal, e.g. public gatherings, conversations in cafés or family talks. These activities and forms of thinking and communication also differ with respect to purposes they serve. They are framed by social positions of interlocutors, by their personal inter-relations, by norms and rules, and traditions. Such diversities of activities and forms stem from their embeddedness in specific local situations (e.g. the family, therapy, social and political group etc.). Voloshinov (1929/1973) noted the proliferation of such activities in life situations. He referred to them as behavioural genres, thus interconnecting communication with action. Behavioural genres are facts of the social milieu, they are conventional and institutional.

In conclusion we can say that it is a challenging task for the researcher to bear in mind all these complexities in the study of dialogue. Not surprisingly, researchers often focus only on some dialogical aspects, e.g. verbal interaction or non-verbal interaction, certain dialogical sequences like adjacency pairs, question-answer-feedback, and so on. Moreover, due to these complexities it has been common in many studies of language and cognition to treat language as transparent and unitary, to conceive of words as simply indexing dictionary meanings and easily identifiable references. Yet, such an easy option is not helpful if we intend to capture, through the study of dialogue (and focus groups) socially shared knowledge or at least some of its characteristics. It remains to be one of the main theoretical and methodological difficulties that dialogical actions, and heterogeneous characteristics of dialogue, interact with one another rather than just co-exist and have an additive impact on communication. Interactive qualities of actions and heterogeneous characteristics cannot be reduced to quantitative and additive effects. Instead, apparently transparent linguistic and cognitive phenomena are no more than the tip of the iceberg hiding an infinite openness of dialogism.

Notes

1   Gellner of course did not share the whole of the Durkheimian ethos. While he believed that humans are in their origin individual rationalists, what he took from Durkheim's position is probably the idea that humans, as individual rationalists,

could not remain solely individuals. They were forced to become 'social' and it was language with its 'astonishingly rich system of socially instilled markers' that helped to keep members of a community 'within their cultural bounds or at least indicating what the bounds are' (Gellner, 1992, p. 176).

2   Schütz (1975) considers three aspects of socialisation of knowledge. The reciprocity of perspectives is the first aspect, involving not only the awareness of past and present perspectives but also anticipations of the future in terms of plans, hopes and fears. Second, the social origin of knowledge, which refers to common-sense knowledge passed over to us by parents, friends, teachers, and so on, in a process over generations. This concerns situations and situation-transcending practices. Not only are we taught how to understand typical situations in the environment but also how typical such constructs must be in order to qualify as being relevant to the individual's activities and reasoning. Finally, knowledge is socially distributed. This last aspect refers to the fact that each individual has precise, clear and distinct knowledge only about a particular sphere of life. At any moment in life, an individual's stock of knowledge structures life in terms of preciseness, clarity and distinctness. And of course, others are specialists in other spheres of life and knowledge.

2 Focus groups through the lens of dialogism

2.1 Introduction

In this chapter, we shall first briefly present what focus groups are, without, however, entering into methodological details. This book is neither a manual telling the reader what to do at various stages of work, nor is it a methodological guide answering practical questions. Instead, we are concerned here to draw attention to communicative and thought processes that are normally involved in mundane thinking and talking and which therefore should be taken into consideration in focus-group research. As a consequence, our limited aim here will only be to recall some main features of focus groups for those who are not familiar with them.[1] This brief presentation will lead us to making an apparently strange observation, namely that focus-group research largely ignores that focus groups are, above all, groups. Researchers do not see communicative activities that take place in a group, where forms of socially shared knowledge, e.g. opinions, attitudes, social representations, etc. circulate and are elaborated. We shall argue that this may be due to the fact that focus-group research is disconnected from research into small group dynamics; in contrast, we consider small group dynamics as an important body of knowledge in the study of focus groups. This is why the first aim of this chapter is to build a bridge over these two disconnected strands of research, by proposing a brief incursion into the classic field of small group dynamics. This incursion will then enable us to stress the group dimension of focus groups and to show that the group has not been fully apprehended in a dialogical perspective. Consequently, the second aim of this chapter is to provide the basis of a dialogical approach to focus groups. More specifically, we shall discuss four analytical assumptions on which our approach is based.

2.2   What are focus groups?

Focus groups are a research method based on open-ended group discussions that examine a particular set of socially relevant issues. In some respects, focus groups are expected to have characteristics that are similar to spontaneous and informal discussions taking place in cafés, in streets and in pubs. As we shall see, it is by no means a new research method in the social sciences.

2.2.1   The past and present of focus groups

The focus-group method was developed during the Second World War and since that time it has been through ebb and flow, decline and rise both in the theory and the method. References concerning group interviews usually go back to the work of sociologists like Robert Merton and Paul Lazarsfeld (Lazarsfeld and Stanton, 1944) during the Second World War. These researchers used focus groups to comment on and to interpret radio programmes, which were concerned with the public's support for the government's war saving-bonds. During the War the US government encouraged people to buy bonds both as a patriotic gesture and to invest money, and bonds were advertised in the same way as other kinds of goods.

Focused interviews and focus groups were also designed to study other issues, like the effect of mass communication during the War, e.g. of War propaganda, patriotism, army feelings and so on. Merton and Lazarsfeld identified public distrust related to a sense of anomie and of real and feigned community values. The work continued after the War and it appeared in the book by Merton, Fiske and Kendall (1956) on 'The Focused Interview'.

After the War, the research using focus groups took a new turn. Focus groups became a popular research method in marketing, which placed emphasis on uncovering the consumers' motivations and on the unconscious sources of their choices for particular products. Until today, market research employs focus groups extensively in order to obtain opinions about products for consumption. Indeed, market research talks about 'focus-group business' helping to plan and assess marketing programmes. Focus groups tend to replace door-to-door techniques of personal interviewing in order to market new products and to encourage consuming.

In the last two decades focus groups have become one of the favourite methods in social sciences, exploring issues of public concern, opinions, beliefs, social representations and otherwise. The 1990s have witnessed more emphasis on qualitative methods enabling the study of the participants' meanings, interpretation and understanding. In this shift of interest, focus groups have attracted more attention in sociology, social psychology and the media. Focus groups have become widely used both in basic and applied research. For example, focus groups have been applied to many issues that are important in people's lives, like democracy, health and illness, disabilities, biotechnology and genetics. These developments have switched, once again, attention to questions like what is the purpose of focus groups, which theoretical ideas underpin the use of focus groups, what is their credibility and dependability as a research method, and so on.

In addition, focus groups as a research method have become popular in other areas. Many organisations like governmental agencies, health education, academics, public relations experts and the media of mass communication have been using focus groups for a variety of purposes. These range from explorations of company policies to health education programmes to extracurricular activities, and so on. One can observe and conclude that in these contexts, the theoretical emphasis that had been present in the original work by Merton and Lazarsfeld, died out. Focus groups are now used largely without any theoretical interest. They only provide quick responses to practical problems.

2.2.2   Setting up focus groups for research

Focus groups usually involve 4–12 persons, who explore jointly certain questions specified by the researcher. In other words, these discussion groups examine questions, which are 'in the focus'. It is important to emphasise that focus groups are set up for the purpose of research. This specification separates focus groups from other kinds of discussion groups like group conversations, group therapy sessions, support groups, committee discussions, brainstorming groups and so on.

Despite emphasis on stringent methodological criteria, researchers are aware of the importance to create a relaxed atmosphere among the participants and to find a suitable context for discussion so that focus groups would become as 'natural' as possible (Kitzinger et al., 2004).

Focus groups can take many different forms depending on the size of the group, its homogeneity versus heterogeneity in the composition of the members, the material which may be used for the organisation of the discussion, as well as the way in which the moderator plays his/her role. All these elements are presented and discussed in a number of methodological kits, manuals and guides describing how to use focus groups (see Appendix 1). The main aim of that extensive literature is methodological. It provides instructions concerning devising and organising focus groups, collecting and transcribing data. It makes researchers aware of sensitive topics and more generally, of the ethical problems involved in focus-group research (e.g. Kitzinger and Barbour, 1999; Kitzinger et al., 2004).

2.2.3   When are focus groups used?

Focus groups are often used in combination with other qualitative and quantitative methods. They can be complementary to ethnographic research, e.g. to observations in hospitals, communities, etc. and to individual interviews. Focus groups are also used on their own, without combination with other methods. Let us consider some ways in which focus groups can be combined with other methods.

First, focus groups are used in the initial stage of research in order to generate ideas and hypotheses and to become acquainted with a new field of inquiry. In this case, it is likely that group discussions will be relatively unstructured and open-ended. Ideas and hypotheses that are generated can be then further tested by other, less intensive methods like surveys, interviews or questionnaires. In fact, this was Merton's (1987) original idea as to how focus groups should be used in research.

Alternatively, focus groups are used at a later stage of research as a way of deepening the understanding of the already obtained data. For example, let us imagine that in using questionnaires, surveys and scales the researcher obtains data on attitudes and opinions. These data provide either 'yes-no' answers to questions in questionnaires etc., or brief answers from respondents. In order to understand meanings of these data and to obtain in-depth knowledge of the issues in question, the researcher can carry out focus groups in which he or she attends more closely to the data obtained in questionnaires. Focus groups can provide insights into the reasons for particular views; they can draw attention to uncertainties and tensions in communication, to the ways in which opinions are formed, and so on.

2.2.4   Analysis of the data

Focus groups are analysed in different ways, depending of the type of problem in question as well as the researcher's theoretical orientation. Sometimes, the analysis is based on a full transcription of the group discussion; sometimes the transcription is partial and serves mainly to making quotations that are used to illustrate the researcher's insight and interpretation.

Since focus groups produce verbal data, they may potentially be analysed by any method that is used to analyse verbal interactions, for example conversation analysis. However, a review of the literature on focus groups shows that few publications give extended information on the way in which data are analysed. The focus-group discussion is mainly used to illustrate some points that the researcher wants to highlight. When more details are given on the analysis of data, the method mainly consists of content analysis which provides a general picture of the contents which have been discussed in the group. We shall return to this point later on.

2.3   Focus groups: where is the group?

Despite a huge number of publications, the literature on focus groups confronts us with a contradiction: whereas the potential richness of group situations is often acknowledged and exploited for practical purpose (e.g. Carey and Smith, 1994; Asbury, 1995), focus-group discussions are very seldom regarded as being the result of group interactions and the group is sometimes considered to be 'a bias' which might have negative effects on the subjects' answers.

2.3.1   A focus group: a group without interactions…

In her review of about 200 publications written between 1946 and 1996, Wilkinson (1999) observed that in most cases, the discursive material collected through focus groups was analysed as if it were made of juxtaposed individual contributions. Similarly, Kitzinger (1994) stated that out of 40 published reports using focus groups, she could not find a single one concentrating on the discussion between the participants and presenting excerpts which included more than one participant at a time. The same statement was made by Myers and Macnaghten (1999, p. 173) who stressed that, when methods of analysing the data were used at all, they mostly consisted of content analysis which, by concentrating on the content, 'lose much of the context (and content) of the interaction: why just this was said just then'. In their view, displayed opinions and attitudes cannot be detached from interactions and situations in which they take place. In contrast, they are interdependent with them; they must not be analysed on their own and cannot be understood apart from interactions and situations to which they belong. As Myers (2004, p. 2) further puts it:

> Opinions are expressed in some interactions between two or more people, and opinions have to be collected and transmitted in some way in order to become public opinion. We need to look at how people say things, and how this saying is transformed, as well as what they say.

By analysing the same excerpt of a focus-group discussion with various tools used in conversation analysis, discourse analysis, pragmatics and rhetoric, Myers showed that we need a range of approaches to deal with these problems.

In brief, the group dimension of focus groups seems to constitute a sort of blind spot within this research field (Wilkinson, 1998).

2.3.2   The group as a bias

When researchers allude to the group aspect, it is mostly in order to stress the possible disadvantages and bias due to a group setting. The contribution by Carey and Smith (1994) is a good example of a frequent mode of dealing with the group issue. On the one hand, the authors stressed that 'the group context cannot be teased out of the focus-group data' (ibid. p. 123) but on the other hand, they considered that 'the major pitfall of the focus-group technique is the potential impact of censoring and conforming' (ibid. p. 124). This claim implies that a group discussion might have undesirable effects, as for example conformism, compliance, polarisation, etc. It then indirectly leads to the following question: how can we avoid or control the bias provoked by the group-effect in a focus group? This assumption becomes quite explicit in other contributions. For example, at the beginning of their chapter, Albrecht et al. (1993, p. 51) announced that 'this chapter is about the process of communication that occurs in the focus group and how this process impacts the validity of the data obtained from focus-group sessions'. They further discussed the way in which it is possible to have 'opinions that are deeply ingrained and personal' (ibid. p. 56) but that might not be disclosed because of a conformity effect. They also described other 'threats to the validity of focus-group data', such as 'social desirability, low level of trust, face-politeness needs, researcher bias, and deception' (ibid. p. 63). This concern for group issues can also be found in the concluding chapter of a classic book on focus groups in which Morgan (1993) stressed that more research about group issues is necessary, and exemplified the kind of studies which are needed on topics such as social desirability and conformity. More recently, the same argumentation can be found in Kidd and Parshall (2000, p. 294):

> Before one can make statements with any confidence about what a focus group or series of groups had to say on a given topic, one needs to assess the extent to which responses may have arisen from conformance or censoring, (…) coercion, conflict avoidance, or just plain fickleness.

Further, they concluded:

> Therefore, the fact that such processes occur in focus groups may raise
> legitimate concerns about the trustworthiness of findings, but in contrast
> to more self-contained forms of unreliability (e.g. inconsistency), it does
> not necessarily vitiate them completely. (ibid. p. 295)

As can be seen from these quotations, in the few contributions that concern the group, reference to work carried out in social psychology concerns the possible negative effects of the group. This negative vision of the group has a long history in social psychology (see for example Morgan and Thomas, 1996). As Graumann (1988) showed, it rests on the assumption that group behaviour can be explained by individual properties of the human mind, such as instincts and suggestibility. In this sense, the main part of focus-group research belongs to what Graumann called 'an individualist conception of social psychology' which, in the view of one of its most well known representatives Floyd H. Allport, coincides with the experimental behavioural approach. This individualistic tradition in social psychology was also stressed by Moscovici and Marková (2006) who recall that for Allport, 'there is no psychology of group that is not essentially and entirely a psychology of individuals' (Allport, 1924, p. 4).

On a theoretical level, the claims that the group is a bias are based upon a dualist vision of the Ego and Alter. They do not take as a point of departure the interdependence between the Ego and Alter, and assume that a so called individual answer is free from any influence; they neglect the dialogism of communication. On the contrary, if we adopt a dialogical perspective, it is no longer possible to make a clear-cut difference between data collected in individual interviews versus group situations. As Kitzinger (1994, p. 117) puts it, it is not relevant to classify the difference between interview and group data in terms of 'honesty' versus 'dishonesty' or 'truth' versus 'falsehood'. According to her, talking of group effects in general is impossible and one should rather examine:

> The composition of the groups and how the characteristics of any
> particular group may influence what is said (ibid. p. 112); (…) Instead
> of disregarding data from group settings we need to acknowledge the
> different types of discourses that may be expressed in the 'private' and
> 'public' arena, or with peers versus with an interviewer. (p. 117)

2.3.3   The gap between focus-group research and group-dynamics research

All these elements show that, strange as it might seem, focus groups have not been fully recognised as being groups. It means that we cannot assume that focus groups, because they have a potential to study communication in its dynamics, are by definition a dialogical method. All too often the analyses apply categorisation and a classic kind of content analysis and disregard the dynamic features that dialogue offers. Content analysis is not specific to focus groups but it is a classic method for the analysis of any text, e.g. of interviews, narratives, newspaper articles and so on. It is a method based on the categorisation of verbal data and it aims to reduce the complex nature of language rather than to use it as an essential resource for analysis. We may raise another question: why does focus-group research seem so often to be blind to the group dimension? One reason for that might be that this research strand seems to ignore research into small group dynamics which has been carried out in the field of social psychology. This situation may be explained by the fact that, as we just showed, focus-group research originated in the field of sociology and mass communication (Kitzinger et al., 2004), whereas research into group dynamics is ascribed to social psychology.

In the following section, we propose to return to classic research into small group dynamics in social psychology with the aim of examining whether the way in which it deals with the group issue might be fruitful for a dialogical approach to focus groups.

2.4   A step back to research into small group dynamics

Let us begin with Kurt Lewin, the main founder of the study of small group dynamics and then examine some developments of research into small group dynamics.

2.4.1   The individual-group interdependency: a Lewinian legacy

Drawing upon the notion of field which he defines as a 'totality of co-existing facts which are conceived of as mutually interdependent' (Lewin, 1946/1951, p. 240), Lewin considered that individual behaviour cannot be understood independently from its psychological ecology or what he also calls the individuals' life space, i.e. 'the person and the psychological environment as it exists for him' (Lewin, 1943/1951, p. 57). Life space is a 'quasi-stationary equilibrium' (or dynamic equilibrium) which results from the joint action of a certain physical and social environment, and a certain psychological state. In

Lewin's view, the individual and the environment are not to be conceived of as two distinct entities but as two elements belonging to the same field. The physical and social environment in which an individual acts limits his/her life space, but life space is not a simple reflection of the physical and social environment. Life space moves along with the changing physical and social environment. A change in the life space is reflected in a change in the individual's behaviour, and conversely the individual's behaviour provokes changes in the physical and social environment. This is why the notion of psychological field is closely linked with time. Any behaviour depends on the psychological field at that time.

Applying the concept of field to the study of groups, Lewin showed that defining a group by the similarities among group members is typical of a 'descriptive classificatory epoch' that should be superseded in favour of a definition based upon interdependency. Claiming that there is no magic behind the fact that groups have properties of their own and that the study of groups should get rid of any metaphysical flavour, Lewin acknowledged that a group has some specific properties that do not simply derive from the participation and behaviour of each member. The group is a dynamic totality. For him:

> In the social as in the physical field the structural properties of a dynamic whole are different from the structural properties of subparts. Both sets of properties have to be investigated. When one, and when the other, is important depends upon the question to be answered. But there is no difference of reality between them. (Lewin, 1947/1951, p. 147)

Lewin's theory requires us to take the individual and the situation as a unit of observation and, hence, to carry out a fine-grained analysis of the situation in which individuals act. Thus, the very notion of 'individual' as it is classically defined in psychology is jeopardised. What Lewin actually proposed was a dialogical stance of the relationship between individual and group (or environment). His model is based upon a holistic vision of the individual and the group. In this view, a group is not a factor which influences individual behaviour. Group processes do not constitute a bias with respect to individual behaviour. The following quotation, which might just as well have been written by one of the more recent systemic theorists (see for example Watzlawick et al., 1967), illustrates the modernity of Lewin's propositions:

> Any kind of group action or individual action, even including that of the insane, is regulated by circular causal processes of the following type: individual perception or 'fact-finding' – for instance, an act of accounting

> – is linked with individual action or group action in such a way that the
> content of perception of fact-finding depends upon the way in which
> the situation is changed by action. The result of the fact-finding in turn
> influences or steers action. (Lewin, 1947/1951, p. 199)

Moreover, Lewin's notion of environment is dynamic and is not reduced to its objective characteristics. In this respect, it is very close to the definitions that are now emerging in the field of ethnomethodology or conversation analysis, in which the context is not defined as an external and stable entity but rather as a resource that subjects are liable or not to consider in their interactions. Context is thus a psychological notion which depends on the meaning that the participants attribute to it (their 'definition of the situation', Thomas and Znaniecki, 1928/1981). In this view, a relevant context is a temporary and emergent result of the participants' interactions (e.g. Goodwin and Duranti, 1992) or, in the terms used by Rommetveit (1992), a temporarily shared state of intersubjectivity in which each subject is temporarily 'attuned to the attunement of the other'. By seeing the context as the result of subjects' activity (or both external and internal framings), Lewin's model took account of social change, as shown in particular in the series of studies carried out by Lewin (1947/1951) and his colleagues on changing food habits.

From a dialogical perspective, there are, however, important limitations in Lewin's work. The first is that even though Lewin's model is an alternative to most models in social science, it nevertheless proposed a vision of social change based on a static model (Marková, 2003a). As Moscovici and Marková (2006) pointed out, Lewin's concept of quasi-equilibrium remains static in that it tends to give precedence to equilibrium rather than to destabilising of the status quo and, by so doing, puts more emphasis upon pressure towards conformity than upon deviance and innovation. This is also the reason why the notions of role and status that stem from this research strand should be apprehended less statically by including the way in which roles are constructed and modified as the interaction goes on, an idea which will be further developed through the notion of activity roles and positionings.

A second limitation is that Lewin and his collaborators did not pay any attention to the study of verbal interactions. For them, communication seemed to be limited to 'moves', 'actions', 'forces', expected and intended 'locomotions'. When communications were thematised at all, it was only done quickly and superficially. For example, in his analysis of the life spaces of a husband and a wife, Lewin showed that the husband's and the wife's expectations and perceptions might not coincide and thus might bring about unexpected outcomes. His conclusion illustrated the way in which he treated language:

> Obviously, husband and wife will soon be in trouble if they do not 'talk
> things over', that is if they do not communicate to each other the structure
> of their life spaces with the object of equalising them. (Lewin, 1947/1951,
> p. 197)

As this quotation shows, reference to talk was made through everyday language
(as shown by the use of quotation marks) and communication seemed to be
reduced to putting one's perceptions into words, coding one's inner mental
states. In other words, we do not find here any dialogical conception of language
and communication.

Our conclusion concerning Lewin's contribution to focus-group research
is thus mitigated: on the one hand, there is no doubt that focus-group research
might benefit from Lewin's legacy by considering that the focus-group method
is not only a way of using the properties of the group to produce data, but also
a way of developing (and maybe challenging) the models of individual psychology which have been established in mainstream psychology. On the other
hand, however, it is also clear that in the present state of knowledge, language
and communication cannot be considered as simple means for information
processing and externalising one's thoughts, perceptions, representations, etc.
Thus, what is needed here is a model which, firstly, considers the individual-
group (or Ego-Alter) interdependency and language as a tool through which
the group and individuals are constructed and dynamically transformed; and
secondly, the model should give more space to tensions, contradictions, and
divergences.

In the next section, we shall limit ourselves to highlighting two main directions that group dynamics studies have taken: interaction-based approaches
which try to give an objective picture of group functioning, and avoid making
interpretations and inferences; interpretation-based approaches which, on the
contrary, claim that an understanding of group processes must be based upon
a theoretical model of the human mind, and entail inferential processes driven
by the participants' behaviour or discourse. One common feature of these
approaches was that all these settings were 'artificial' since they had been
especially constructed in order to observe group interactions. Similarly to
focus-group settings, they could thus be considered as a sort of laboratory in
which group processes manifested themselves within a certain framing.

Our aim is not to review this expanded literature but to draw attention to
two divergent, yet not necessarily incompatible, methodological approaches to
group dynamics, and to discuss them from a dialogical perspective.

2.4.2   Interaction-based approaches

In the aftermath of Lewin's work, during the 1950s and 1960s, Robert Bales and his collaborators carried out numerous studies with the aim of analysing the interactional processes at work in small groups, and describing different modes of group interaction (Bales, 1950; 1951; Bales and Strodtbeck, 1951). They analysed many small groups in different situations and were among the first who paid close attention to group communication and who categorised the various types of contributions made by group members. In this context, they developed a coding scheme ('Bales' coding scheme') which has been frequently used for the analysis of group interaction. Based upon the coding of observable actions, this coding-scheme consists of coding the actions carried out by each group member and summing these contributions in order to draw a general picture of the interactional processes at work in a group. The coding scheme itself is made up of twelve symmetrical pre-defined categories which are divided into two clusters of six categories: the first cluster describes a member's action when s/he asks for information (e.g. 'asks for an opinion'); the second refers to a member's action when s/he 'sends' a message (e.g. 'gives an opinion'). With this method of analysis, it is possible to quantify the level of participation of each member, to categorise his/her mode of participation and to differentiate general characteristics of members' conduct: emotionally-oriented versus task-oriented. More specifically, it shows how roles (for example the leader's role) are distributed between the different group members. Bales' coding scheme (and many other coding systems, see Linell and Marková, 1993; Marková and Linell, 1996) was based on individuals' contributions. Verbal interactions were seen as a chain of individual utterances with unambiguous meanings. As a consequence, despite the fact that it started from a definition of the group which stressed the special characteristics of the group as a whole, this coding scheme was basically designed to 'diagnose' the communicative achievements and/or capacities of individuals, rather than the properties of the joint dialogue.

2.4.3   Interpretation-based approach

Interpretation-based approaches pertain to many different theoretical trends. Let us discuss two of them which illustrate contrasting perspectives. The first trend is based on the study of small group dynamics as it was introduced by Lewin and his collaborators Kenneth Benne, Leland Bradford and Ronald Lippitt in 1946 (Benne, 1964). It emerged from the idea that the best way of learning about groups is to be personally involved in a group and to observe its functioning from inside. The settings which were designed for this purpose and which were called T-groups (for Training-groups) present many similarities with focus-group settings. They basically consisted of small groups made up of 8–12 persons who met for a limited period of time (generally for one to three-week seminars) and had regular group sessions. In order to create heterogeneity, the groups were in general composed of people who had never met before and who had different social backgrounds. The groups were led by a moderator (or one moderator and one observer) whose role was not to be a leader but to guide the participants towards an understanding of the processes at work in the group. In the classic setting of T-groups, there was generally no task to be carried out. Participants were involved in an open situation which obliged them to decide how to use the time they were to share together. The moderator was thus a sort of non-directive facilitator who also interpreted the member's contribution as a product of the group. At the beginning these groups were mostly based on Lewin's theory but over time they developed in various directions and drew their sources in various theoretical fields, Carl Rogers' (1961) theory for example.

The second trend draws upon psychoanalytical theory. Psychoanalytical work on groups took a particular turn in England just after the Second World War. It has been considerably developed within the Tavistock Institute of Human Relations by scholars such as Elliott Jaques, Michael Balint and above all Wilfred Bion (1961) a pioneer in group psychotherapy, and in France, by psychoanalysts such as Anne Ancelin-Schützenberger (1972), Didier Anzieu (1971; 1984) and René Kaës (1976; 1993). Starting from settings comparable with those of T-groups and drawing upon psychoanalysis, scholars working in this vein emphasised the emotional dimensions of group processes. They proposed certain concepts that account for emotional alignments and identification between the individuals. They showed how group members come to share assumptions, emotions and phantasms that give them the feeling of forming a group, and tend to 'reduce the boundaries between individuals and bring together the group as a whole' (Morgan and Thomas, 1996). Bion (1961), for example, showed that the development of a group is based upon reference to three basic assumptions which go back to primitive defences (in the psychoanalytic sense of the word): dependency, fight-flight, and pairing. Anzieu (1971; 1984) described the same sort of mechanisms and showed that the feeling of forming a group goes hand in hand with the appearance of a sort of 'honey-moon'-like atmosphere that he called 'group illusion' characterised by the members' feeling of forming a unified and homogeneous group. Other concepts referred to the construction of a group psychical entity which, as it develops, enables group members to articulate the feeling of being both unique and being part of a group.

According to these scholars, groups develop specific psychological modes of functioning ('groupishness' or 'groupality' for Bion, 1961; 'a groupal psychic apparatus' for Kaës, 1976) which, at certain conditions, enable group members to share a feeling of forming a group without losing the advantage of individual resources. Finally, the notion of group not only refers to an observable entity (a gathering of more than two individuals) but also to a psychical structure. In other words, this research trend dealt with the two poles which are implied in the notion of Ego-Alter interdependence: on the one hand, preservation of the individual's sense of uniqueness, on the other hand, preservation of the individual's sense of being part of a group and being capable of innovating and constructing in joint action and communication.

2.4.4   Language and communication in research into group dynamics

Altogether, the mass of observations which have been collected through these different approaches showed that group behaviour, attitude and discourse have their own characteristics and are not mere expansions of individual functioning. More specifically, they showed that being part of a group is the result of a developmental process which goes through different phases that are recurrent across various groups (see for example Anzieu (1971) for interpretation-based approaches and Tuckman (1965) for interaction-based approaches). Through this developmental process, members of a group come to display behaviour and discourse that make sense as group productions. Therefore, despite their important theoretical divergences, despite their limits, too, interaction-based and interpretation-based approaches converge on one point: the group is not a bias. Context is not a 'nuisance factor' in communication. Individuals and groups are two sides of the same coin, with moments in which the individual tries to detach him- or herself from the group, and moments in which he or she seeks to merge within the group.

However, despite its merits, research into group dynamics may be subjected to many criticisms. One important criticism concerns the methods used to study group communication. In fact, interpretation-based approaches draw upon discourse and other means of communication in order to get access to psychological functioning and assign meanings to subjects' actions. In order to do that, they have a broad set of concepts which refer to intra-psychical as well as to inter-psychical functioning. However, as was the case with Lewin's work, they lack an explicit theory of communication or language. Language is viewed as a means which gives access to internal aspects of human activity, but it is not analysed in itself. It is conceived of as being transparent and is ignored in its materiality. As regards interaction-based approaches 'à la Bales', they worked with a communication model which, explicitly or not, viewed communication as information-processing. At that time, this view was in line with the model proposed by Shannon and Weaver (1949). Since then, these types of model have been subjected to a number of criticisms showing that they pertain to a monological stance on language (e.g. Linell and Marková, 1993; Marková, Graumann, and Foppa, 1995; Grize, 1996; Rommetveit, 1998; Linell, 1998a; 2005). In fact, by treating discourse as a chain of individual utterances and by attributing to each utterance a code chosen as a function of the content and form of the utterance, the method suggested that meaning lies within the utterance itself and is, thus, independent of the context in which it is produced and of the subjects' activity of interpretation. It also completely neglected the fact that meaning is derived from the positioning of a contribution in a sequence.

2.5   Focus groups and dialogism

From our brief incursion into research into small group dynamics, two main conclusions may be drawn: the first is that a group is a dynamic entity which has specific properties. As regards focus-group research, this means that we need theoretical models that conceive the group and the individual as complementary, and we require methodological tools that account for the construction of shared assumptions, attitudes and knowledge, as well as the emotional and unconscious alignments in focus groups. The second conclusion is that this field of research is lacking explicit theory and disregards language and communication. Altogether, this step back into classic research into small group dynamics enabled us to propose a dialogical perspective on focus groups.

Focus groups may be regarded as socially situated interactions, with this aspect being the defining feature of focus-group research. Interactions between the participants form both a means of generating data as well as a focus of analysis (Kitzinger, 1994; Kitzinger et al., 2004). The context in which focus groups take place is essential to their analysis. Meanings and contents of the participants' communicative interactions derive their significance from situations in which they take place as well as from many related and socially relevant phenomena. It is because of these characteristics that focus groups can generate rich verbal and interactional data and this is why we can say that they are potentially more 'social' than other methods in social sciences. They allow the researcher to examine dynamic interactions that take place during communication as well as the formation, maintenance and change of socially shared knowledge.

Why do focus groups have a special potential for studying dialogically socially shared knowledge? A focus group can be characterised as being 'a thinking society in miniature' (Farr, personal communication). This characteristic alludes to the supposition that a society as a whole is 'a thinking society' (Moscovici, 1984) and that, in observing society – or focus-group discussion – one can study the formation and transformation of knowledge as well as other social psychological processes. In addition to being 'a thinking society', a focus group is of course 'a talking society'; participants think together and talk together and are stimulated in their thinking when listening to other people's ideas. It is as if the 'strange perspectives' of others (Bakhtin, 1986/1993) stimulate individuals to mobilise their own potentials to develop new insights and associations, and recall those which they have encountered on previous occasions.

Just like different thinking and talking societies, focus groups too are dissimilar in many respects. Even though focus groups are assembled with a demographically homogeneous membership, the group and its members will show heterogeneities of thinking and talking. Partly in opposition to contentions that group processes hide or distort thinking and talking, we argue that socially shared knowledge is by its nature characterised by tensions, contradictions, vagueness and ambiguities, as well as by regularities and recurrent themes that are often exhibited in focus-group data. These analytical aspects have already been documented in focus-group explorations of social representations. For example, these studies include the environment and environmental changes (e.g. with respect to issues of sustainability; Myers, 1998; 1999; 2004), democracy (Moodie et al., 1995; Marková et al., 2001), medical confidentiality (Marková et al., 1995; Grossen and Salazar Orvig, 2000; Salazar Orvig and Grossen, 2004), AIDS (Kitzinger, 2004), genetically modified food (Wibeck, 2002; Wibeck et al., 2004), and the public space in Brazil (Jovchelovitch, 1995; 2007). In these studies, focus groups have often been used together with alternative or supplementary methods like the analysis of media/newspaper articles, questionnaires etc.

Through the study of communicative processes in focus groups, we also learn how people interpret and re-construct social phenomena, change their meanings and create new meanings. Our ideas, images and social realities are more vivid when society undergoes a crisis or a change due to a political, economic or other kind of upheaval. Under such circumstances communication becomes particularly rich.

This complex and social nature of the data in focus groups is both the source of richness of ideas and interactions and a challenge for the researcher. As a source of richness of ideas and interactions, focus groups can provide us with insight into the formation and change of social representations, beliefs, knowledge and ideologies that circulate in societies. In focus groups people elaborate on and thematise particular social objects. But the richness of language and interactions in focus groups also presents challenges for the analysts; language and interactions are not transparent and they can reveal as well as hide the participants' social representations, beliefs, emotions and otherwise. Each participant brings into the focus group his/her own experience, whether linguistic, topical, emotional, social and otherwise, thus contributing to it something new and indeterminate. At the same time dialogue reflects the participants' socially shared knowledge, whether of the topic, or of relevant social skills, relationships and otherwise. This also means that a single dialogue is never a finished product and while embedded in the past, it is open towards the next encounter.

If dialogism conceives communication as the primary feature of language, then focus groups are a method to study communication in interaction. In and through communication participants convey their thoughts about social realities, and feelings of their past and the present experience, as well as anticipations of the future. They draw upon and transform social knowledge when they talk and think together. We assume that natural conversations and focus groups can provide us with essential data for research into socially shared knowledge and that they have a potential to take on board different forms of socially shared knowledge. These data, it is to be hoped, can examine how focus groups can realise this potential.

Moreover, focus groups illuminate the holistic aspects of symbolic communication. We assume that what is said and argued about is not only a local activity here-and-now but that language in real social interactions and sense-making involves socio-cultural aspects of dialogue; the ways in which people generate meanings in the group dynamics of multi-party interactions; the kinds of communicative activities that participants in focus groups perform. For example, giving a name to something or to someone may involve complex social psychological processes like prejudice, discrimination, ceremonies and so on. Through these the participants in focus groups may hide and reveal their religious beliefs, ideologies, scientific convictions and social representations.

Finally, communication in focus groups displays manifold heterogeneities. These involve different kinds of temporary and more permanent 'identities' and perspectives expressing the participants' relations to third parties like other co-participants, invisible groups and societies. As the participants co-author their dialogical positions, they deepen their understanding and misunderstanding and negotiate their positions through hidden and open polemics, as well as external and internal dialogues with one another. These invisible loyalties do not make the task of the researcher easy but it is important to bear them in mind when carrying out focus-group research. Communication continuously moves in several directions. On the one hand, participants take over perspectives from one another and aim to develop their intersubjective understanding and closeness of perspectives. At the same time, they set their own perspectives through which they affirm themselves and strive for their social recognition. In focus groups participants confront their ideas and let them clash in open and hidden polemics and in internal and external dialogues with one another. Taking the perspective of the other and setting one's own perspective go hand in hand.

2.6   The use of analytical tools in the study of focus group: four main assumptions

The above dialogical considerations about focus groups have specific consequences for the analytical tools that could be used in order to analyse focus-group discussion and to account for the construction of socially shared knowledge. We have identified four main assumptions on which analytical tools should be based if we want them to be congruent with a dialogical approach to focus groups.

2.6.1   Considering focus-group discussions as group discussions

This principle means that two fundamental elements have to be taken into consideration. The first is that a group discussion does not develop in a social vacuum and that the context in which the participants of a focus group interact is not transparent. More particularly, the specific way in which a focus group is set up constitutes an external framing which orientates the participants' actions. However, talking of external framings does not mean that the participants' actions are determined by the objective characteristics of the group or the context in which it takes place. The interactions as they develop within the group also create a context, or what we shall call an internal framing. The subtle interplay between external and internal framings gives way to specific communicative activity types that need to be analysed in themselves. The second element to consider is that focus-group discussions are not totally comparable with dyadic interactions. They allow specific modes of interactions that can be partly grasped with the notion of multi-party talk. Thus, analysing focus-group discussions requires us to take into account the potentialities of multi-party talk and to closely examine what Goffman (1981) calls the 'participation framework'.

2.6.2   Considering the subject's heterogeneity

This principle is based upon the notions of double dialogism and internal dialogism that have been introduced in Chapter 1 and leads to assuming that the subject (or what will be called the 'speaking subject') is heterogeneous, that is to say has different social identities and may talk from different positions. As a consequence, even when there is only one person speaking in a group, it becomes relevant to ask an apparently self-evident question: 'who speaks in a focus group?' Asking this question will require us firstly to account for the fact that dialogue refers not only to an actual discussion between co-present participants, but also to dialogues with absent or virtual participants, or even to dialogues with oneself; secondly to identify the different voices in the discourse (even in that of one participant) and the different positionings that a single participant is liable to adopt in his or her discourse.

2.6.3   Considering a focus-group discussion as circulation of ideas

Drawing upon Bakhtin's dialogism, this assumption states that discourse is always addressed to somebody but that it also can be considered as a response to previous discourse, which has occurred before and elsewhere. This double-faced notion of addressivity/responsivity means that the analysis has to consider the way in which discourse is constructed: how participants interpret each other's discourse, how they link their own discourse with the discourse of the other participants, how they create new and original ways of putting a certain argument into words, how they bring certain topics to the floor, develop and transform them in the course of their discussion, how they come to agree or disagree with certain topics, etc. In other words, any analysis of data has to consider phenomena of agreement-disagreement, as well as all the discursive means that are used to reach states of mutual understanding. As a consequence, analysis of focus-group discussions has to account not only for what is said but also for how it is said, for whom it is said, and in which communicative activity types.

2.6.4   Considering a focus-group discussion as a situated activity which relies on historically and culturally shared social knowledge

This assumption, which concerns the relationship between situated discussions and socially shared knowledge, might be regarded as more controversial. In fact, considering that focus-group discussions are not mere externalisations of prefixed socially shared knowledge might lead to opting for a 'here-and-now' analysis of the participants' discourse. Rejecting classic content analysis because it assumes that discourse is literally the 'ex-pression' of 'contents' (presumably 'contents of the mind') would then lead to analysing the discursive data as if they were mere products of the ongoing interactions. By so doing, it would disregard that the participants are members of larger and various groups which are historically situated. Considering discourse as a 'product of the mind' or considering it as the immediate product of the interaction leads in both cases to a decontextualised view of human cognition. In our view, taking full consideration of the context in which focus groups take place and of the discursive processes at work in no way excludes the fact that participants of focus groups, as members of various social groups, share a great deal of social knowledge and participate in social life on the basis of implicit knowledge and routines. In what follows, we shall examine how these four assumptions might apply to focus-group data.

Notes

1   See the list of selected literature on methodological issues in Appendix 1.

3 Dialogical analyses of focus groups: data and analytical approaches

3.1 Introduction

As we saw in Chapter 2, the focus-group method provides rich material but the ways in which focus-group data are analysed (if analysed at all) often reduce this richness to a list of contents which participants have discussed. So, the analytic challenge is to maintain the dialogical complexity of the focus-group discussion, while we move to the analysis. Practically, one way of coping with this demand is to analyse the material with various analytical tools and from different angles. Before developing in detail the various analytical approaches in the next chapters, we shall present a brief comprehensive overview indicating how our analytical assumptions could be put into practice. We shall start from a long excerpt of a focus-group discussion that aims to identify the types of observations required to account for these assumptions and to provide some pointers to the empirical chapters. By presenting these analytical assumptions at work, we do not intend to provide methodological tools but to point to various features of interactions and discourse that could be captured if we adopt a dialogical stance. Moreover, we do not claim to cover all the aspects which could be captured through a dialogical lens. More modestly, we shall present only those analytical assumptions with which we are familiar through our own work.

Let us first present the focus-group data used in this book.

3.2   Presentation of the focus-group data

The focus-group material which is discussed in this book was collected in several countries (United Kingdom, France, Sweden, Switzerland and Czech Republic). The focus groups discussed different topics which have some relevance in our social world, such as genetically modified food, democracy and medical confidentiality. They involved members of different social groups. The focus-group material was collected by various methods. They included, on the one hand, talks about moral dilemmas, namely situations constructed by the researcher in order to stimulate a debate and on the other hand open discussions and debates prompted by material such as newspaper articles, advertisements (for details, see Appendix 2).

3.2.1   The moral dilemma focus groups

In this first corpus of data, all focus groups have been set up according to a procedure which consisted of presenting the focus-group members with a series of vignettes containing a 'moral dilemma'. The group members had to discuss this dilemma and to make a decision on how it could be solved.

One part of the corpus contains data on moral dilemmas exploring social representations of responsibility (Marková et al., 2000; Orfali and Marková, 2002; Collins and Marková, 2004). An example of such a moral dilemma is the following:

> You are Chief Medical Advisors in the Ministry of Health. Your primary task at present is to contain the spread of HIV/AIDS. People with HIV and AIDS are protected by medical confidentiality. This means that the doctor must not tell either his/her professional colleagues or the patient's spouse or anybody else that the patient has HIV. However, if the patient does not behave responsibly he or she can infect other people. As a group of advisors you are responsible for the health of the public. What advice would you give to the Minister in resolving this dilemma?

Most examples used in this book come from another corpus of data. They are taken from a study carried out by Grossen and Salazar Orvig (see Grossen and Salazar Orvig, 2002; Salazar Orvig and Grossen, 2004). In this study, each group was presented with five vignettes and asked to make a decision on a topic of medical confidentiality in relation to HIV-positiveness. This topic introduced a dilemma between the patient's right to privacy and the protection of public health. The participants of this study were French speaking university students from Paris (France), Lausanne and Neuchâtel (Switzerland) (for more details, see Appendix 2). The formulations of the five moral dilemmas, which were slightly adapted to the specificity of the cultural context, were the following:

'Day Nursery' dilemma

A little two-year old girl, Elodie, became HIV-positive after a blood transfusion. The girl is in treatment and is well. In order for her to have contacts with other same-aged children, her parents regularly put her in a day nursery which cares for about twenty children. The paediatrician who is consultant for this day nursery knows that Elodie is HIV-positive but the other parents do not. Should the paediatrician inform the other children's parents?

'The Couple' dilemma

Jean and Pauline have been married for a long time. For several years, Pauline has regularly had extra-marital affairs in which she only occasionally protects herself. After she asked her doctor for a HIV test, it came out that she is HIV-positive. But she did not tell her husband. Now, it happens that her doctor is also her husband's doctor. The latter has known the couple for a long time and has a trust relationship with both of them. Should the doctor tell Jean that his wife is HIV-positive?

'Work' dilemma

You have a basic training in medicine and are the head of the health department of [the canton of Vaud, Neuchâtel or the French DDASS]. You find on your desk a letter signed by several hospital directors who ask you to allow them to require HIV-tests when they hire new people. As the person responsible for the health department, should you give them this permission?

'Dentist' dilemma

You are a patient of a dentist you appreciate very much and who is well known for his competence. Now, this dentist became HIV-positive and continued working without taking any particular care when he treats his patients. Should the doctor who follows this dentist report this case to the dentists' professional order?

'Sport' dilemma

George has been playing in the [Boxing Club for the focus groups in Lausanne and Neuchâtel] versus [Rugby Club for the focus groups in Paris] of his town since he was an adolescent. Now, he became HIV-positive after a blood transfusion. He is under treatment and is well. George does not want to tell the other members of the club. Doctor Dominici, who is the consultant of the club, is the only one who knows. Should Doctor Dominici tell the other members of the club?

The moderator first read out the dilemma, then distributed a printed version of the dilemma, and finally opened the discussion. He or she tried to intervene as little as possible in the course of the discussion. The groups were all conducted in French (see original in Appendix 3).

3.2.2   Open discussion focus groups

Another procedure often used in focus-group studies is staging a fairly open discussion among participants around the issues in focus. Usually, the moderator presents the group with some stimulus material, such as a newspaper article or a set of general questions and then retracts to a peripheral participation. We shall use data from a number of studies which were carried out in Sweden. Two studies focused on genetically modified organisms (GMO): Wibeck (2002) studied genetically modified food in what we shall call the GEF study ('genetically engineered food'), and Bakshi et al. (2000) focused on genetic therapy as applied to humans (the GTD study: 'genetic therapy and diagnostics'). Two other studies based on other kinds of issue will occasionally be referred to: Levin (2003) dealt with major changes in a large public workplace (a reorganisation of a military garrison: the ROM study), and Åkerblom (2003), in the WPC study, discussed more general attitudes to change in the working life and workplace of one particular industrial company.

These different studies had much in common, something which justifies their classification into 'open discussion' focus groups. However, there were also divergences and heterogeneities, some of which are of principled interest, and will therefore be explored in the communicative activity analysis in Chapter 4. Technical details about the number of focus groups and their composition can be found in Appendix 2.

3.2.3   Why two sets of data?

Throughout this book we shall present excerpts taken from one or the other of these two corpora to illustrate various aspects of dialogism. As the reader will see, some excerpts will appear more than once since the 'thickness' of discourse and its multi-layeredness opens it to different kinds of analysis. Hopefully, it will also familiarise readers with some of our data so that the interdependence of our analytic points can be seen more easily.

The fact that these two corpora have been collected by each of us in various independent studies led us to paying serious attention to the variety of focus-group discussions. A quick glance at the way in which the literature on focus groups deals with variety of discussions shows that in most studies, the mode in which the focus groups have been set up, is reported in a section concerning the empirical procedure. However, it is rarely thematised as an issue which needs to be considered if we want to make sense of the participants' discursive production. The underlying assumption of those studies is that the context in which the participants talk together is a sort of scenery which deserves to be described but which is not directly relevant for the topic under study.

As we have shown in Chapter 1, this assumption can be challenged from a dialogical perspective. The interdependence between the Ego and Alter also refers to the interdependence between the subjects' discursive production and the context in which they talk. Without presenting details at this point, let us emphasise one issue that we shall conceptualise: the relationship between the mode of conducting focus groups and the subjects' discourse. This will be examined in Chapter 4 through the notion of framing.

3.3   Dialogical analytical assumptions at work: a first overview

How can we account for the dialogical complexity of focus-group discussions? In order to answer this question, we shall refer to the moral dilemma corpus and discuss a long excerpt taken from 'The Couple'. 'The Couple' dilemma is the third vignette that the participants in this group, Anabelle, Monique and Joël, who are all students in psychology, are requested to discuss.

Excerpt (1) LAU1A: 'The Couple' dilemma; translated from French[1]

```
1    Moderator  [...] should the doctor tell Jean that his wife is
2               HIV-positive? (7 sec) ((laughter of several
3               participants))
4    Several
5    persons    Mmh
```

```
 6   Anabelle   and I think yes ((brief laughter))
 7   Monique    I think so too ((brief laughter))
 8   Anabelle   because there is already- there's no more trust in the
 9              couple, anyway because well uh as she has been having
10              extramarital affairs for several years now, I think
11              a third person should intervene
12   Joël       for myself it's yes but (.) ((general laughter)) yes but
13              ((general laugher))
14   Joël       because first of all when you say that the trust
15              relationship is broken, it's yes and no in the sense
16              that it's you who's making a judgment about the broken
17              trust relationship [but I think]
18   Anabelle   [but if she doesn't say it] because [(xxx)]
19   Joël       [yes but] but it's it's I think it's also up to her to
20              bring herself come to the point of saying it, I don't
21              think that it's up to- I don't think you can just
22              simply say (Anabelle: yes but) it, just like that
23              I think the doctor must-
24              has one possibility, it's again- like re-discuss this
25              with Pauline, and bring her to realise the risks she's
26              exposing her husband to and I think that in a certain
27              number of cases, it's impossible to get a person to
28              admit that well it must be said anyway even if it's
29              hard and secondly if there's still resistance at
30              that point there is another way, it's to arrange a
31              meeting between Pauline her husband and uh [of of]
32   Moderator  [with the doctor?]
33   Joël       with the doctor and to say simply 'well uh uh I
34              recently had Pauline uh as as uh a patient (.) and
35              uh I discovered something quite delicate' and to see
36              what Pauline's reaction is, and then to little by
37              little maybe simply explain that the test is
38              positive without necessarily saying that well-
39              ((takes a deep breath)) revealing her private life
40              because there are many ways there is blood
41              transfusion there's (Moderator: mmh) there's there's
42              I mean maybe that she uh
43              well it seems difficult to me because one ought to
44              hide the fact that one injects oneself but let's say
45              there's drugs there are many possibilities
46              yes I agree with you but one should proceed gently
47   Anabelle   well I I am maybe a little bit hard because ((general
48              laughter)) but well I start from the fact that a
49              couple- and well I think that there must be trust
50              within a couple and for myself it seems to me from
51              what's been said that first of all she's an
52              irresponsible woman who - ell if she's already had
53              extra-marital affairs and she didn't protect herself
```

```
54          uh (.) perhaps she needs support yes from somebody
55          else maybe it's true that one should maybe at the
56          beginning get her to admit it herself to her husband
57          but I mean in the meanwhile he doesn't know anything
58          and the relationships keep going on and before he
59          didn't have it and during these last two months he he
60          can catch he could have caught it (.) it's also serious
61          I think (.) because the doctor could have saved his
62          life because well uh she has it already but (.)
```

This excerpt is representative of what a focus-group discussion might ideally be. The participants seem to be willing to cope with the situation, to make sense of the dilemma constructed by the researcher and to consider it as a sensible question. They engage in a free discussion in which they talk together. Having read the dilemma, the moderator intervenes only once with a clarification request ('with the doctor?' line 32).

In this excerpt, some participants are more active than others. Monique, having expressed her opinion just after the reading of the dilemma ('I think so too', line 7), does not take the floor for a while. Consequently, the conversation looks like a face-to-face interaction between Joël and Anabelle with Monique taking the position of a witness of their discussion. However, this does not mean that Monique does not participate: her laughter (lines 12–13, 47–48) shows that she is involved in the discussion.

As regards Joël and Anabelle, they enter a discussion which is close to a widespread communicative activity type, that of a debate where people propose arguments and counter-arguments. For example, Anabelle expresses the view that the doctor should tell Jean that his wife is HIV positive, and argues that there is 'no more trust in the couple' (lines 8–9) and Joël provides a counter-argument based on Anabelle's own argument ('when you say that the trust relationship is broken…', line 14). They express divergent opinions (for example, Joël: 'I don't think you can simply say…', lines 21–22). They bring a number of arguments and their exchanges give way to new arguments and solutions which are in turn submitted to discussion (Joël: 'secondly, if there's still resistance at that point there is another way, it's to arrange a meeting between Pauline her husband and uh…', lines 29–31). They also build new arguments by analysing the consequences of their partner's solution (Anabelle: 'but I mean in the meanwhile he doesn't know anything and the relationships keep going on and […] during these last two months he he can catch he could have caught it', lines 57–59).

Despite their divergent opinions, there is a friendly group 'climate' or 'atmosphere' (Lewin, 1947/1951) which is based upon cooperation. The participants listen to each other, as shown by there being only a few overlaps; they orientate their discourse to each other by linking their intervention with what was said before or by anticipating possible counter-arguments (Joël: 'I think that […] it's possible to get a person to admit that well it must be said anyway even if it's hard…', lines 26–29) or by anticipating clarification requests and reformulating their own discourse (Anabelle: 'well I start from the fact that a couple- and well I think that there must be trust within a couple…', lines 48–49). They make concessions (Anabelle: 'well I I am maybe a little bit hard because', line 47) or mitigate their opinion (Joël: 'yes I agree with you but one should proceed gently', line 46). They also reformulate their partner's discourse (Anabelle: 'perhaps she needs support yes from somebody else maybe it's true that one should maybe at the beginning get her to admit it herself to her husband but I mean…', lines 54–57).

However, apart from the fact that there are numerous mutual references to each others' talk, Anabelle and Joël also draw upon bodies of knowledge which circulate outside this setting as socially shared knowledge (Joël: 'because there are many ways there is blood transfusion there's […] let's say there's drugs there are many possibilities', lines 40–41). They do not only take up each other's discourse but refer to discourses they have heard elsewhere or perhaps just imagined (Joël: '… and to say simply "well uh uh I recently had Pauline uh as as uh a patient and uh I discovered something quite delicate"', lines 33–34); they also allude to taken-as-shared social values such as trust (Anabelle: 'I think there must be trust within a couple', lines 49–50).

In sum, the whole discussion gives the impression of a highly coordinated activity. It contains many intertwined sub-activities: aligning with the moderator's definition of the situation and request, coordinating the turns, managing a relationship with the other participants, managing each other's identities, reasoning about the dilemma, bringing in (or anticipating) arguments and counter-arguments, constructing new solutions, questioning one's own assumption or trying to make them explicit for the others, using discursive strategies to convince the others, etc.

From the brief description we just offered, it is self-evident that any specific analysis, or even a set of analyses, will necessarily be quite limited. Consequently, in the remainder of this chapter, we shall concentrate upon our dialogical analytical assumptions and with the help of the same excerpt, briefly illustrate how they can be applied to focus-group material.

3.3.1   Focus-group discussions as group discussions

Our first analytical assumption is that focus-group discussions have external and internal framings and are multi-party talk. However, since the issue of external and internal framing of the group requires a comparison between different types of focus groups, we shall leave it for Chapter 4.

A focus group is not just a group of which individuals are simply members. Instead, the interactions in different (focus) groups unfold in different ways, depending on which communicative activity types they enact. Therefore, we shall develop several notions to account for the specificity of different kinds of focus groups. These are, in addition to 'communicative activity type' (Chapter 4), 'participation framework' and 'multi-party talk'. While the former will enable us to show how the group discussion offers participants opportunities to participate in the discussion in different ways, the latter will compel us to realise that the members of a group are also members of larger social communities.

Goffman (1981) used the term 'participation status' to refer to the way(s) in which a participant relates to the others and to the ongoing activity, as speaker or listener, as ratified participants, overhearers, eavesdroppers, etc. Participation statuses can shift from moment to moment, or at least from episode to episode. The related notion of 'participation framework' refers to the total configuration of participation statuses at any given time (Goffman, op. cit., p. 127; see also Duranti, 1997, p. 297).

We can of course also talk about the overall participation framework during a focus-group session. Accordingly, 'at any given moment' each group member has a certain 'participation status'. For example, in Excerpt (1), Joël and Anabelle are those who take the floor, so that we might think we are witnessing a dyadic verbal interaction. However, this would neglect the fact that there are different manifestations of the audience: backchannelling (listener support items) after the moderator's question; Monique's support to Anabelle's 'yes' response (line 6); the audience's laughter during Joël's and Anabelle's turns (lines 12–13, 47–48); the moderator's clarification request (line 32) as well as her backchannelling ('mmh', line 41). All these elements show that Joël and Anabelle address their contributions not only to each other, but also to the other participants who, as ratified participants, are liable to monitor their interaction, by explicit support, clarification requests, laughter, or other non-verbal reactions that a simple verbal transcription cannot grasp.

In this context, Joël's response ('yes but', line 19) is not only an objection to Anabelle's and Monique's responses but an anticipation of the audience's reaction (he has already produced this type of response before). This is shown by the way he pauses, and by the general laughter which follows (line 12). In other words, the participants' anticipated reactions regulate the way in which

Joël addresses the other members of the group, and lead him to using certain discursive and relational resources to bring a divergent opinion.

This example also shows that one important characteristic of a group discussion is that the participation framework is very flexible, with moments in which everybody speaks together, moments of monologically organised talk (long turns), moments of split floor discussions with different subgroups speaking together, moments in which nobody wants to take the floor (or dares to do it), etc. Consequently, as Grosjean and Traverso (2002) showed, a group discussion does not necessarily mean that the group members share a common focus of attention and are involved in joint actions. Various degrees of focus of attention can be observed among group members, ranging from no shared focus to a collective focus and joint actions.

Moreover, the flexibility of the participation framework, as well as the presence of an audience, makes it difficult to determine precisely who speaks to whom. A group discussion allows certain interaction games to be played that are impossible in dyadic or even in triadic interactions, in particular addressing someone with the aim of being heard by someone else in the group (a 'conversational trope' according to Kerbrat-Orecchioni, 1997). What Sacks, Schegloff and Jefferson (1974) called the speaker's 'recipient design' (or other-orientation) is complex since the same speaker can address different parts of his or her utterance to different addressees. Groups might thus give place to 'split recipient design' (see also Linell, 1998a, p. 106, on the notion of 'split addressivity' and 'split audience'). In a similar vein, Linell and Korolija (1995) showed that successive topical episodes (local sequences that are topically coherent, see Chapter 6) often differ in their participation framework; participants may occupy different discursive roles, such as instigator, main speaker, main addressee, indirect addressee, and other ratified or non-ratified listeners.

Considering a group discussion as a multi-party talk draws our attention to the fact that speaking of a 'group discussion' by no means refers to an equally balanced and non-conflicting discussion.

However, despite its interest, the notion of multi-party talk has some limitations, at least if it is meant to refer only to the internal dynamics of a group discussion. We shall therefore use it in a broader sense which includes the relationship between the internal dynamics of the group and external social dynamics. If we turn again to Excerpt (1), it enables us to see that Joël is simultaneously a member of several larger groups or social categories: a man, a student in psychology, a former law student, etc. So the question is: how do these social roles (Chapter 4) in different groups influence the way in which the participants will take on certain roles and identities within the group (in other words their positioning, see Chapter 5)?

The answer to this question is not simple since we cannot assume that the participants 'import' their social identities within the focus group. In fact, these social identities are liable to be negotiated and even put in jeopardy by the actual interactional group dynamics. This means that one and the same subject may take on different roles during the same situation (both different activity roles and different orientations to social roles, see Chapter 4). This is precisely what the notion of positioning invites us to observe: the dynamics of the various activity roles that a participant is liable to take on during a focus-group discussion. The observation of the speakers' positioning, the dynamics and heterogeneity of their positionings (see Chapter 5) will enable us to examine how roles are performed (and not simply taken on) throughout the interaction.

Using the notion 'party' to relate the internal dynamics of the group to larger social dynamics also means that we need to consider that a participant's discourse may be addressed to absent or virtual parties, e.g. the researchers who organised the focus groups in the first place and will now analyse the data. For instance, the fact that the subjects in our example are students frames their discourse in a certain way and directs it towards possible addressees: in particular towards the researchers who are also their teachers and who set up the situation and asked for their participation.

3.3.2   The subject's heterogeneity

Our second analytical assumption claims that the term 'dialogism' cannot be restricted to interactional dimensions but refers to different aspects which are, among other things, related to double dialogism and internal dialogue. More generally, it refers to the idea that any individual utterance is intersected by the words (or voices) of other speakers and involves various kinds of tension between these voices.

This dialogical assumption leads us to propose the notion of 'the heterogeneity of the speaker'. Some pragmatic and linguistic conceptions in the French-speaking tradition are critical of the idea that an utterance originates in the individual mind of the speaker and that it has a unique and homogeneous meaning. Following Benveniste's (1977) theory of enunciation, as well as Ducrot's (1984) polyphonic theory of enunciation, Vion (1998a; 1998b) defined the notion of positioning as the expression of the way in which a locutor presents, or puts his or her own discourse on stage. With different variations depending on the authors, French linguistics makes a distinction between the locutor, the one who says 'I', and the enunciators who correspond to the different points of view, or voices which are expressed in an utterance. This distinction will be further developed in Chapter 5. Within the limited scope of this chapter, it will suffice to stress that heterogeneity means here that a single speaker is liable to build on different voices in the construction of his or her argumentation. These various voices might refer to different pieces of discourse, but they might also correspond to the manifestation of the subject's own heterogeneity: when one speaks, one does not do it from a unique perspective. For example, in the moral dilemma focus groups, some participants had a former training in education, or in health care, some of them were also mothers, still others had completed previous studies in law or in architecture, etc.

The consideration that the speaker presents heterogeneous features has a dramatic consequence, which has been neglected by previous research into focus groups. In fact, it means that it is not self-evident to identify who is speaking in a focus group. Any speaker can take on different identities, speak from different perspectives and evoke voices which refer to other discourses, be they discourses that have actually taken place at other occasions, or virtual discourses that the speaker only imagines. The subject's positioning during the focus-group discussion is tightly intertwined with the notions of discursive role and activity role. However, the notion of 'positioning' draws our attention to the fact that a role is not fixed once for ever, it is dynamic and changes throughout the group discussion. Hence, an important analytical tool is to examine the subject's positioning.

While these theoretical notions will be fully developed in Chapter 5, let us now briefly turn back to Excerpt (1) and examine it with this new analytic lens.

After the moderator's reading of the dilemma, Anabelle (line 6) provides an explicit 'yes' answer. However, she does not just say that the doctor should tell Jean, but indicates that she positions herself as 'I' ('and I think yes'). So do also Monique ('I think so too', line 7) and then Joël ('for myself it's yes but...', line 12), so that at this stage, each participant has given his or her opinion in a way that explicitly indicates that they assume the responsibility of what they say.

However, Joël's answer is, as he says, a 'yes but' which brings a restriction to the clear-cut 'yes' answer given by Monique and Anabelle (who at this point form a party in the sense discussed above). We can then see how in the formulation of his disagreement, he leans his discourse on the answer given by

Anabelle and reaffirms his opinion with respect to his own I-positioning: 'when you say… (line 14) … in the sense that it's you who's making… (line 16) … but I think (line 17) … I don't think you can simply say… (line 21)'.

Now, Joël's positioning appears to be more complex. In fact, his argument against Anabelle's argument ('there is no more trust in the couple', lines 8–9) implies that Anabelle should not make a 'judgement about the broken trust relationship' (lines 16–17). By making a judgement about what Anabelle should or should not do and by adding that it should be up to Pauline to tell her husband, he implicitly takes a doctor's positioning, that of a generic physician who obeys a more or less explicit professional rule: neutrality with respect to the patient's decision. Note that this rule belongs to most of the deontological codes of psychologists or psychotherapists and that therefore, as a future psychologist, Joël might know about them. In other words, he implicitly invokes the voice of professional deontology which stipulates that a health practitioner should not influence his or her patients.

In the following part of his discourse (lines 22–41), it becomes more and more evident that Joël takes the doctor's perspective. This time, however, he identifies himself not with a generic physician but with Jean's and Pauline's doctor by telling what he should do and even by reporting what he should say. He lends his own voice to a virtual doctor's voice by using reported speech ('well uh uh I recently had Pauline uh as as uh a patient and uh I discovered something quite delicate', lines 33–34). In this piece of reported speech the 'I' is now the doctor and this shift from an 'I' referring to Jöel's own opinion to an 'I' representing a doctor, can be seen as an identification move: now Joël is, in some sense, the doctor who meets Jean and Pauline and has to talk with them.

If we move further in Excerpt (1) and look at Anabelle's last turn (line 47), we observe a similar identification move which has, however, different points of departure and arrival. Anabelle first formulates a general rule that was implicitly present before ('there is no more trust in the couple', line 8). This rule does not belong to the medical institution but to another social sphere, marriage as an institution: 'there must be trust within a couple' (line 49). It leads her to make a judgement on Pauline ('she's an irresponsible woman', lines 51–52), to make a concession for Joël ('perhaps she needs some support', line 54) and, as a last resort, to take the husband's perspective by invoking his situation 'who doesn't know anything' (line 57), who 'could have caught it' (line 60).

This analysis shows that the dialogue between Joël and Anabelle can be apprehended at least at two levels: at that of their actual discussion in the focus group and at that of a dialogue between two institutions: the institution of health professions (which sees neutrality as a valuable deontological rule) and the institution of marriage (which sees trust as the very foundation of a close relationship.)

3.3.3   A focus group as a circulation of ideas

What we get in Excerpt (1) are not isolated utterances but questions, responses, self- and other-reformulations, oppositions, agreements, concessions, repetitions, echoings, etc. which are both responses to previous discourse and initiatives to what may follow. Thus, each contribution is the result of a step-by-step and collective construction which dynamically creates the context for the next contributions (internal framing). During this discussion, the response to the dilemma is examined from different viewpoints. The discussion takes up various topics, brings in different arguments and counter-arguments and provides space for agreements and disagreements. The participants also tend towards certain communicative activity types depending on their own framing or definition of the situation. Their contributions draw upon contextual resources which are constructed by the dynamics of discourse, as well as upon external resources, for example medical knowledge about AIDS and its mode of transmission, moral assumptions concerning what a couple should be, or the way one should behave when having extra-marital intercourse (Anabelle: 'she is an irresponsible woman', line 52), role expectations (what is the physician's role in such situations), etc.

So, in Excerpt (1), Anabelle's argumentation for her 'yes' response (line 6) shows that her interpretation of the specific communicative activity type is what could be expected in this context; one should provide arguments and not only give responses to the dilemma. However, her contribution is also an anticipation of a possible disagreement. Joël actually expresses his disagreement (line 21) in a way which even makes it into a sort of moral disapproval of Anabelle's opinion. He calls into question Anabelle's assumed contextual background of the situation (lack of trust in the couple) and offers an alternative solution which makes it possible to have the husband informed and to protect Pauline's privacy. By so doing, he argues for a compromise, namely for a solution other than a simple 'yes/no' response, but nevertheless proposes a response which is close to that of Anabelle: if Pauline does not agree to tell her husband, then the physician could tell him, provided that he did not disclose the contamination mode. In response to Joël, Anabelle reformulates her main argument ('there is no more trust in the couple anyway', lines 8–9) in a slightly different form. Instead of focusing upon the couple Jean and Pauline, she produces a generic and mitigated discourse about trust in a couple ('and well I think that there must be trust within a couple', lines 101–103) and adds an argument (the risk of contamination) which is new in this dilemma but was already discussed in the two previous dilemmas, and which makes her solution more acceptable for Joël.

This example shows that a focus-group discussion is not simply an arena in which the participants display pre-existing (or preformed) ideas, opinions, representations, etc. Confronting the other members of the group, the participants are provided with an opportunity to construct new forms of reasoning and to make them explicit for the others and for themselves. In this regard, disagreement is an interesting phenomenon to observe.

As we shall see in Chapter 6, a focus-group discussion deals with various themes that can first be analysed through a dialogical analysis, and can then be further analysed by considering how they are transformed throughout the interaction, and how they are brought onto the floor through various discursive devices, such as analogies, metaphors, metonymies, prototypical examples, etc.

3.3.4   Knowledge taken-as-shared

Excerpt (1) shows in a very clear way that Joël's and Anabelle's argumentation is organised around the notion of trust, even though they do not thematise it in the same way. In fact, the resources that they use to defend their opinions and construct their argumentations are based upon a social value (trust) that they interpret and contextualise for the purpose of their discussion and the specificity of the situation in which they participate.

For this group, as for others, the notion of trust plays a central role in the participants' approach to discussing the dilemma. It is associated with an evaluation of the risk that someone in contact with a HIV-positive person runs of being contaminated. In Excerpt (1), trust is discussed in the context of relationships within married couples. Starting from the information that Pauline had extra-marital affairs, Anabelle infers that 'there's no more trust in the couple, anyway' (lines 8–9). By so doing, she not only displays her assumption, she also refers to knowledge taken-as-shared (trust in a couple) which is also one of the institutional bases of marriage.

This is precisely the assumption that Joël questions. In fact, he puts emphasis neither on trust in the couple, nor on trust between Jean and the doctor (as does Anabelle). Instead of stressing the lack of trust in the couple, he stresses the need to use the existing trust between Pauline and the doctor in order to escape the dilemma. His expected 'yes' or 'no' response becomes a compromise (leading to Pauline herself telling her husband) that preserves medical confidentiality.

So, even though the notion of trust is the base on which their argument is constructed, Anabelle and Joël do not contextualise trust in the same way: for Anabelle 'trust in the couple' is an overarching principle which justifies the breach of medical confidentiality, while for Joël medical confidentiality is the overarching principle and trust becomes a means for maintaining it.

More generally, this example shows that as is any discourse, focus-group discussions are based partly upon explicit elements and partly upon implicit assumptions that form a taken-for-granted background for communication (Marková et al., 1995). These implicit assumptions, which may concern values, bodies of knowledge, social rules, etc., form part of relevant social contexts in which the participants of focus groups live. Therefore, we need a theoretical tool that may help us to consider socially shared knowledge; for this reason we shall attempt to develop the concept of themata (Chapter 7) that may enable us to satisfy this requirement.

3.4   Conclusion

The aim of this chapter was to illustrate, in an excerpt of a focus-group discussion, how our analytical assumptions could be concretely used.

First of all, we have shown that a group discussion has specific features that cannot be found in dyadic face-to-face interactions. The participation framework, in particular, puts the members of the group in different participation statuses that may change in the course of the discussion and, in some conditions, give way to phenomena such as split floors (or split recipient design), conversational tropes, aside conversation, etc. Moreover, focus-group discussions are composed not only of 'multi-person' talk, but also of multi-party talk, namely of discussions, in which many participants may form a 'party' or, conversely, in which one participant may embody, or voice, different parties. Highlighting the notion of multi-party talk we have shown that focus-group discussions are not free from the social asymmetries, power relationships, alliances, coalitions, etc. that might be observed in any group. In a dialogical approach, the participants of a focus group are considered to be both members of the group in which they are currently involved and social actors who have various social statuses and roles in their everyday life. In this context, the question is: what is the interplay between pre-existing social roles and statuses, and the dynamics of the focus-group discussion? We have suggested that roles and social identities are not fixed characteristics of the subjects but are on the contrary negotiated throughout a focus-group discussion. In order to account for the dynamics of role and identity construction, we suggested the notion of activity and discursive roles which will be further developed in Chapter 4.

Secondly, we have introduced an idea which will be fully discussed and illustrated in Chapter 5, namely that the speaker takes on heterogeneous positionings. The main idea here was that the same speaker might take on different perspectives when he or she asserts something. A participant in a focus group could, for example, speak from the perspective of a woman, a mother, a professional, etc. In other words, she could take on different enunciative positionings. As we shall show later, taking into consideration the speaker's heterogeneity means that many persons may speak through the same speaker. One important consequence is that the notion of social representation itself cannot be conceived of as a set of homogeneous, static and decontextualised 'ideas' that a subject (or a group of subjects) has on a given topic. As we shall see throughout this book, social representations circulate through communication and, therefore, are embedded in social activities which are always contextualised and draw upon various resources of a subject.

Thirdly, we have shown that a focus-group discussion is not a juxtaposition of individual contributions which simply display some pre-established mental states, e.g. opinions, attitudes, beliefs, etc. Ideas circulate, are constructed and transformed in the dialogical process of the discussion, and their circulation is closely intertwined with the way in which the participants manage their relationships, negotiate their identities, are emotionally involved in the discussion, and use some discursive figures and rhetorical tools to construct their discourse and position themselves in the discussion. In other words, it is impossible to make a distinction between what is said (the content of discourse) and how it is said, in which context, for which purpose, etc. In this sense, the issue the participants are asked to discuss is what we call an issue-in-focus, namely a 'content' which is expressed in a certain place, at a certain time, by a speaker who adopts a certain positioning, with certain expectations, etc. In other words, 'issues-in-focus' are embodied and situated; they imply different degrees of personal involvement and identification with the topic under discussion (in our example: the risk of HIV contamination) which contribute to creating a group climate.

Fourthly, drawing upon Bakhtin's dialogism, we have considered different aspects of the notion of dialogue showing that it cannot be restricted to the analysis of the here-and-now interactional dimensions. In considering these forms of dialogue we are raising an issue that was left unquestioned by classic research into small group dynamics, as well as by most research into focus groups: who speaks?

As we have already pointed out, these four aspects form the red thread of this book and will now be developed in the following chapters. However, by stressing these four aspects, we hope to show how a dialogical perspective could be applied to focus groups (and more generally to discourse) and to foster new research in this field.

Notes

1   Transcription conventions

(.)	denotes a micro-pause, a short untimed pause
(1.1)	denotes a timed pause in seconds and tenths of seconds
=	(equal sign) marks latching between utterances, i.e. there is no interjacent pause whatsoever between two adjacent utterances
° °	(degree signs) denote speech in a low volume ('sotto voce')
LOUD	CAPITALS mark words spoken in a loud volume or with emphatic stress
[	(left brackets) on two (or sometimes three) adjacent lines, the one placed right above the other(s), mark the approximate beginnings of simultaneous (overlapping) talk by two (or more) speakers
]	(right brackets) on two adjacent lines mark the end of simultaneous talk (not always marked)
-	(single dash) indicates a halting or abrupt cut-off in the flow of speech
:	(colon) indicates the prolongation of a sound
* *	(asterisks) indicate laughter in the speaker's voice while pronouncing the words enclosed
hh (.hh)	indicates breath (exhalation vs. inhalation)
(A: yeah)	denotes the occurrence of a listener support item, i.e. something said (here: yeah) by a person (A) who does not hold the floor and whose utterance is not perceived as claiming and/or acquiring the floor; the parenthesised utterance is put approximately at the place in another speaker's (the current floor-holder's) talk where it occurs
(may seem)	(words within parentheses) denote an uncertain transcription
(xxx)	denotes speech that cannot be deciphered
(( ))	((material within double parentheses)) marks comments on how something is said or on what happens in the surrounding situation

4 Focus groups as communicative activity types

4.1 Introduction: communicative activity types

One of the basic assumptions of dialogism is that actions and utterances are interdependent with the overarching activity of which they are part (Bakhtin, 1984; Todorov, 1986). At the same time, superordinate activities are of course made up of their constitutive acts and utterances (Linell, 1998a, p. 87). This assumption of act-activity interdependence will serve, in this chapter, as a backdrop for a discussion of focus groups in terms of communicative activity types.

Communicative activity types are defined in terms of, among other things, their specific tasks and framings (situation definitions), activity roles, participation frameworks and discourse types. The concept of communicative activity type is quite closely related to that of communicative (or speech) genre. These concepts have sometimes been used interchangeably in the analysis of talk-in-interaction, despite the fact that they have different provenances. The notion of genre originates in literary theory and the classification of written texts, and has been adapted for application to talk by dialogists and analysts of talk-in-interaction, notably by Mikhail Bakhtin (1986: 'speech genre'; cf. Todorov, 1986), Thomas Luckmann (1992; 1995; 2002; 'communicative genre') and Ivana Marková (2000; 2003a; cf. 'communicative genre'). Luckmann talked about a communicative genre as a routinised solution to some kind of recurrent communicative problem in social life.

The notion of (communicative) activity type, on the other hand, comes from social theory and the philosophy of action. It was introduced into the pragmatics of language first and foremost by Stephen Levinson (1979/1992), who explicitly refers to Ludwig Wittgenstein's (1958) notion of language game[1]. At an early stage, the notion was further developed by John Gumperz (1982), particularly within a cross-cultural perspective.

Despite the obvious similarities between communicative genre and communicative activity type, the former tends to be more focused on forms of talk (discourse) and the latter more orientated to actions, situations, social encounters and settings (Sarangi, 2000, p. 2). One can say that communicative activities comprise more than forms of talk; we are concerned with 'the social situation that the talk is conducted within' (Levinson, 1983, p. 279). Another difference is that many theoreticians seem to think that one could develop a theory of a limited number of genres, whereas it is generally assumed (cf. Wittgenstein, 1968/1958, p. 11, on language games) that cultures have developed an unlimited number of activity types (Gumperz, 1982, p. 166). Thirdly, Bakhtin, Luckmann and others included several kinds of speech events in their notion of '(speech, oral, communicative) genre', such as minor genres like forms of greetings and congratulations, military commands, proverbs and parables, which are different from communicative activity types.

For the purpose of this chapter, we shall develop the notion of communicative activity type. These are social, rather than individual, types of activity. What, more specifically, are they? For a start, we can say that communicative activity types belong to the class of joint human activities (Clark, 1994). Such activities are organised sequences of actions, carried out for particular purposes and accomplished by people together, or at least partly together, in situated encounters in real time. Most, but not all (Clark, ibid.), kinds of joint activities involve some – sometimes a very considerable amount of – talk, and they are 'focused interactions' (Goffman, 1961); in a focused verbal interaction, all participants attend to the same conversational floor. We will call these talk-dominated encounters (and other social activities in which communication plays a major role) 'communicative activity types'. Central concepts in the analysis will be 'situation definition' and 'framing', to which we will soon turn.

Yet recent theorising about genres and activity types exhibit many similarities. This includes the emphasis on dynamics (participants in communicative activities or social encounters are not entirely constrained by norms and expectations, but often have considerable wiggle room), and on hybridities and heterogeneities (Bakhtin, 1984; Marková, 2000). Gumperz (1982, p. 166) claims that '[a]ctivities are not bounded and labelable entities but rather function as guidelines for the interpretation of events which show certain general similarities when considered in the abstract but vary in detail from instance to instance'.

This chapter will, accordingly, be concerned with the nature of focus groups as communicative activity types. In fact, we shall argue that focus groups do not constitute one single typified communicative activity. Rather, there are hybridities, and participants orientate towards several activity norms and genre expectations, responding to varying sets of contextual factors. As an upshot of this analysis, we shall also probe the issue if, as is often claimed, focus groups simulate ordinary mundane conversations.

4.2   Framings and activity roles in communicative activity types

Activities, including communicative activities, are often typified by participants and analysts by reference to 'framings'. This goes back to the analytic notion of 'frame' as proposed primarily by Erving Goffman (1974), who, in turn, built upon other thinkers, notably William James, Alfred Schütz and Gregory Bateson. However, since the Goffmanian notion can be rightfully criticised for being rather static, we will prefer the more dynamic term 'framing' (MacLachlan and Reid, 1994).

Activity framings are 'situation definitions' governing people's understanding of 'what's going on' in the situation, therefore also guiding their expectations of what will or will not, and may or may not, happen there. Goffman (1974, p. 8) says:

> I assume that when individuals attend to any current situation, they face the question: 'What is it that's going on here?' Whether asked explicitly, as in times of confusion and doubt, or tacitly, during occasions of usual certitude, the question is put and the answer to it is presumed by the way the individuals then proceed to get on with the affairs at hand.

Gumperz (1982, p. 101) writes the following about participants' assumptions about how to proceed in a given situation:

> Knowledge of the conversational activity entails expectations about possible goals or outcomes for the interaction, about what information is salient and how it is likely to be signalled, about relevant aspects of interpersonal relations, and about what will count as normal behavior.

References to assumed situation definitions will thus help participants bring some kind of order into their joint interaction; in ethnomethodological jargon, we can say that they 'orient to' the interactional and discursive orders of activity types.

Framings define many aspects of the communicative activities, among them their purposes and activity roles, which are often asymmetric and complementary, with different sets of rights, responsibilities and obligations (Levinson, 1979; Sarangi, 2000). Communicative activity types with different situation definitions ('framings') are court trials, clinical interviews, speech therapy sessions, employment interviews, school lessons, academic seminars, focus groups, as well as different types of informal mundane conversations, such as intimate phone calls, family dinner table conversations, café discussions, dentist's waiting-room talks, car-ride conversations, occasional chats with the neighbour over the fence, etc. Note, with regard to the last-mentioned examples, that the dimension of framing is present in 'ordinary conversations' too, and that there are many kinds of 'ordinary conversations' (Wilson, 1989). Different communicative activity types typically recruit certain discourse types (or genres), such as narration, argumentation, instruction talk, and small talk. Empirical research supports the contention that we should distinguish between different communicative activity (sub)types within most of the above-mentioned categories of (institutional as well as private) talk-in-interaction. That this holds for focus groups too is both an important premise and a conclusion in this chapter.

When the notions of frames and framing have been used in the literature, the reference has primarily been to social framing (Bateson, 1972; Goffman, 1974; MacLachlan and Reid, 1994), that is, how participants understand the social situation and its central activities, how they actually go about organising their interaction and the treatment of topics. But framing has also been a central concept in cognitive theories (Bartlett, 1932; Minsky, 1975; Schank and Abelson, 1975, etc.), within which they deal with how thoughts and topics are perspectivised, or put into a larger context ('cognitive frame') (Tannen, 1993). In practice, for example in focus-group discussions, the social and cognitive dimensions of framing are intertwined.

Another distinction is between 'pre-interactional framing' and 'on-line interactional framing'. The former concerns how participants' apprehensions have been pre-formed or shaped beforehand, for example, in the case of focus groups, through the researcher's instructions and other ways of organising the setting (see e.g. Grossen and Salazar Orvig, 2000, for an account of how the design of moral-dilemma focus groups could be experimentally varied). On-line interactional framing is about how participants actually build their discourse from moment to moment in and through the ongoing interaction, once it is in progress and actually staged ('mise-en-scène'), performed and accomplished. These two aspects are interlaced too. We shall call them 'external framing' and 'internal framing', respectively. While external framing, e.g. the instructions given, the physical locality picked for the focus-group session, and the seating arrangement chosen, is important and must be scrutinised in the analysis, we must primarily start from and work with the internal framing. The reason for this is that for participants, internal framing takes precedence over external framing, or, in other words, the external contexts, such as the pre-forming arrangements, become relevant and effective only if participants actually orientate to them 'internally' (Schegloff, 1991). That is, actual framings (and patterns of positionings, see below) are emergent rather than pre-determined. Issues related to external versus internal framing have been raised by Grossen (1998); among other things, she brings up the question what dilemma is actually discussed in 'moral dilemma focus groups' (see Section 4.5.1 below).

Communicative activity types involve participants exploiting 'social roles' and adopting 'activity roles'. Social roles are patterns of positioning that people orientate to in social life, irrespective of their participation in specific activities, such as focus groups. Examples are role expectations, norms and patterns of conduct linked to being a man, a woman, a middle-aged person, a teenager, an Englishman, a medical doctor, a lawyer, a married person, a widow, a parent and countless others. The membership in such categories may be oriented to, by self and others, in specific activities, such as focus groups. Thus, social roles and identities are differentially imported into situations and to varying degrees reflected in situated behaviours (Zimmerman, 1998).

Activity roles, by contrast, are specifically associated with situated activity types, and concern the shifting positions that participants actually take and give each other in the dynamic interaction. One may want to distinguish between such roles at (minimally) two different levels (cf. Thomas, 1986; Sarangi and Slembrouck, 1996). First, we have (communicative) activity roles proper, such as – in different types of focus groups – chairperson, retracted moderator, active discussant, person playing 'the devil's advocate', interviewer, interviewee, expert (who indulges in conversational teaching), etc. Secondly, there are discursive roles, that is, speaker-listener alignments such as instigator of a topic, main speaker, active (main) addressee (who provides responses, acknowledgements, short evaluations), indirect addressees, mere overhearers, etc. Both communicative activity roles and discursive roles may shift and be exchanged from one sequence or episode (or even single turn) to another, but it is particularly discursive roles that are locally determined. In their self-presentation or alter casting at the local level, participants often draw upon social roles or identities.

The notion of role is, like that of frame, loaded with static associations. In a dialogical conception of the world, we may therefore want to avoid such static notions. Yet, roles can just as well be dynamically conceived, and we could hardly do entirely without the notion. People have had their life's experiences before they come to participate in the focus groups, and as a result of their experiences, they have come to occupy, or be ascribed, social roles or social identities. But they orient to roles in a dynamic way; the expectations, obligations and rights associated with roles allow for situated accomplishments, variation and choice. Participants orient to, or identify with, roles partly and temporarily, as they position themselves to each other, to topics and purposes, across phases and episodes in the interactions.[2] Seen in this way, what actors do in interaction is to position themselves, and their 'positionings' are interdependent, on the one hand, with (partly pre-given) expectations (which is what 'roles' actually are), and on the other, with opportunities that emerge on-line with the situated interaction itself. In other words, roles – just like activity types, framings and social representations – must be conceptualised in terms of what kind of manifest actions in the interaction actualise and stage them (cf. the above-mentioned dialogical principle of 'act-activity interdependence', Linell, 1998a, p. 87). In the analyses of focus groups below, we shall make reference to two kinds of roles, social roles and activity roles.

4.3   Focus groups as communicative activity types

What kind of communicative encounters are focus groups? Are all of them instances of the same communicative activity type? Judging from the literature on how to organise focus groups, you may perhaps get the impression that the answer is yes. However, the main bulk of the 'tool kit' literature (cf. Appendix 1) contains few real-data excerpts from actual focus-group discussions. But if you listen to tapes from actually staged focus groups, or look at transcripts of group discussions from different focus-group studies, you will soon be convinced that such groups display a great deal of variation.

Focus groups can be organised for different purposes (see Chapter 2), and as a consequence, in different ways. For example, in marketing and public-opinion research, they have often had the character of group interviews with one or two moderators adopting a rather interventionist style, often using, for example, multi-unit questioning strategies (Puchta and Potter, 1999). In studies of social representations, on the other hand, focus groups have often been staged in partly different manners, with participants having been assigned other kinds of tasks and with a non-directive moderator occupying a rather quiet, retracted position. However, here too, there are considerable variations. In this chapter, we will discuss in particular the two types of focus groups, 'the moral dilemma' and 'the open discussion', which were introduced in Section 3.2. Using our empirical data, we will exemplify and discuss some of their similarities and differences. After that, we will discuss whether focus groups can simulate natural (informal) group discussions.

4.3.1   Focus groups as embodying a communicative dilemma

Focus groups can be, and have indeed been, organised in many different ways. What they have in common is that they are ad-hoc groups, assembled and organised by a researcher. Therefore, they are in one sense 'artificial', and yet far from as artificial as, for example, the T-groups described in Section 2.4.3. Other features that distinguish focus groups from many informal multi-party discussions, for example, in cafés or during lunch breaks, are that participants may often be strangers to each other, and that the discussion gets tape-recorded. Usually not much attention is paid to the latter condition, but one can nevertheless hardly exclude the possibility that it stays in the backs of participants' minds that their opinions are on record and can be researched. As a consequence, participants may become 'personal' but hardly 'private'. (This is true of most other multi-party situations too.)

Participants in focus groups are often instructed to aim for a free discussion. At the same time, the discussion should be topically focused, and is often monitored by a moderator. Krueger (1994, p. 6), a much used handbook, defines a focus group as follows: 'A focus group is a carefully planned discussion designed to obtain perceptions on a defined area of interest in a permissive, non-threatening environment'. Commenting on this, and following other commentators,[3] Myers (2004, p. 93) notes that this involves a tension between control (careful planning, design by researchers) and permissiveness. We shall return to this predicament of focus groups several times in the ensuing sections and chapters. The tension involved amounts to a kind of communicative dilemma; researchers want to learn about participants' own views and opinions, not those encouraged or elicited by the ways in which the focus group itself has been staged, but at the same time, they need a sufficient focus on relevant issues, not the undisciplined digressions into all sorts of topics that may characterise many informal free-floating conversations (cf. below). The dilemmas involved may pave the ground for a good deal of hybridities in the communicative activities that actually unfold when focus groups are carried out in practice.

4.3.2   Aspects of the external and internal framing of focus groups

A communicative activity type analysis would potentially comprise all relevant aspects of the social, cognitive and interactional contexts of activities, as well as all the discursive and interactional dimensions of the talk embedded within those contexts and making the activity manifest. The theory of communicative activity types can be seen as an attempt to integrate analyses of the 'interaction order' with the 'institutional order' (Sarangi, 2000). Here, however, we will be content with noting a fairly limited number (11) of points of special relevance for the analysis of focus groups. First, these points (marked with # and a number) will be introduced in the present section, and then be referred to in the following sections on our two divergent kinds of focus groups. These latter sections will allow for a comparison across types of focus groups, and they will also make the points considerably more concrete.

#1: Purposes and tasks: The purposes stated before-hand and/or tasks actually adopted and carried out in the activity are of course always of central importance. The external framing concerns, among other things, how exactly the moderator presents the tasks (cf. Myers, 2004, p. 58–59). However, the aspects of internal framing are more important, for reasons already discussed (cf. Section 4.2). Parts of the actual outcome can be indirectly accessed through post-interviews; how do participants describe their own interaction afterwards? However, this method involves certain pitfalls, since participants are often not capable of retrospectively describing their own prior activities in a veridical manner.

#2: The composition of the group: Is the group homogeneous or heterogeneous with respect to cultural background (or age, sex, occupation, etc.)? Do participants know each other from before, and if so, in which capacity? Is the focus group an already existing group, say a work group within an organisation or a group of close friends? If so, is the issue-in-focus related to the group's ordinary tasks and usual activities? That is, does the focus group have a common interactional history beforehand, especially as regards the issue-in-focus?[4] Are participants directly affected by the issue, or are they just members of a society in which the issue is socially important at a more general level (cf. #10 below)?

#3: Social roles (on activity roles, see #8 below): This point is interdependent with both the preceding points. There are at least two types of social roles which may prove to be relevant. On the one hand, participants may orient to expectations having to do with the way the group has been composed (#2 above); in the GEF study (see Appendix 3, and Section 4.4.2), for example, participants could, at least in theory, identify themselves as farmers, GreenPeace members, Christian students, etc. In other cases, participants could identify with roles evoked by researchers' definition of the task; good examples appeared in the moral dilemma groups discussed in Section 4.4.1.

#4: Setting and time: How is the physical scene organised, and what are the time constraints? Can the physical arrangement (character of locality, seating arrangement) be assigned some symbolic meaning, and therefore potentially have an impact on the discussion practices?

#5: Stimulus materials and other cognitive artefacts: Moderators often use stimulus materials as prompts to get the discussion started. What is the nature and impact of the stimulus material or instructions given?[5] Sometimes pictures or texts are distributed, or given out beforehand, in other cases participants are instructed to sort cards, etc. Are texts available and used as references or tools in the argumentation?

These points pertain mostly to the external framing of the encounters (but cf. #1). The remaining points are more directly related to the actual staging of the focus group ('internal framing').

#6: The overall character of the interaction as a communicative encounter: Focus groups are not only (supposed to be) focused in terms of topics, they are also 'focused interactions' in Goffman's sense. But within these limits, there may be variations in terms of 'participation framework' (Goffman, 1981, p. 127) in any interaction at any given time (see also Chapter 3). For example, with regard to focus groups, do we get an open discussion without definite conclusions, or a decision-making session? Do participants talk with (amongst) each other, rather than to the moderator (as in a group interview)? Do they work in order to reach a consensus decision, or to arrive at a common understanding, or are they more aiming for a discussion in which argumentation and counter-argumentation themselves are assigned a high value? Are there other activity types, say a work group, an academic seminar, a school lesson (with the moderator as the teacher-discussion leader), or even a talk show, which may spring to participants' minds and to which they might orient? We shall return to such possible participants' orientations in Section 4.6.

The interaction patterns adopted by the group may of course be influenced by the moderator's interventions: What kinds of questions does she use (Puchta and Potter, 1999)? Does the moderator actively encourage disagreements? But also with a very retracted moderator, participants may orient to expectations that they have implicitly or explicitly adopted, whether these are in accordance with researchers' intentions or not.

#7: The phase structure of the session: An encounter often consists of partly different activities, and these are sometimes ordered sequentially as 'phases'. In the case of focus groups, one would assume the discussion of the issue-in-focus as such to be the main activity, but there is often also a first phase in which participants discuss the premises, the nature of the task, and what they are supposed to do. Furthermore, do argumentation and decision-making end up as different phases? Can arguments raised and opinions stated by participants be assigned the same import, irrespective of which phase they appear in?

#8: The activity roles adopted by the moderator and participants during the main activity: Activity roles may be, for example, discussion facilitator and group discussion participant, chairperson and committee member, interviewer and interviewee, etc., respectively. What are the participation framework and turn-taking patterns actually transpiring?

#9: The (dominant and subordinated) discourse types actually used: What framings (#1–5) will induce participants into recruiting which discourse types, such as small talk, story-telling, seminar discussion or goal-directed decision-making talk? Are these types realised in different phases, or are they rather mixed into hybrid activities? Can goal-directed talk develop into, for example, gossip? Do different discourse types make different kinds of social representations relevant?

#10: The nature of topics: Topics, that is, basically the content of the discourse, or what participants actually talk about, are always of central concern. Focus groups can of course evolve in quite different ways, if their topics are of widely different kinds. We shall deal with topics and themes (at several levels of abstraction) at length in Chapters 6 and 7. Here, however, we want to point out a few aspects of considerable importance: Are participants directly affected (or not) by the issues-in-focus or other topics brought up? Do interactionally delicate topics (Kitzinger and Farquhar, 1999) appear?

Here we come close to yet another of Goffman's (1981) concepts, which we will have reasons to return to later: that of 'footing', which refers roughly to interlocutors' displayed attitude to other participants and to current topics. Duranti (1997, p. 296) defines footing as 'the position or alignment an individual takes in uttering a given linguistic expression'. Hence, footing is related to participation framework (#6) (Levinson, 1988), but we shall use the term in a more special sense related to participants' (displayed) seriousness and involvement: Are participants serious, or are their contributions meant or taken up as joking or ironic? Do they come forth as authentic, or do they merely engage in rhetoric (saying what is politically correct) or 'ventriloquation' (Bakhtin)?

#11: Invocation of absent parties: To what extent is the interaction not only a discussion between the persons present, but also an expression of different interests in society, whether group members portray themselves as spokesmen of these interests or they are opposed to them? Do participants orientate to 'remote audiences' (Linell, 1998a, p. 107f) and other 'third parties', and do they invoke 'virtual participants' (Adelswärd et al., 2002)?

We have now asked a large number of questions. These, and other similar, questions should be explored for each type of focus-group study. Obviously, we can do no more here than illustrate some points. This we will do by comparing, in some respects, the two focus-group types described in Section 3.2, that is, what we have called 'the moral dilemma' type and the 'open discussion' type. After that, we shall discuss whether focus groups simulate informal multi-party conversations.

4.4 Communicative activity type analysis of two kinds of focus group

4.4.1 The moral dilemma focus group

The focus-group studies by Marková, Moodie and Collins (2000) involved a number of moral dilemmas constructed around issues of democracy and confidentiality and administered to focus groups in several West and East European countries. In a partly similar way, Grossen and Salazar Orvig (2002) and Salazar Orvig and Grossen (2004) used a broad array of experimentally varied dilemma descriptions all pertaining to medical confidentiality as applied to circumstances having to do with HIV/AIDS.

In the studies by Grossen and Salazar Orvig, different groups of students were consecutively given a number of moral dilemmas to discuss and decide upon. We shall refer to this focus-group study as representing a 'serialised moral dilemma' type of focus groups. The moderator read each dilemma, and after that, the participants also received a printed version of the vignette. Here, we will draw upon only one of these dilemmas, the one named 'The Couple'. For reasons of convenience, we repeat here the dilemma as it was given to the focus-group participants (translation from the French):

> Jean and Pauline have been married for a long time. For several years, Pauline has regularly had extra-marital affairs in which she only occasionally protects herself. After she asked her doctor for a HIV-test, it came out that she is HIV-positive. But she did not tell her husband. Now, it happens that her doctor is also her husband's doctor. The latter has known the couple for a long time and has a trust relationship with both of them. Should the doctor tell Jean that his wife is HIV-positive?

The discussion of the outcome of this focus-group study will follow the sequence of points stated above, in Section 4.3.2.

#1: The task was explicitly stated as one of resolving a number of moral dilemmas. The participants knew from the outset that they would discuss several dilemmas, but not exactly how many. The instruction called upon the participants to discuss the dilemma amongst themselves. For example, in the case of 'The Couple', they were asked to give their opinion about what decision the physician should make, but it was not stated explicitly that the group should come up with a common opinion or a shared decision. Nevertheless, many groups interpreted the task in that way. In addition, many participants did not just take the dilemma as formulated, but reconstructed it in ways that proved useful for their discussion.[6]

The fact that several dilemmas had to be discussed one after the other frequently led to references between the dilemmas. For example, in (1), the group has just finished 'The Couple', and the moderator has read the second dilemma, in this case 'Day Nursery' (see Section 3.2.1):

Excerpt (1) LAU2B: 'Day Nursery' dilemma; translated from French[7]

```
1    Liliane that's even more complicated than before
2            ((4 seconds; laughter))
3    Florian I think I think that it isn't, see this
4            thing here seems to me less complicated,
5            y'know
6    Pauline mm
7    Liliane no?
8    Florian no I think it is not, yeah, because I find
9            that- (.) after all, my mother is a teacher,
10           she often tells me that parents are more
11           difficult than-
```

Here, Liliane makes a comparison with the previous dilemma, suggesting that the new one is 'more complicated' (line 1), something that is immediately contested by Florian (lines 3–5). This will, at least for a start, frame the discussion of 'Day Nursery' in a manner that was not stated in the instruction, even if it may or may not have been implicitly premeditated by the researchers.

#2: In many of the groups, the participants (students) knew each other from before. In some, they even knew the researchers.

#3: In this setting, task-evoked social roles were clearly more important than external social roles (basically, participants were all students). For example, members of some groups discussing 'The Couple' could identify with the role of the medical doctor or with the husband (Jean). The general point is discussed at length in Chapter 5, where several examples will be given.

#4: The time actually spent on discussing each dilemma (e.g. 'The Couple') was 10–15 minutes. Five different dilemmas were covered in an hour's time.

#5: The group had at its disposal a printed text containing the description of the moral dilemma to be discussed, but this was only occasionally used and referred to in the actual discussion.

#6: For each dilemma, the group had a relatively focused problem to work with. However, the groups defined the task in different ways, some taking it to be one of coming to a (possibly consensual) decision, others one of simply conducting a good discussion (as a kind of experiment). The different, implicitly adopted orientations could therefore be said to be 'The more easily we can decide, the better we are' and 'The more arguments we can produce, the better we perform'.

Sometimes, a single group oriented to both interpretations. If so, the progression of the talk often had some resemblance to a decision-making session, in which participants perhaps tried out some understandings of the premises, then covered a number of arguments and discussed various solutions and obstacles to solutions, and then focused the discussion on forming a consensual decision. Perhaps, one can liken this to a jury deliberation. However, other groups went rather straight to a decision, and only then reformulated their task as one of covering as many arguments as possible, thus attenuating the character of decision-making. For example, here is an excerpt from 'The Couple' dilemma, where the group has just reached a decision (that the doctor should make Pauline disclose her status to Jean):

Excerpt (2) LAU2B: 'The Couple' dilemma; translated from French

```
1    Florian [but precisely that's it that's it it's it's
2            once again a conflict of opinion, it's a
3            new approach well an ideological debate but
4            in a good cause, I dunno I don't think
5            that it's necessarily bad well-
6    Liliane =when you say eh change of conduct would be
7            general it would not be only one thing, so
8            it would result in a change of mental
9            attitude. it's a new [or (xxx)
10   Florian                      [no coz she- well one
11           cannot] it wouldn't be it wouldn't be
12           another person a change of character=
13   Liliane =no I don't mean a change of mental attitude
14           but a change of ideas at least on this topic,
15           for example eh maybe yeah=
16   Florian eh maybe yes=
17   Liliane =at the level of trust relationships
18           etcetera [of being secretive
19   Florian          [maybe yeah but then I don't know
20           at all how to set it up and everything it's-
```

Florian's comment on lines 1–5 may be heard as a kind of summarising remark on the decision taken. However, it is delivered in a partly hesitating mode. This may contribute to inviting after-thoughts, which is what Liliane comes up with (lines 6ff.). This in turn invites a new exchange on a new aspect of the problem, namely, how far-reaching the wife's change of mind would be.

As another example, consider the following excerpt, which is taken from a group discussing the 'Day Nursery' dilemma (Section 3.2.1). The group has discussed the dilemma at some length, and in lines 1ff. below, the moderator summarises the discussion, thus trying to imply that the discussion is closed:

Excerpt (3) LAU1A: 'Day Nursery' dilemma; translated from French

```
1    Moderator  so then you you are for the in effect
2               for maintaining the medical confidentiality
3               in this case, and then it's rather eh it's
4               it's the parents themselves basically if I
5               sum up a bit your your different positions
6               it's it's the parents who who ought to be
7               brought around too to reflecting a bit eh
8               about the relations that that
9               [their daughter should have
10   Anabelle   [there I'd say that if the people in charge
11              know, coz it's after all a situation
12              handling twenty children I think, if there
13              are many eh, well one can just as well check
14              if just this child has got an injury, I'd
15              say twenty children that's still
16              a manageable situation (Moderator: mm),
17              it's clear that then if there are fewer
18              people in charge there, well
19   Moderator  mm and then the eh it it well the- you said
20              that the staff of the nursery ought to be
21              eh informed about it by the physician? by
22              the the parents? eh
23              (.)
24   Joël       I think together
25   Monique    [yeah
26   Anabelle   [yeah
27   Joël       there must be a meeting they must call
28              a meeting for all of them certainly eh
29              (2.0)
30   Joël       and especially remind the staff properly
31              that they themselves are precisely subject
32              to a form of professional confidentiality
32              (Moderator: mm) that they don't have the
33              right to disclose to just anybody
34   Moderator  mm
35   Anabelle   definitely, so that they have the somewhat
36              more personal views of both parents and
37              then (Moderator: yeah) really the medical
38              view
39   Moderator  okay
```

After the moderator has made a 'formulation' (Drew, 1998) initiated with 'so' (French: donc) (lines 1–9), clearly an attempt to summarise the group's stance on the dilemma, Anabelle comes up with additional considerations that will substantially change the decision. She suggests that the personnel be informed about the medical case, thus breaking medical confidentiality, or rather extending it to non-medics.

#7: The sessions exhibited a partly sequentialised phase structure. Often, the groups had difficulties in getting started, and participants were cautious not to threaten each other's faces. This may reflect the nature of the group as an ad-hoc group and the task as one of taking a difficult decision. Some groups had two phases of the core activity, first a deliberation aimed at decision-making, then a more free discussion of producing arguments and counter-arguments (#6).

#8: The moderator acts like a discussion moderator and facilitator, inserting questions to the group.

#9: The discourse type is usually of a hybrid type, aiming for argumentation but also for decision-making. Since the group had a series of (partly similar and partly different) dilemmas to discuss, their treatment tended to change over the series. Later dilemmas could sometimes be treated more cursorily, by reference to the suggestion that the group had already gone through the arguments in connection with the previous dilemmas. However, the particular way of presenting several dilemmas in a sequence also led to some discussions of why the researchers had constructed the specific dilemmas in different ways.

#10: The students were not directly affected by the situations presented in the dilemmas, at least as far as we know. However, in 'The Couple' dilemma, the participants often identified differentially with characters in the story, that is, with the doctor, the husband or the wife. Chapter 5 will explore in detail how participants may position themselves with respect to their social roles and the characters depicted or implied in the dilemmas given.

Participants sometimes slipped into topics that were interactionally marked as delicate. Such sensitive topics could both promote and impede the flow of ideas.

#11: References were made to constructed third parties, as well as to concrete individuals outside the group, for instance, the researchers. As a case in point, we saw in Excerpt 1 above how the participants initiated a discussion of the possible intentions behind different dilemmas as formulated by the organisers-researchers. Thus, the group in a sense acted as if the researchers were an absent third party.

4.4.2   The open discussion focus group

As examples of the 'open-discussion' focus groups, we will exploit data from the four studies carried out in Sweden, as described in Section 3.2.2. We recall that one study, the GEF study ('genetically engineered food'; Wibeck, 2002), focused on genetically modified food (or 'organisms', GMO), and another study (GTD = 'genetic therapy and diagnostics'; Bakshi et al., 2000) focused on genetic therapy as applied to humans. The ROM study (Levin, 2003) dealt with major changes in a large public workplace (the downsizing of a military organisation), and, finally, the WPC study (Åkerblom, 2003) was concerned with more general attitudes to change in working life and workplace organisation (although this study actually concerned one particular industrial company) (for information on all the studies, see Appendix 3). Even though all these studies fall within the category of 'open discussion focus groups', they exhibit differences, due to various factors, including of course the issues-in-focus and the social representations connected to them. In addition, we can say that most of the participants in the GEF study had had no particular concern or familiarity with the issue-in-focus (GMO), whereas the participants in the ROM and WPC studies discussed issues that directly affected them in their daily working life. In the GTD study, there was a considerable variation between the groups as to whether participants were directly affected by the issue-in-focus or not.

We shall now return to our 11 points of external and internal framing (Section 4.3.2) and this time apply them to the open-discussion focus groups. (The reader might want to compare the points to the corresponding ones for moral-dilemma focus groups, as outlined in the previous section):

#1: The moderator stressed that the group discussion should be open, and no evaluation of opinions as being right or wrong would take place.

#2: The GEF groups were homogeneous, but members usually did not know each other, at least not as a group (some knew of each other), and they were differentially affected by the phenomenon of GEF, although none of them had had reasons to discuss the issue systematically beforehand. In ROM and WPC studies, the groups were also homogeneous, and in addition, participants were directly affected in their daily working life by (the type of) reorganisation measures to be discussed.

#3: Unlike in the moral dilemmas, the tasks of these groups did not define any particular roles to identify with. On the other hand, the groups were composed of members of certain social categories (farmers, Christian students, etc.), something which participants were aware of most of the time. Participants could occasionally orient to this membership, particularly if the group was directly affected by the issue-in-focus (#10 below).

#4: With a few exceptions, the focus-group sessions lasted between 50 and 65 minutes.

#5: In the GEF study, the group was given a stimulus material consisting of some newspaper articles on GEF, distributed in advance. When the group met, a tin of tomato paste made from genetically modified tomatoes was passed around. The moderator gave a short introduction instructing the participants to discuss what 'genetic engineering' could mean, and what they thought about it. It was stressed that there were no opinions that were right or wrong.

#6: Each session was fairly homogeneous with no clear phases (except for a short warming-up sequence, see #7). Mostly, the sessions approximated a relatively unconstrained group discussion. Most of the time available was used for trying out attitudes, opinions and understandings (Chapter 6), and no attempts were made to sum up the discussion.

As mentioned (#5), the moderator did not, at the outset or later, issue any explicit demand for a firm opinion or evaluation. Despite this, in the course of their discussions, participants regularly interpreted the task as one of producing arguments for or against the acceptance and adoption of GEF. Indeed, as we shall see in Chapter 6, underlying the discussions was evidently the will to take a stance on the moral issue: is genetically modification good or bad? In other words, sometimes a kind of implicit decision-making, or rather, opinion-making, took place. (And naturally, the moderator did not do anything to obstruct such a discussion.)

It may well be that focus-group discussions as such implicitly invite some kind of evaluation and decision-making. After all, participants in our open-discussion focus groups too were asked what they 'thought of' the issue-in-focus, whether this was gene technology or work organisation changes.

#7: There was less of a phase structure like that of the moral-dilemma sessions above. Often, there was a short starting-up phase, in which there was usually a good deal of pausing, hesitation, laughter and some meta-talk;

some participants stressed that they did not know anything about the issue-in-focus. Yet, they invariably produced a lot of argumentation later on. Thus, participants used most of the time arguing and displaying opinions, sometimes behaving a bit like a seminar group, sometimes more like an informal leisure-time ('café') discussion. The sessions were often closed rather swiftly, typically at the suggestion of the moderator who felt that the discussion seemed to have come to a natural end-point, as no new ideas were spontaneously offered.

#8: The moderator acted as a discussion facilitator, intervening with questions, especially when the debate seemed to have come to a temporary standstill. However, she often occupied a very retracted position, in some groups saying very little.

#9: The discourse type was mainly an argumentative discussion. Some of its discursive figures will be discussed in Chapter 6. However, the different focus-group studies were partly divergent. Those in which the participants were more directly affected by the issues-in-focus naturally engendered more of anecdotes and personal (biographically based) stories. This applied to some groups in the GTD study, for example, one with parents of disabled children (Chapter 6, Excerpt (3), lines 31, 42). Some groups, in particular in the ROM and WPC studies, in which participants were most often affected by the issue-in-focus, included many features of an informal multi-party conversation, at least at the level of a subordinated (marginal) discourse type. See examples and discussion in Section 4.6.

#10: There seemed to be differences between groups directly and not directly affected by the issues-in-focus. The work organisation changes in the ROM and WPC studies belong to the issues having affected the focus-group members. By contrast, the GEF issues belong to the latter, although there were differences between individual groups. The GTD study exhibited most variation on this point. These differences will also be discussed in more substantial terms in Section 4.6.

With regard to sensitive topics, it was especially in the GTD groups that participants sometimes disclosed personal information, such as experiences of miscarriages, in-vitro conception, and thoughts about having an abortion.

#11: Participants often referred to stake-holders in society, and constructed them and referred to them as collective agents, e.g. 'the media', 'the industry', 'the researchers', 'the man in the street' (cf. Adelswärd et al., 2002).

4.5   Hybridities of framing

Even this short review shows that focus groups have not solidified into one stable communicative activity type. Elaborating on this point a bit more, we can say that when subjects have been recruited to focus groups, they often do not know how to perform. The arrangement is not necessarily readily recognisable for them as a known communicative activity type. Therefore, when faced with the task to start talking, participants may have to use knowledge about other more or less established activity types as resources. For example, referring to our previous points, especially #6–8, we propose that focus-group participants may organise their talk-in-interaction in ways that may remind us (and the participants themselves) of communicative activity types such as the following:

- a teacher-led group discussion in school, which may happen if the researcher, say, assembles a group of secondary school students, letting them interact in their own classroom;

- a university seminar, which is near at hand for a group of undergraduates, whether meeting on the university's premises or somewhere else;

- a group interview, in which participants behave as or are interactionally managed into the activity role of interviewees; individual participants are perhaps active only in specific sequences, and in dyadic episodes with the moderator-interviewer, and often the same questions by the interviewer are answered separately by different participants;

- a business meeting of a team in an organisation; in some studies, the same groups can be working teams in normal organisational life too, outside the focus-group study;

- a work group set up ad-hoc in an organisation to discuss and perhaps decide upon an issue of current relevance for the employees at the workplace;

- an informal, though topically focused, multi-party conversation, with non-regulated turn-taking and a moderator in a retracted role.

The basic idea behind the focus-group method would seem to be to exploit the dynamics of a reasonably free, though focused, group (or more precisely, multi-party) discussion. The evidence for this case will therefore be further explored in the subsequent sections of this chapter. However, already here we may point out that there have been many examples of focus groups that have developed in other directions. For example, in marketing research, many focus groups have been staged more or less as group interviews (Puchta and Potter, 1999).

Participants in different focus groups, or even in one and the same focus group, may orient to several different interactional orders (e.g. a decision-making session or a free argumentation), either sequentially or simultaneously in different kinds of interactional blends; this is what has been called communicative activity hybridity (Sarangi, 2000). Some focus groups may indeed be similar to ordinary group conversations (cf. Section 4.6), involving a rather unconstrained interaction and attaining some kind of openness, but in other cases the moderator may find him- or herself negotiated into an activity role (e.g. teacher, interviewer, formal chair) that he or she did not wish to occupy. Some focus groups are more like Socratic dialogues, where the moderator (more or less clearly) guides members into producing stances that are somehow preferred or anticipated by him or her, with features of producing the 'correct' text (like in the traditional classroom, cf. Anward, 1997), thus exhibiting closure rather than openness. In situations like these, the group can display conformity effects; members may be worried to say things that they suspect might be disruptive. Another possibility is that participants may voice different identities, coming out sometimes as professionals, sometimes as individuals talking in a biographical mode, etc. (Hydén and Bülow, 2003).

Even within one single focus-group study, there may develop differences in communicative activity type across individual groups. For example, in the study on genetic therapy and diagnostics on humans (GTD, see Appendix 3) reported in Bakshi et al. (2000), we found that three groups (persons with disabilities and relatives of such persons, members of a parents' union in a secondary school, nurses in a neonatal ward) approximated the focused multi-party conversation, while a fourth group (Master's students in communication) staged more of an academic seminar. The former discussed the issue-in-focus with more of concrete examples, while the latter tended towards discussing conceptual issues and problems of definition, with the moderator acting a bit like a seminar chair.[8]

Naturally, a focus group – like any other multi-party encounter – can involve internal differences among participants, for example, with regard to their commitments to the task and common activity. Some members may change footings to more of non-serious talk or to adopting a rhetorical situation, merely ventriloquating conventional or politically correct talk on issues (Marková, 2000, p. 440). When threatening situations and sensitive topics appear, individuals' ways of relating to each other and to particular topics may change. For example, this was the case in some of the focus groups on moral dilemmas conducted in different European countries by Moodie et al. (1995). While such heterogeneities surface as individual differences in footing, they may point at the same time to larger contexts of political history. Thus, in some countries, particularly those with a totalitarian past, recourse to politically correct talk has been mandatory in many contexts. In other words, focus groups are not necessarily a window to people's true opinions.

4.6   Focus groups as informal conversations

As we remarked in Chapter 2, a focus group can be regarded as a 'thinking and talking society in miniature'. Socially shared knowledge is primarily produced, circulated, negotiated, modified and consolidated in ordinary conversations, as well as in the media, when and where people talk together. Therefore, it does not come as a surprise that in basic social research, there has been a methodological preference for staging focus groups as relatively free multi-party discussions. But the situation is compromised by the fact that focus groups are 'carefully planned' focused interactions 'designed' and staged by researchers. Is it reasonable, then, to say that focus groups simulate informal conversations?[9]

Myers (1998, p. 103) proposes that focus-group participants:

> display a range of opinions – by playing devil's advocate, attributing opinions and accounting for disagreements. These moves show their orientation to making the group work in terms of what they have been told is its purpose: to display opinions, not to pass the time, develop relationships, arrive at consensus, or make decisions.

However, we would argue, on the basis of our empirical evidence, that focus-group participants sometimes do almost all these things that Myers claims they don't do.[10]

4.6.1   Informal multi-party conversations: handling the interaction

For a start, we will use an example from our 'moral dilemma' focus-group studies. It comes from the dilemma called 'Sport', which we repeat here for the sake of convenience (see also Section 3.2.1):

> George has been playing in the [Boxing Club for the focus groups in
> Lausanne and Neuchâtel] versus [Rugby Club for the focus groups in

Paris] of his town since he was an adolescent. Now, he became HIV-
positive after a blood transfusion. He is under treatment and is well.
George does not want to tell the other members of the club. Doctor
Dominici who is the consultant of the club, is the only one who knows.
Should Doctor Dominici tell the other members of the club?

The following excerpt shows how the group reaches a decision. (It should be
mentioned that the group has earlier done the other dilemmas, including 'The
Couple'.)

Excerpt (4) PAR2B: 'Sport' dilemma; translated from French

```
1    Noël      but from (Sylvie: yeah) the moment when
2              there is no risk (.) if you want the doctor
3              is no longer obliged to tell it (1.5).
4              from the moment when there is a risk he
5              is obliged to inform the patient in order
6              (.) just to stop him from falling ill
7    Carine    yeah but the patient! but not the others!
8    Noël      okay if the [the potential patient
9    Marine                [the patient (1.0) right! there
10             you are, the patient not the others! (.)
11             that's what you are saying! [so he doesn't
12             inform
13   Noël                                 [well! because
14             in principle [in principle all  [the people
15             are patients, (.) but (.) there is—
16   Marine                 [NO!
17   Carine                                   [YES!
18   Carine    in fact it's it's surely the same
19             (to Marine:) view-point as the first case in fact
20   Marine    yes indeed exactly!
21   Noël      [but it's it's it's it]
22   Carine    [he says that well one must inform the other
23             players]
24   Noël      what I'd like to say
25             (1.0)
26   Sylvie    [he must tell-
27   Noël      [all the players all the players are pati- are
28             all the the players are patients of the doctor >do
29             you agree with me<=
30   Marine    =so then the other people need not know about
31             it, only the first one=
32   Carine    =that's it!
33   Noël      there is (.) in principle no eh (.) major
34             risk
35   Marine    yes! (.) when (Carine: there you are) in the
```

```
36                first case he said that it was necessary for
37                the husband to know=
38   Noël        =yes! [because there was ] a major risk
39   Sylvie             [there was more of a risk]
40                (1.5)
41   Sylvie       that he would be contaminated but the
42                players were not, (1.0) in any case less!=
43   Noël        =there is I don't know my parents have been
44                married for twenty-one years, if you want
45                in my view it's a long time since they
46                dropped the condom you see!
47                ((2 seconds, general laughter))
48   Noël         in principle you no longer protect yourself!
49   Marine       yes of course! but um ((3.0)) I dunno
50   Noël         whereas here, well in the end you put a
51                a condom on the rugby ball here!
52                ((laughter))
53   Carine       *you put a condom on yourself like that and
54                you'll run no risk*
55   Noël         yes! but it's a hell of a lot less easy to
56                run
57   Carine       (laughingly, makes a gesture as if putting
58                something on her head)) *yeah must* (.)
59                that's when there is a risk
60                (3.0)
61   Carine       well that's it!
62   Noël         that's it!
63   Sylvie       no!
64   Marine       no.
65   Moderator    no?
66   Serge        no.
67   Moderator    oh, that's funny. you arrived at a consensus
68                (1.0) very well (.) why not?
```

Here, the group discusses the dilemma of the doctor of the sports team, when
Carine suggests that the dilemma is similar to 'The Couple' dilemma ('the
first case', line 19), in which the wife had become HIV-positive through
sexual intercourse. The discussion homes in on the problem which cases
face 'major risks'. Sylvie (lines 39, 41–42) concludes that the rugby players
run no, or 'in any case less', risks. It is here that Noël makes a digression,
a rather typically conversational association, linked to the sexual-relations
case, when he alludes to his parents' marital life, which does no longer, he
thinks, involve the use of condoms. This serves as a starting point for a joke
on Noël's part; he suggests that by contrast ('whereas here', line 50), the
rugby players should put a condom on the ball (line 51). There follows a
joking and laughter sequence (which exploits the ambiguity of the French

term for 'condom' in the original: 'capote', which also means 'top, hood', cf. Carine's lines 57–58), surely a time-out from the dilemma discussion. When this episode, which has had a footing different from most of the group discussion, is ebbing out, the moderator steps in with a contribution (lines 67–68), possibly also with a double-barrelled meaning, but this time at the level of the different communicative projects that the participants have been pursuing for the last few minutes. He points out that the participants have both proposed a solution and reached an agreement ('a consensus') (one, or both, of which is 'funny', line 67), and perhaps he proposes that this agreement may also serve as a consensus on the dilemma.

The excerpt illustrates the opportunities given to (and taken by) the group to orient to different communicative activity types within the same focus group. The hybridity of the communicative activity (Section 4.5) is shown in the group's discussion of the dilemma at hand as a problem-solving task, and in their staging of the session as an opportunity for having fun, as in a 'café discussion'. In addition, they introduce a comparison of the dilemmas 'Sport' and 'The Couple': they seem to feel challenged to find out what might have been the researchers' rationale for constructing the dilemmas the way they did.

Apart from the group's change to a footing of non-seriousness for a while, there are other conversational features in (4). One of them would be the frequent moments of simultaneous talk (cf. the overlap marked by [in the transcript) and rapid turn-taking (latched turns being marked by equal signs (=)), and many exclamations ('that's it', 'there you are!', French: 'voilá').

Orientations to framings of informal multi-party conversations can also be seen in our next excerpt, which comes from one of the open-discussion focus-group studies (GTD). The following is an excerpt from a focus group with nurses from a neonatal ward. In this episode, they have just talked themselves into a discussion of eugenics and the reproduction of strong and healthy children:

Excerpt (5) GTD2: 269ff.: cf. Bakshi et al., 2000; translated from Swedish

```
 1    Ylva    yes but your husband is perhaps a bit sickly
 2            so he won't do as a father of children, but
 3            then one would have to take Charlie then
 4            (Anne: but oh yes) ((Linda giggles)) who
 5            lives four houses away like, it can
 6            of course- that scenario may come like in
 7            a future in [that case
 8    Ulla                [yes but this we have got in fact,
 9            I s'pose, in those sperm banks, (Ylva: yes)
10            don't you find it you [there you can
11    Ylva                         [but it is, can
```

```
12              still optional I s'pose
13  Ulla        where you can all the time ah come an' choose
14              what you'd [like to have
15  Ylva                   [yes but it's you who decide
16              anyway, it's not little- there's nobody
17              telling you that now you must see to
18              it now we have had a lottery for you
19              coz you will have a child with x y z here
20  Ulla        but this is of course happened many
21              hundred years ago
22  Linda       *mm* this is old [after all
23  Ulla                         [yes that that's old
24              of course this thing that somebody else-
25              implants something and you shall give
26              [bir- yeah
27  Linda       [mm yeah
28  Ylva        and like in the Nazi [time then
29  Anne                             [surrogate
30  Ulla                             [God *Jesus*
31  Anne        surrogate oh I see I thought
32  Ulla        no [I just
33  Ylva           [during the Nazi time there was y'know
34              homes really really (Ulla: mm) for German
35              women (Ulla: mm mm) where one yes in fact
36              picked (Linda: mm) out ah good (.) women
37              so-to-speak and good men then (Ulla: mm)
38              these children they were born y'know
39              at in these homes beautiful Aryan children
40              so there one didn't have there, one didn't
41              have y'know this technique, then one had
42              y'know to rely on nature and look at
43              people that they (Ulla: yeah) looked
44              alr[ight
45  Linda          [limping ###
46  Ulla          [but it is a little scaring then that
47              that they can't keep it in mind (Anne: mm)
48              this thing about how it was but but they
49              go on in this way
50  Ylva        yes it y'know this=
51  Ulla        =but the researchers [must
52  Ylva                             [that's y'know the
53              evil side then and then it's the good one
54              that one goes tries to develop (Linda: mm)
55              ((short pause))
56  Ulla        yes one can of course hope that from the
57              beginning it was thought so (.) with the
58              gene technology that one would then be
59              able to cure diseases and then what the
```

```
60              other thing
61  Ylva    the other thing you get in the same [bargain
```

In the beginning of this excerpt, Ylva contemplates the idea that only some people should be allowed to become parents. She suggests that this might become a reality in some imaginary future society (lines 6–7). Ulla objects that this is already a possibility, since you can get almost what you want from a sperm bank (lines 8–10). In her turn, Ylva counters that this is still 'optional' (line 11), that is, the individual's own decision, rather than something decided upon from above (lines 15–18). After this, Ulla comes in with yet another counter-point, sticking (it seems) to her prior position (lines 8–10), or rather she strengthens her position that selecting parents does not belong only to a future scenario; she claims that 'this' actually happened many hundred years ago (lines 20–21), and Linda supports her claim (line 22). Exactly what 'this' 'old' thing is may not be quite clear from the beginning (lines 20–21), but it seems to involve the idea of somebody else choosing who shall be the father of your child; thus, Ulla and Linda seem to oppose Ylva's idea of the individual's own choice (lines 15–18). The sequence has so far shown the use of analogies and distinctions, organised in sequences and cycles of different kinds, a topic that we will further discuss in Chapter 6.

What is indeterminate around the turn on lines 20–21 will soon be made even more ambiguous. Interestingly, there are three different examples coming up almost simultaneously, expressed in overlapping utterances. Ulla thinks of the conception of Jesus (line 30), anticipated in lines 25–26 in the formulation 'you shall give bir-(th)', whereas Ylva (line 28 and the long turn of lines 33–44) talks about the production of Aryan children during Nazi times. Anne, on her side (lines 29 and 31), mentions surrogate mothers, but interrupts herself (line 31), when she hears about the other ideas. After this brief passage of schisming – concurrent discourses and competing interpretations – in the multi-party discourse, the group goes back to discussing today's research on gene technology. Ulla uses the Nazi analogy to warn of the present tendencies (lines 46–49), while Ylva points to a distinction ('one didn't have this technique' in the Nazi period, line 41). Then, Ylva and Ulla try to remind themselves of the 'good side' of the development. You get both good and evil things 'in the same bargain' (line 61).

Excerpt (5) shows a case of a small 'thinking society' which manages to come up with several relevant ideas in a very short time. We can see how associations, analogies and distinctions are used continuously (see further Chapter 6). Sometimes, participants team up with one another or against each other. At the same time, the discussion has several features of an informal conversation.

For example, it involves some instances of simultaneous talk, and topics are developed in several directions more or less simultaneously.

Let us first try to list some features of the interaction in (at least some) focus groups that one might associate with informal multi-party conversations (not all these features are necessarily substantiated solely by the two examples just given, but see also examples in Chapter 6):

- action is mostly relatively spontaneous, i.e. not so controlled, edited, censured, or diplomatic, as in contexts where you would be held responsible for what you say after the encounter (this holds provided that the moderator occupies a retracted position). Participants have fairly similar activity roles (disregarding some differences in amount of talk). They do not act as 'experts' or 'chairpersons', which are activity roles that would have been more typical of institutional or professional encounters. (This holds with the exception of the moderator's occasional interventions as chair). This is not to say that specific individuals may not 'own', i.e. be primary speakers in, specific episodes. A related feature is that participants regularly give feedback in terms of 'continuers' or listener's support items (such as 'mm, yeah, yes, no, okay, exactly' etc.) to each other, rather than to one person with a particular activity role, such as that of chair or moderator. As Myers (2004, p. 29–30) points out, such continuers directed to other group members are common in focus groups.

- Alliances as well as competing subgroups may be formed, at least on certain topics and topical aspects. However, at least as far as open-discussion focus groups are concerned, arguments are seldom developed into real attempts to persuade (Myers, 2004, p. 180). This may be a feature distinguishing focus groups from genuine decision-making meetings.

- There are occasional passages with overlapping talk, or competing topical developments. But the interaction remains a 'focused interaction', that is, it does not split up more definitely into parallel conversations with separate floors (what Egbert, 1997, calls 'schisming'). Tendencies towards such splitting are generally dispreferred, or sometimes even sanctioned by the moderator.

- Participants may sometimes partly leave the task temporarily to indulge in telling an anecdote, joking, and cutting loose in laughter. (However, moderators can of course step in and try to restrain this too, but this was seldom done in our studies) Moreover, good stories are usually not produced for their own sake, but are used to illustrate arguments (see Section 6.6).

- Participants can sit back and reflect, and come back with interventions. (As we observed in Chapter 3, a multi-party interaction involves other opportunities than dyadic exchanges.) This opportunity for participants to position themselves as 'observers' for some periods of time and then come back as speakers is typical of multi-party conversations that are relatively disciplined in terms of turn-taking.

- There may sometimes be a consensus-orientation, and finding counter-arguments is not always quite as central as in, for example, some seminars. (But confer the points below.)

Some of these points will be further substantiated in Chapters 5 and 6. However, we should point out already here that the list above must be counter-balanced by a couple of non-conversation-like features that often occur in focus groups and are related to participants' orientation to the encounter as a chaired meeting:

- Topics are not allowed to wander off completely, as they can do in impromptu conversations (Erickson, 1982). Rather, moderators often exercise some topic control, often initiating and closing topics, sometimes also steering topics through their progression.

- There is more of an orientation, often encouraged by moderators, to expressing counter-arguments and disagreements, for example, playing the devil's advocate, than in casual conversations. Yet, Myers (1998), who discusses this point at length, notes that the well-known mundane preference for agreement, which serves to diminish face-threats (Pomerantz, 1984), still tends to be reflected in focus groups, albeit in more indirect ways. Disagreements often come with hedges, first-positioned weak agreements and prefatory concessions ('yes (I agree) but…'). Sometimes, when more explicit concessions and disagreements are expressed, these contributions, unlike genuine agreements as well as more passionate disagreements, are sometimes (at least pro-forma) addressed to the moderator, rather than to the co-participant one is disagreeing with (Myers, 1998, p. 97 and 102; 2004, p. 126). In another paper, Myers (2000, p. 132) observes that '[a] sense of confrontation is avoided because the participants relate their contributions to the group using collaborative construction, echoes, formulations, and hypothetical stories'. These, again, reflect conversational attitudes.

By way of provisional summary, there are many features that make focus groups conversation-like in terms of their interaction. At the same time, several of the points above were appended with some riders, which point in the direction of focus groups being partly hybrid-like activities.

4.6.2   Informal multi-party conversations: handling the content

We will now turn to the content side of multi-party conversations, keeping in mind that this can hardly be understood independently of the interactional dimensions that we have just attended to. Let us begin with an example:

Excerpt (6) ROM1, cf. Levin, 2003: 169–170; translated from Swedish. This is a focus group of civilian administrators at a military garrison; the study deals with people's understandings of what is involved in the then current reorganisation of the national military

```
1    Andrew   if we all did exactly the same, ordered our
2             travellings as you say well in advance, conscripts
3             were exemplary did exactly right every time,
4             right?, then there were no problems but it isn't
5             like that, you cannot have all people cast in
6             exactly the same mould, it won't work, but that's
7             how they want it, banks have turned pro[11] on that,
8             banks are so good there, y'know, so (Angela: mm)
9             people have to do more and more, and they have to
10            pay *for doing it ha ha* and it's such a success
11            how they managed, it's like if we had to pay
12            for going *to our workplace ha ha, like*
13            but that's the way the banks have been doing it,
14            twenty years by now winding up, offices and
15   Amy      winding up themselves
16   Andrew   .yeah they do it
17   Amy      °.mm°
18   Andrew   and make customers pay for it that they do
19            things for the bank clerks who disappear *ha ha*
20            so that's a bit of what we are doing
21   Amy      °mm°
22   Andrew   we are busy eliminating ourselves
```

In his rather long argument by a single speaker, Andrew is thinking aloud, working himself up to the conclusion that the military employees are in fact deliberately – as it seems – eliminating their own job opportunities. This sequence has many traits of an improvised reasoning in which topics glide (the partial contradiction on lines 6–8 is surely not impeccable logic but does still not appear as topically unmotivated), and the talk slips rather seamlessly into new topics; one may perhaps talk about a topical derailment. Basically, the topical trajectory is the following (here the > sign means 'develops into'): people are not the same (generally, and in the military organisation) (lines 1–6) > but banks make people become the same and behave in the same ways (lines 7–8) (note the distinction involved here, cf. Section 6.5) > banks make people do the job themselves and yet pay for it (lines 9–13) > this also eliminates the bank employees' jobs (lines 14, 21) > military employees also eliminate their own jobs (lines 20–22) (note the analogy here, cf. Section 6.5). The episode contains a good deal of self-irony and rather black humour. The speaker laughs several times, evidently at the fact that people, including his own group, let themselves be fooled.

Moving now to some generalisations with regard to the semantics and pragmatics of language, we find that free-floating conversations may include features that we will also find in focus groups with reasonably free discussions. Thus, we expand our list above with some further points: (again, only some of these pertain directly to the examples given in this section, but see also examples in Chapter 6):

- The discourse is often replete with topical glides, contradictions, ambiguities, and partial derailments. These derailments are not unmotivated, but their reasoning does not stand out as impeccable logic.

- Participants typically try out rather than expound stances; they do not act as 'experts', cf. above. Informal conversations disprefer 'conversational teaching' (Keppler and Luckmann, 1991).

- The discourse contains different voices; participants construct hypothetical quotes, thereby ascribing stereotypical opinions to virtual participants/speakers (see Section 6.8). That is, participants use quasi-reported speech to distance themselves from stances they nevertheless – in and through the quotes – express; they insulate something they say from some possible consequences for themselves (this will be further analysed in Chapter 5).

- There is a preference for 'we'–'they' dichotomies, rather than 'one' or impersonal constructions. Thus, the talk displays some affinities with gossip. Sometimes, participants make personal or even private associations, moving the issues into their own 'small worlds'.

- A related feature is extreme case formulations (exaggerations) (Pomerantz, 1986), that is, claims are often made without reservations (for example, claims about 'everybody' or 'nobody').

- We often find irony, emphasis on the discrepancies between (other) people's rhetoric and the actual reality (as depicted by participants), as well as pessimism couched in (black) humour.

It seems that some of the features of the list above, especially the last four points, 'we-they' dichotomies, irony, black humour are, at least in our Linköping studies, more typical of groups in which participants were directly affected by the issue-in-focus (ROM, WPC).

4.6.3   Goal-directedness versus sociability

Despite some important divergences, many focus groups, especially perhaps among the 'open discussion' type, embody features of informal free-floating multi-party conversations. It seems that participants cannot help using those interactional routines, the 'logic' of ordinary conversation, with which they have become familiar in their normal social life. Our ad-hoc groups are 'invaded' by the social forms of their societal environments. Hence, we can indeed look upon focus groups as 'thinking societies in miniature' which function as arenas for the production and circulation of social representations, largely in analogy with what takes place in 'naturally occurring' conversations.

But focus groups are by definition ad-hoc groups set up for research purposes, and they have to be topically focused. None of these conditions pertain to informal leisure-time group conversations. Also, focus-group members are often strangers to each other.

Linell (1998c) has suggested a typology of communicative activity types in terms of a few underlying dimensions. Perhaps the most fundamental one of these is that of 'play' versus 'decision making'. Casual conversations exhibit a good deal of non-goal-directed play-making. On the other hand, it is an almost ubiquitous property of 'institutional' encounters, that is professional–lay interaction and interprofessional talk, that they involve some kind of decision-making. In other words, the distinction is related to those of 'conversational' versus 'transactional' and 'free-floating' versus 'focused' that have been part of our discussion in this chapter. Georg Simmel (1949/1910; 1950) insisted that a theory of society must recognise the role of a 'social game' involving play, as an important genre or function that diverges from those transactions which pursue economic and political interests. In discussing focus groups, Myers (2004, p. 112) talked about this 'social game' involving play as 'sociability'. Indeed, it seems that focus groups exhibit a good deal of variation on a scale from play-forms to decision-making (or opinion-making).

By way of summary, we should remind ourselves again that 'ordinary conversations' are not one single communicative activity type. Nor are informal multi-party conversations always of the same kind. In most of our data, the open discussion is salient, as if it were the dominating discourse type. However, a gossip genre surfaces occasionally, as a subordinated discourse type. However, one must of course warn against drawing general conclusions about informality from examples derived from just a couple of specific conversational cultures. The ways in which interlocutors interact in northern Europe, for example Sweden or Britain, are partly different from those in, say, southern Europe or Latin America. Standards of informality and turn-taking are different. What in Spain may be a rather disciplined group discussion may appear to northern outsiders to be a quite informal multi-party conversation (Gille, 2001). Moreover, as Jovchelovitch (2004) demonstrates, there are important cross-cultural differences in how participants act as focus-group participants.

4.7   Summary and discussion

In this chapter we have adopted a micro-sociological and social-interactional perspective, looking at focus groups as communicative activity types, that is, special kinds of multi-party encounters, with specific tasks and framings. In this perspective, focus groups are not just small groups *tout court*, i.e., groups with a number of members. Instead, focus groups are – as indeed, virtually all groups are – socially structured constellations of participants, who adopt different roles with a social – and usually partly asymmetrical – distribution of responsibilities, knowledge and participation.

However, there is not one single, specific communicative activity type. On the contrary, focus groups can be organised in different ways and develop into fairly different activity types, depending on a host of external and internal factors. There are also many groups that display hybridities in terms of communicative activity types.

We have also argued that some focus groups display interactional characteristics of fairly free-floating group discussions, at least as long as they have a relatively retracted moderator. At the same time, unlike most informal conversations, focus groups are partially (externally) framed by outsiders, that is the organisers. This may introduce orientations to other framings, such as those of group interviews or seminars.

Notes

1   Another related notion is Hymes's (1972) 'speech event'.

2   On 'phases', see #7 in the list of Section 4.3.2 below, and on 'episodes', see Chapter 6.

3   For other comments on focus-group research, see Chapter 2.

4   Our hunch is that a group with a comprehensive common history is not ideal as a focus group, since the members of such a group sometimes tend to remain silent or indirect about shared, cultural or idiosyncratic premises for their argumentation.

5   Another simple example of cognitive artefacts is the use of pen and paper, as exemplified in Chapter 6, Excerpt (9).

6   For example, it was argued in Section 3.3 that the issue of medical confidentiality in 'The Couple' was sometimes, as in Excerpt 1 (Chapter 3), reformulated as a dilemma about trust and lack of trust, and about exactly which relation of trust (Jean and Pauline, Jean and the doctor, Pauline and the doctor) was primarily at stake.

7   Many examples used in this book have been translated from another language than English, notably French and Swedish. All the original analyses that we build upon were of course made on the original data. The originals are available from the authors.

8   It should be admitted, though, that the stimulus conditions were not quite identical; the former three groups had read a couple of newspaper articles on the issue, while the students had no material to read but only got an oral introduction introducing a number of issues that they could choose to discuss.

9   In tackling this question, we should first note that there is of course neither any homogeneous speech genre nor any single communicative activity type to be called 'ordinary' or 'natural' conversation, despite the often unquestioned assumption to this effect within, for example, Conversation Analysis (Wilson, 1989; Linell, 1998a, p. 241). Rather, informal conversations can be framed by participants in several different ways, for instance, in family dinner-table conversations, intimate talk between friends, social small talk in a train compartment, or fun-making talk among adolescents.

10   However, Myers himself (2000; 2004, p. 112) emphasises the role of sociability too.

11   I.e. 'professional'.

5 Who is speaking in focus groups? The dialogical display of heterogeneity

5.1 Introduction

So far, we have seen that one of the main reasons for using focus groups to study social representations or socially shared knowledge is that they are comparable to ordinary talk. That is, they enable us to grasp the way in which different perspectives come into oppositions with each other, are negotiated and co-constructed. In the previous chapters, we have also seen that participants in focus groups define and reframe the communicative situation in which they find themselves and it is in so doing that they adopt particular positions[1] and enter into a debate.

This is also why deciding whether we should choose a homogeneous or a heterogeneous group can be a central methodological question (Marková, 2003b). By making such a decision, e.g. by choosing homogeneity, we determine the characteristics of the group according to certain 'external' or 'a priori' criteria, such as age or sex, a common life experience regarding the discussed topic, or even a shared culture (Ashbury, 1995).

However, external framing evolves in the actual interaction and gives way to internal framings. Myers (1998, p. 89), for example, has pointed out that framing is not merely a phenomenon determined by external factors, but that it also depends on the way in which the participants view themselves through the dialogue:

This homogeneity could have affected the way participants expressed agreement and disagreement – not so much because they had something in common, but because they soon saw themselves as having something in common.

Wilkinson (1999) emphasises that identities are constructed through discourse. Speakers present themselves as X, speak from the position X (as a housewife, or a highly educated person and so on). In fact, they often build their identity in opposition to the way they present others in discourse.

However, the literature on this subject has paid very little attention to the ways in which participants commit themselves to interaction in focus groups or to the specific aspects of their identity activated in this task. The prevailing assumption in setting up and studying focus groups – as well as in many other research methods (see Grossen, in press) – is that participants approaching the task engage themselves in dialogue and negotiate the meanings from a position that is uniform. This assumption relies on another one concerning the subject. According to this view the subjects are coherent in the way they take a stance, presenting themselves in front of other interlocutors, report experience or emotions and account for specific events. These approaches rely on the presupposition of the homogeneity of the subjects.

This issue arises together with that of the relationship between the identity and participants' social role, which is quite familiar in sociological research. Indeed,

> it becomes difficult to sum up the heterogeneous set of attributes that attaches itself to each person through a unique symbol [.] Nowadays the person and status tend to be regarded as separate. (Boudon and Bourricaut, 1982, p. 568, our translation)

Without entering into the debate about such notions as status and identity (Gergen, 1972; Elster, 1985), it is relevant to point out the discrepancy between the way in which the focus group is set up (and therefore the criteria determining the homogeneity of the group), and the way in which participants interpret the situation, the instructions and the interlocutors' discourse. In other words, it is very often forgotten that it is the participants' interpretations that bring out the multiplicity of their identities.

Nevertheless, if focus groups enable us to capture the dynamics involved in the construction of socially shared knowledge, it is precisely because it is within such groups 'that the participants' ideas come into confrontation, collide with each other in overt or hidden polemics, in internal or external dialogue' (Marková, 2004, p. 233). Notions such as 'hidden polemic' or 'internal dialogue' refer to the fact that subjects are not only involved in a dialogue with the other, but also in a dialogue with themselves, with common sense, and with other discourses that are not necessarily directly or explicitly displayed. Consequently, such subjects should not be considered as being homogeneous, but rather, once inscribed within the whole complexity of dialogism, as presenting multiple characteristics.

5.2   Positioning in dialogical dynamics

Let us pause on an excerpt from a focus-group discussion taken from the research presented in Chapter 3 in order to provide some concrete characteristics to this perspective:

Excerpt (1) LAU1A: 'Work' dilemma; translated from French

```
1    Moderator  [...] and we'll get to the second uh
2               second situation (10s) so it's a
3               situation, I'll read it out to you: 'You
4               have a basic training in medicine and are
5               the head of the health department of the
6               canton of Vaud. You find on your desk a
7               letter signed by several hospital
8               directors who ask you to allow them to
9               require HIV-tests when they hire new
10              people. As the person responsible for the
11              health department, should you give them
12              this permission?'
13              (3s)
14   Anabelle   well I've already got a question uh
15              (Moderator: yes), you have a basic
16              training in medicine and you are head of
17              department, does that mean that she is
18              only an admin person? OR does she have
19              contacts with the=
20   Joël       =no, he is he is the political chief if
21              you like he is =
22   Anabelle   =yeah, so in the end=
23   Joël       =(the higher)who who makes a political
24              decision, so, (.) here precisely
25              ((laughter))it's somehow ((general
26              laughter))somehow the lawyer is
27              going to who is going to who is going to
28              who is going to to feed, who is going to
29              say that (.) anyway he- uh, because he
30              will call on lawyers who will tell him
31              that it might be possible to imagine such
32              things but there is already a federal law
33              on data protection, so that means that
```

```
34               every fact that is gathered must be uh uh
35               without the identity of the person in
36               question being necessarily identifiable
37               outside the- these health professionals,
38               isn't it ?, (?: right) so (.) it's
39               necessary- it seems to me it see- it
40               seems to me first of all a very
41               COMPLICATED thing to imagine in the sense
42               where we are-there is the principle of
43               protection of identity and data
44               (Moderator: hmmm) which which is quite
45               close to the principle of medical
46               confidentiality (Moderator: all right)
47               which is (Moderator: hmmm) already in
48               place, so uh (3s) yeah concerning the
49               principle, one should see in which way-
50               the datum is very vague, one should see
51               in which professional area [because]
52  Moderator   [yeah well for many]
53  Joël        there are also areas of risk so=
54  Anabelle    = that's it that is what (Moderator:
55               that's it) because if: if it's really a
56               doctor field doctor uh, it's still AIDS
57               which is contagious, I don't know
58               how (.), I don't know how it goes, if in
59               fact doctors are positive, if gloves, I
60               really don't have a clue.
61  Moderator   hmm, I I don't have any more information
62               here than=
63  Anabelle    =in this situation I would be asking more
64               questions (I don't know/I'm not)
65  Monique     I think it's trivial to to to yeah
66               immediately test the employees like that
67               (Anabelle: yes absolutely) to say 'so
68               from the beginning we don't trust you and
69               we will check', and on the other hand
70               it's clear that: well OK (Joël: but
71               but) it's true that some people could be
72               led to hide their HIV status because they
73               know that they run the risk of not being
74               hired, so it's: true, but on the other
75               hand, I think it's a little trivial to go
76               about it like that=
77  Joël        = yes but there is the famous little
78               group of people who 'have it without
79               knowing it',
80  Monique     also ((slightly muffled laugh))
```

```
81  Joël        so uh but indeed, it's true that there is
82              that famous problem of the protection of
83              identity, if I don't necessarily feel
84              like saying uh: that I am HIV positive
85              and so I imagine that one can imagine at
86              the very least giving permission in those
87              very few professions that are very high
88              risk because [ some ]
```

One can notice from the outset the richness in the ways in which the participants stand in relation to each other, since each of them turns him- or herself into a spokesperson for a different opinion.[2] However, a closer examination of the dialogue shows that each contribution does not merely correspond to the possible individual answers to the question. So, for example, Anabelle raises the issue of medical practices by following up the breach opened up by Joël when he modulates his own discourse by 'one should see in which professional area because [.] there are areas of risk so' (lines 49–51). Monique speaks out against uniform HIV testing (lines 65–76) at the very point when Joël's and Anabelle's discourse seems to converge towards agreeing with uniform testing. Thus the evoked themes necessarily inscribe themselves in the argumentative dynamics and function as responses in opposing each other's perspective, rather than simply expressing the speakers' views about the problem. According to François (1982) this is the characteristic of a true 'efficiency of dialogue': what one says in dialogue is very different from what one might have uttered as an individual. Instead, in a dialogue speakers jointly contribute to a common discourse (Rommetveit, 1990; 1991).

However, what this excerpt mostly shows is the complexity of the moves accomplished by each of these speakers within this dialogical dynamics. Let us briefly present this point before entering into details.

First of all, we can observe that before she commits herself to an answer, Anabelle wishes to know what is the role of the doctor who will make a decision concerning a systematic testing of HIV. In other words, she wants to know to which position she is being summoned. In the same way, before he answers, Joël invokes his past as a law student which he mentioned at the beginning of the recording. These two interventions show one aspect of the dialogical complexity in focus group discussions: the question of knowing 'as who' is the participant speaking. This, of course, raises the issue of the complexity and the heterogeneity of the subjects' identity.

We can also note that the speakers take on different roles during the entire exchange: Joël takes on first the role of a lawyer, but then he explicitly puts into words his identification with a person who is HIV antibody positive ('if I don't necessarily feel like saying uh: that I am HIV positive', lines 83–84).

Therefore, the subjects manifest a kind of empathy with the characters that they depict and accordingly, they construct the positions from which they argue.

In addition, while they argue, the participants call upon other real or virtual discourses: thus Joël portrays the speech of lawyers (lines 30–38) and Monique that of the hospital administrator (lines 67–70). Hence we can say that voices of others merge into the speaker's voice thus intertwining different kinds of relationships. This interweaving also applies to utterances of the interlocutors, who are used as resources for the wording of each participant of the group.

Finally, various types of modalisation can be observed: for example, while she powerfully argues in favour of generalised testing, Anabelle restricts what she is saying (lines 54–60 and 63–64). The subjects are not only in a dialogue with their interlocutors or with fictional voices (see later) they are also in a dialogue with themselves (Bakhtin, 1984). This example shows that the discussion is not constructed by homogenous individuals but that each carries different voices and positionings.

5.3   The heterogeneity of the speaker

The aim of this chapter is therefore to study the ways in which the participants mobilise the multiple aspects of their identities in focus-group discussion. We shall attempt to examine how the subjects address the dilemmas with which they are presented. In the framework of discourse analysis, this means that we shall view the notion of 'subject' not as a psychological or social entity. Instead, the subject manifests him- or herself in the discourse in his or her role as a speaker, for example through the different means by which speakers talk about themselves or about the objects in the world. This idea relates back to rhetoric and to the notion of ethos (Amossy, 1999) and can be explored in different ways. In the first instance, following Bakhtin (1981b; 1986) let us recall that the words of other speakers necessarily resonate in everyone's discourse.

> Each utterance is filled with echoes and reverberations of other utterances to which it is related by the communality of the sphere of speech communication. Every utterance must be regarded primarily as a response to preceding utterances of the given sphere (we understand the word 'response' here in the broadest sense). Each utterance refutes, affirms, supplements, and relies on the others, presupposes them to be known, and somehow takes them into account. (Bakhtin, 1986, p. 91)

Taking this perspective leads us to note that there is no strict correspondence between individual subjects and their discursive production. Speakers are not necessarily the authors of their discourse. Through their discourse, other voices and discourses can be heard. This observation has prompted linguists and discourse analysts (Ducrot, 1984; Vion, 1998a; 1998b; Bres, 1998; 1999) to propose the distinction between locutor and enunciator.[3] The locutor is the one who utters the words, that is the one who says 'I', while the enunciator corresponds to a point of view presented in the utterance, a point of view that may or may not be taken on board by the speaker. Consider the following utterance:

Excerpt (2) LAU1A: 'Work' dilemma; translated from French

```
1    Monique    yeah I think that there is the big
2               question of professional confidentiality
3               so, since it isn't maintained anymore at
4               all, because if you you say yes if you're
5               a (woman) patient you would like to know,
6               patients should know.
```

The speaker, Monique, unfolds her point of view by saying (lines 1–2) that she thinks that the issue of professional confidentiality is at stake. But at the same time, she takes up, by quoting it, her interlocutor's argument ('if you you say yes if you're a (woman) patient you would like to know, patients should know', lines 4–6) an argument that she clearly attributes to her interlocutor ('you say') and therefore she does not take any responsibility for it. Thus, in this utterance, there is one locutor, corresponding to the speaker, i.e. to Monique, and two enunciators that correspond to the points of view expressed by Monique and her interlocutor.

We can therefore adjoin some other aspects of dialogism to interactional dimensions that we have encountered in previous chapters. According to Bakhtin, every utterance is characterised by a tension arising from an internal dialogue between one's own words and others' words. What the literature has mainly retained of this Bakhtinian idea is that in every utterance there are traces of previous (oral or written) discourses. It is what Bakhtin calls 'the dialogue with the cultural sphere'. Our words are always marked by this relationship to what has been written about or spoken before, whether we take it up and agree with it or enter into a polemic with it, and whether we take it up consciously or not. Our speech is therefore construed and filled with a variety of voices and discourses in relation to which we position ourselves.

Bakhtin has also insisted that utterances in face-to-face interaction are characterised by this tension, which means that we can analyse under this perspective the different language games of repetition, polemic, agreement and disagreement, all identifiable in the dynamics of verbal interaction. We have seen an example of this, and we will get back to it in Section 6 below.

Finally, even if this is a point less often cited, Bakhtin (1984) also reminds us that subjects carry on a dialogue with themselves (François, 1982; 1990). For example, through the use of modalisations, speakers may take some distance from what they are actually stating. Thus, the discourse manifests two different and contrasting relationships to what is being uttered: an assertion and a backwards glance on that assertion. We shall come back to this aspect of dialogism and to the way in which it permits us to approach the subjects' heterogeneity.

In addition, Ducrot (1984) readily insists on the fact that the locutor is also a discursive construct. Speakers manifest themselves within discourse in different ways, not only as actors but, most importantly, they put into words, in different ways, their discursive activity (Vion 1998a; 1998b). The discourse can thus present what is said as either something self-evident, or as a manifestation of doubt, or as originating from another discourse, or as the result of a polemic.

Even if we do not consider psychological and sociological factors, it is difficult to think of the speaker as a homogeneous or monolithic entity. A three-fold complexity is at stake: the fact that discourses involve different voices (and as we shall see shortly, these different voices are resources for argumentation); the fact that speakers sketch different images of their self; and finally, the fact that they position themselves in different ways in relation to their discourse.

5.4   From where is one speaking?

Every discourse constructs its objects from a certain point of view. In this context the notion of 'point of view'

> implies on the one hand the existence of a common reality and on the
> other hand, the notion that this reality is presented in different ways, that
> there is no overarching perspective capable of providing a synthesis for
> all points of view. (François, 1994 p. 22, our translation)

This is to say that while focus-group participants are guided by the researcher's instructions to adopt a certain position, their discourse also shows, directly or indirectly, the perspective(s) from which they consider the topic under discussion. This takes place within a complex interplay between the subjects' multifaceted identity and the way in which these facets are invoked by the setting of the discussion.

Although focus groups are expected to create conditions approaching those in everyday life, we must not forget that it is the researcher who constructs them with certain aims in mind. The way in which the group is composed might, for example, favour identification between participants. I could favour different attitudes of identification, indifference or rejection with respect to the theme.

At the moment when the participants are about to answer, they can potentially do so from different perspectives, all of which can more or less become activated. For example, these could involve the position of a lay subject; the opposite position of an expert; the position of a person inclined to be moved by the dilemma in a particular direction; and so on. Naturally, not all these positions are always explicit but the participants often invoke their understanding of positioning as part of the interpretation and framing of the communicative situation.

We have seen in Excerpt (1) how Joël reminds the group of his status as a former law student. This kind of phenomenon occurs frequently and most often it derives from the fact that participants make use of an expertise that differs from the one on the basis of which they were invited to participate in the focus group.

Excerpt (3) PAR1 A: 'Day Nursery' dilemma; translated from French

```
1    Claire   […] I I have worked in the medical
2             sector, it's not a d-, (..) and::: (..)
3             I think that it's more in the: in the
4             human sector, and I say that-. (.) I just
5             give my opinion straight out, (..)
```

This is a good example of the way in which subjects respond from two different and complementary perspectives. Claire (line 1) appeals to her experience in the medical field in order to reframe the presented dilemma and to situate it in the domain of something 'human' (lines 3–4), and as something that can, therefore, be addressed from the position of a lay person (line 5) rather than of an expert. By contrast, some subjects may cast doubt on their legitimacy or their capacity to answer:

Excerpt (4) PAR1 A: 'Day Nursery' dilemma; translated from French

```
1    Natacha there is one point that bothers me, my
2             opinion is asked for, well, my personal
3             opinion about what a (.)doctor should do
```

```
4        (..)well I:: I consider that I'm not a
5        doctor, (...) and that: it seems
6        difficult to me, (..) of- of course I
7        have an opinion but I cannot replace (.)
8        uh the doctor, (.) and in as much as I
9        haven't studied medicine uh::, I- I know
10       this: this problem well, (.) well I'm a
11       teacher and: I know: I know that there
12       can be a discrepancy, (..) between the
13       different points of view uh (.) well all
14       absolutely uh (..) relevant of certain
15       parents but who don't have all the facts
16       (.)uh:: of the facts of: of (...) the
17       profession the activity of teaching (.)
18       the facts on the field, (2s.) and who are
19       not really in a position (.) of
20       addressing a problem. (..) I-I will uh
21       (.) however give my opinion, but: I -it
22       seems I difficult to be able to replace
23       (...) the- the opinion of a doctor.
```

In this passage, Natacha makes two different moves. On the one hand (lines 4–9) she wonders whether she is capable of giving an answer, in as much as she cannot put herself, she thinks, in the place of the doctor. But this line of questioning is not done from the perspective of a 'non-expert' speaker. On the contrary, she invokes (lines 9–20) her status as a school-teacher who has to deal with the opinions of other non-expert subjects (the parents) in order to address such kinds of questions. The identities that are assembled in this talk are complex: we have here an answer produced by someone who was invited to take part as a student and who refuses as a lay person to put herself in the place of an expert, a doctor, because as a school teacher she herself has expert knowledge of dealing with these kinds of situation.

Such interplay of different facets of the participants' identities does not concern only the speaker as an individual. Even if less frequently, it can also manifest itself through the ways in which the interlocutors mutually address one another.

Excerpt (5) LAU2B: 'Day Nursery' dilemma; translated from French

```
1   Liliane    but would you then let your children go
2              there if you knew? (you have (xxx)
3              children) ((general laughter and noise))
3   Moderator  (you) or not?
4   Liliane    no I[personally I don't know]
5   Moderator  [doesn't it make you think?]
```

```
 6   Liliane    well I don't have children [but I mean I
 7              don't know, I: if it made me think yes
 8              well yeah (Moderator: hmm) [whether the
 9              risk is less]
10   Moderator  [would you (xxxx)?]
11   Liliane    I really don't know =
12   Moderator  =hmm
13   Maude      [I think that]
14   Liliane    [I'd have to be in the situation] for me
15              to know what I'd do (Moderator: hmm) here
16              I don't see
17   Florian    I I I just imagine, I play basketball and
18              in basketball there are also all the
19              time contacts and there's a rule it's
20              that if there's a player
21              (3 sec)
22   Maude      well I wonder to what extent, well I have
23              a [child] (.) uh (.) ]
24   Liliane    [well yeah I was wondering what you think
25              about it] ((laughter))
26   Maude      I I have the impression that in terms of
27              risks, what terrorises me these days, is
28              that he'll get run over when crossing the
29              road, (Liliane: oh yeah it's greater uh)
30              my impression is. that if there was such
31              a situation at the day nursery where he
32              goes and that I was told about it (.)well
33              it's not the case I am not told about it
34              I don't know about that but if there was
35              such a situation I imagine that I'd
36              continue thinking that he runs more risk
37              while crossing the road (.) (Liliane:
38              hmm) than [catching AIDS like this]
```

In the discussion, Liliane tries to push her interlocutors into a certain kind of identification with one of the characters in the dilemma, i.e. the parents of the other children. Considering discussions of the 'Day Nursery' dilemma in all groups, it is interesting to realise that participants seldom identified with those parents' position. Generally, they tended to adopt the point of view of the child who might be excluded and marginalised if her HIV antibody positive status became known. Therefore, appealing to someone who could speak as the mother of a child attending a day-care nursery makes it possible to reinforce different positions concerned.

Finally, it can be also noted that the participants themselves might wonder about the relevance of their participation in group:

Excerpt (6) LAU1A: Beginning of the meeting

At the beginning, the moderator asks everyone to introduce themselves.

```
 1   Joël      so I would maybe just like to clarify
 2             (Moderator: yes) that seems to be
 3             slightly important, I actually studied
 4             law, I did not get the degree of bachelor
 5             but I studied (Moderator: yes) law which
 6             might affect my reasoning, my reasoning I
 7             thought it would be important to
 8             (Moderator: yes!) point this out before
 9             entering into a discussion
10   Moderator yeah
11   Moderator OK well it's it's it's good to know
12             actually to know that you have taken
13             these law courses (Joël: right) and then
14             that: you you # also base in in part on
15   Joël      on this
16   Moderator on this knowledge hmmmm
17   Anabelle  just one question (Moderator: yes) you
18             have chosen only people with a psychology
19             background
20   Moderator yes
21   Anabelle  yes
22   Moderator yeah
23   Anabelle  ((loud)) why
24   Moderator oh there's no reason it's one - practical
25             reasons of recruitment in fact but it's
26             true, like I said, we are just at the
27             beginning and it would actually be
28             interesting to discuss these cases with
29             people who who who do something else than
30             psychology=
31   Anabelle  = yeah because I mean we are maybe more
32             prepared (Moderator: hmmmm) for these
33             kinds of situations
```

Joël brings up information that he considers relevant (lines 1–9): the fact that he can also adopt the perspective of a lawyer. This clarification seems to provoke a more general questioning about the relevance of the participants' status. Anabelle asks (lines 17–20) why the researchers had chosen psychology students and later she argues (lines 31–33) that this social role could bring out some kind of expertise to the debate. More generally, this way of defining the status from which they speak determines one of the ways in which the participants position themselves during the exchange, as Joël's intervention shows a little further on.

Excerpt (7) LAU1A: 'The Couple' dilemma; translated from French

```
1   Joël    [...] and then there is something very
2           important that you shouldn't forget AS a
3           doctor or as a psychologist or whatever,
4           one does not have the right to judge
5           people's behaviour.
```

If the dilemma invites them to take on the role of a 'doctor', these subjects associate it with the role of a psychologist. This could be due to the emphasis on their status (as psychology students) in the preamble to the discussion.

These different examples show the plurality and diversity of the participants' positioning. They explicitly state that they do not speak from a single and uniform identity. They show their complexity as individuals in the ways they answer a research question and make use of the conjoined resources of these different positions.

Therefore, if one of the (explicit or implicit) questions recurring in the focus groups that we have been able to observe regards the status from which one speaks or 'as who' one is summoned, it appears that the subjects do not limit themselves to any static positioning. Instead they are in a 'dialogue' with the external framing in which the discussion takes place, as well as in dialogue with other interlocutors and with themselves. This dynamic is also manifest in the relationship that they establish with the characters in the dilemmas.

5.5 The play of identification through wording: coding and slippages

As we have seen, the expression of position from which participants discuss can be introduced by explicit statements. What is in play in these declarations is the way in which the participants describe themselves as speakers. As we have seen, the presentation of the problem favours such a description. But at the same time, in the case of Salazar Orvig and Grossen's (2004) study, the dilemmas create an imaginary setting that the participants take as the starting point for their discussion. They are constructed in such a way as either to induce or to prevent identification with one of the characters. For example, in some dilemmas, the participant is an outside witness, asked to give an opinion on a situation presented to him as in 'The Couple' dilemma where the question is 'Should the doctor tell Jean that his wife is HIV positive?' But in other cases, the formulation of the dilemma invites the participants to identify with one of the characters. Thus, in the 'Work' dilemma they are required to put themselves in the place of the doctor: 'You have a basic training in medicine and are the head of the health department of the canton of Vaud'. On the other hand, in the 'Dentist' dilemma, the participants are called upon to identify themselves with the position of a potential victim of HIV infection: 'You are a patient of a dentist you appreciate very much and who is well known for his competence. Now, this dentist became HIV-positive and continued working without taking any particular care when he treats his patients'. But more generally, whether the dilemmas spell out the identification or not, they put highly typical, ordinary characters into play, thus allowing the participants to make a link between them and their own experience.

Therefore, in their discussion and attempt to interpret the dilemma, focus-group participants are likely to be engaged otherwise than as witnesses and arbiters. Their positioning does not feature only as having this or that status corresponding to the needs of a given study. Discourse contains numerous traces showing that, in their reflection and discussion, the participants not only manipulate rules and given principles but they put themselves in the place of the invoked characters.

Excerpt (8) LAU1A: 'Work' dilemma; translated from French

```
1    Anabelle    yeah absolutely, well I would really say
2                uh that in cases where one (Fr.on⁴) knows
3                exactly in situations where there are
4                high risks, I think that it it's still
5                good to know well I don't know, it seems
6                to me: in terms of honesty towards the
7                woman patient (Fr. la patiente) also
8                (Moderator: hmmm) because I mean that if
9                one goes to get treatment one trusts
10               (Moderator: hmmm) and but it's true that
11               you have to distinguish between the
12               different- different areas, because I
13               think there are areas where there I would
14               say General Practice there is no risk,
15               but some some cases (.) yes, an
16               operation: uh I don' t know whether I
17               would first of all be asking myself more
18               questions, ME for instance if I was a
19               patient I would like to know (Moderator:
20               hmmm) ((very softly)) I don't know°
```

Anabelle starts her reasoning by putting herself in a generic position (through – line 2 – the French pronoun 'on' ('one') and the lack of determinacy in the construction – lines 4–5 – 'it's still good to know') which may be the position of the discussing subject. But very quickly, in the statement that follows, a feminine coding emerges ('la patiente', 'the woman patient', line 7) which is not the usual way in French to refer to a generic individual. The recourse to the feminine (whether conscious or unconscious, it matters little here) concords with the fact that Anabelle speaks here mainly from the point of view of patients. She represents the patients. This can be seen, in the following utterances, in the way in which the first person is used ('I would be asking myself more questions', lines 16–18), which in this case acquires a different value. So far, 'I' refers back to the subject in its role as speaker ('I think', lines 4 and 12–13; 'I would say', lines 13–14), whereas in 'I would be asking myself more questions' it expresses the subject as a potential patient. Finally, this move is confirmed through a hypothetical utterance ('if I was a patient', lines 18–19) which makes explicit the position through which Anabelle develops her line of argumentation.

Identification can be explicit, through a statement like 'if I was a patient' (lines 18–19) or through fictional discourse, as we can see in next excerpt

Excerpt (9) PAR2B: 'The Couple' dilemma; translated from French

```
1    Noël      well ok ! imagin- imagin-
2              let's imagine that your boyfriend tells
3              you today that he - that he has cheated
4              on you
```

In other cases, the identification is progressively built up in the discourse, leaning on the potential values of the linguistic devices, and specifically on personal pronouns. Let us analyse how this is done in another excerpt

Excerpt (10) LAU1A: 'The Couple' dilemma; translated from French

```
1    Joël      = I can make two small precisions
2              ((laughs)) maybe, in the first place
3              I cannot very well imagine the doctor
4              let time go along for two months, if
5              he has to deal with such a case he will
6              do everything to say to Jean AND to
7              Pauline that that it's important that he
8              must see them, and if REALLY uh if he is
9              confronted by Pauline's refusal, so then,
10             he must maybe tell Jean 'I have something
```

```
11          urgent to tell you we must see each other
12          immediately'. and then, there is
13          something very important that we
14          shouldn't forget, AS a doctor or as a
15          psychologist or whatever, one does not
16          have the right to judge people's
17          behaviour, because this is what really
18          surprised me in what you said, it's that
19          you made a value judgement. now the
20          doctor who has or - the psychologist or
21          some person in this kind of professional
22          capacity, one does not have the right to
23          make value judgements, one just has to
24          avoid that (.) my other patient with who
25          I maintain a relationship of trust
26          catches that illness. so I have to do
27          everything to disclose it but WITHOUT
28          making a value judgement and WITHOUT
29          precisely uh pfff, I also have to take
30          into account more or less, (that) Pauline
31          has the right to follow a certain rhythm
32          and in a certain way, I mean,
```

First the doctor is encoded as a third party (line 3), then potential identification is expressed through words such as, 'as' ('en tant que', line 14,) and, 'one' ('on', line 15). The pronoun 'on' ('one') which is polysemic (being equivalent to 'we', to 'I' or to 'anyone') gives way to a direct embodiment in an utterance where, in fact, both positionings are combined ('one just has to avoid that (.) my other patient with who I maintain a relationship of trust', lines 23–25). Joël encodes himself as a doctor. And the first person pronoun becomes in that way a generic 'I', an 'I' that is potentially able to take the place of someone else. In this way, a linkage is made between the two entities: Joël speaks at the same time as himself and as a potential doctor/psychologist.

These two examples correspond to coherent identification moves and they progress from an implicit to an explicit mode of identification. But at this level as well, the participants' discourse shows the heterogeneity involved in the positioning.

Let us go back to Excerpt (1) and consider the complexity of positionings in Joël's discourse. This excerpt is a good example of the way in which subjects adopt various points of view as they reflect on the problem and discuss it. In the 'Work' dilemma, Joël speaks from at least three different perspectives: he speaks, as he explicitly says, as a lawyer ('somehow the lawyer', lines 25–26); and then, slowly, his discourse slips towards a less determined position ('it seems to me it seems to me it seems to me first of all a very COMPLICATED thing to imagine', lines 40–41) which could just as well be that of the doctor as that of the speaker. In fact it is impossible to answer with any degree of certainty the question: 'who imagines?' Indeed, this indeterminacy is induced by the text of the dilemma that proposes the identification ('you have a basic training in medicine', lines 4–5). But a little further on (lines 83–84), in his discussion with Monique, we have seen that with the help of the generic 'I' ('if I don't necessarily feel like saying uh: that I am HIV positive'), Joël puts into play much more markedly another identification move, this time that of an applicant for a hospital job who has an HIV. In this case ('so I imagine that one can imagine', line 85), it is once again the French pronoun 'on' ('one') that amalgamates the position of doctor and that of the speaker.

These various examples show that what is being enacted, i.e. the speakers' interactions with their interlocutors and with the researcher (and his representative, the moderator), doubles up with another kind of relationship. It is the relationship with the characters depicted in the dilemmas, i.e. characters that function as exemplars facilitating thinking and discussion among the participants. These characters are also alter-egos with which the participants in focus group establish (or fail to establish) intersubjective relationships. The participants can therefore put themselves into the shoes of these characters and speak (give opinions, argue, take a decision) from their positions. However, this relationship is not univocal: as our analysis shows, such discussions are not dominated by a unique move of identification. On the contrary, the participants run through different positions in the course of the same debate: they take on different types of identification, combine them with the different statuses for which they have been selected (or think they have been selected) and respond to the positionings that their interlocutors exhibit in the same way.

5.6   Relations between discourses

Any discussion is underpinned by the fact that everyone's discourse leans on the discourse of the other. Therefore, we never speak about objects or events in ways that would be independent of what others said or could have said about them. Let us return to one part of Excerpt (1):

Excerpt (11) LAU1A: 'Work' dilemma; translated from French

```
1   Monique   I think it's trivial to to to yeah
2             immediately test the employees like that
```

```
 3                 (Anabelle: yes absolutely) to say 'so
 4                 from the beginning we don't trust you and
 5                 we will check', and on the other hand
 6                 it's clear that: well OK (Joël: but but)
 7                 it's true that some people could be led
 8                 to hide their HIV status because they
 9                 know that they run the risk of not being
10                 hired, so it's: true, but on the other
11                 hand, I think it's a little trivial to go
12                 about it like that=
13  Joël         = yes but there is the famous little
14                 group of people who have it without
15                 knowing it,
16  Monique      also ((little muffled laugh))
17  Joël         so uh but indeed, it's true that there is
18                 that famous problem of the protection of
19                 identity, if I don't necessarily feel
20                 like saying uh: that I am HIV positive
21                 and so I imagine that one can imagine at
22                 the very least giving permission in those
23                 very few professions that are very high
24                 risk because [some]
```

In a concessionary move, Monique evokes a given referent: 'some people would want to hide their HIV status because they know that otherwise they run the risk of not being hired' (lines 7–9). In the same vein Joël makes two separate moves. First, in lines 13–14 he evokes a second referent: 'the famous little group of people who 'have it without knowing it'. Second, in lines 19–21, he refers again, though in a different way, to the previously evoked object: 'if I don't necessarily feel like saying uh: that I am HIV positive'.

We wish to point out three things. First, the wording of one speaker is related to the wording of the other speaker. Consequently, the arguments and the contents of one speaker are related to those of the other. Thus Monique speaks of people 'who know' and Joël answers in terms of 'those who do not'. He turns Monique's argument around by making use of her wording. Secondly, it means that the changes in encoding constitute positioning moves. Using the wording of others implies in some way accepting or adhering to their perspectives. Thus, whereas Monique makes a concessionary move ('because they know', lines 9–10), Joël uses the same argument by playing with identifications through the pronoun 'je' ('I'). The fact that he makes use of this particular wording, gives his own concessionary move (which runs counter to Monique's) a greater strength right before evoking the possibility that testing might be authorised.

If we accept that there is no neutral or objective discourse, then every discourse presupposes a positioning of the speaker in relation to the content of talk. However, such positionings are also achieved from the perspective of a particular relation to the discourse of the other.

Locutors can point to such discourse in terms of contrasts, but they can also quote it explicitly. Let us take up again some excerpts that we have already examined from a different perspective.

Excerpt (12) LAU1A: 'Work' dilemma; translated from French

```
1    Anabelle   yeah absolutely, well I would really say
2               uh that in cases where one knows exactly
3               in situations where there are high risks,
4               I think that it it's still good to know
5               well I don't know, it seems to me: in
6               terms of honesty towards the woman
7               patient [Fr.la patiente] also (Moderator:
8               hmmm) because I mean that if one goes to
9               get treatment one trusts (Moderator:
10              hmmm) and but it's true that you have to
11              distinguish between the different-
12              different areas, because I think there
13              are areas where there I want to say
14              General Practice there is no risk, but
15              some some cases (.) yes, an operation:
16              uh I don' t know whether I would first of
17              all be asking myself more questions, ME
18              for instance if I was a patient I would
19              like to know (Moderator: hmmm) ((very
20              softly)) I don't know°
21   Monique    yeah I think that there is the
22              big question of professional
23              confidentiality so, since it isn't
24              maintained anymore at all, because if you
25              you say yes if you're a (woman) patient
26              you would like to know, patients should
27              know. but then in fact if one does this
28              test but who is qualified to see the
29              result afterward? (Joël: yes) the people
30              who are doing the hiring? the colleagues?
31              (Joël: I think) or else the personnel?
32              you aren't going to advertise [ the fact
33              that she is HIV positive] so what will be
34              done with the results afterwards?
```

In this example, Monique not only directly quotes what Anabelle has just said but she also attributes to Anabelle a point of view that is not necessarily hers. If we consider strictly Anabelle's words, we can see that she has not said, at least not explicitly, that patients should know (about HIV positive status). This position is constructed by Monique who infers it from Anabelle's discourse. We can see that what is in play is the heterogeneity of utterances in this talk: the heterogeneity of utterances for which Monique takes the responsibility and the heterogeneity of utterances that she attributes to her interlocutor.

5.7   Other voices

Focus-group discussions are inhabited by different voices, those of the various participants and those of other sources, called upon and brought to discussion by the speakers. These voices manifest themselves in different ways (as reported speech, as virtual discourse, quotations, and even stereotypical expressions) that correspond to various enunciators that take part in the debate. Thus, the participants' voices are mixed with these virtual and actual resources. Subjects also position themselves in relation to these.

5.7.1   The voices of absent or virtual speakers

Just as they rely on the discourse of their interlocutor, participants call upon what others have said on other occasions.

Excerpt (13) PAR2B: 'Work' dilemma; translated from French

```
1    Noël     they treat all patients as:: [ as ]
2             potentially HIV positive.
3    Marine   [ they t-]
4    Marine   they told me 'do you coagulate well?' I
5             said 'yes', he told me 'OK, thanks! and:
6             (.)on to the operation!' ((Carine
7             laughs)) they didn't ask me anything!
8             [they won't do anything for me! and
9             that's it!]
```

Due to her experience, Marine talks about the healthcare staff ('they told me', line 4). Staff no longer refers to a generic entity but to particular individuals, whom she has met and who have spoken to her. Marine's discourse is firmly based in this recourse to reported speech. Her voice (and her position) is confirmed by that of another voice.

Most often, however, those 'others' who are evoked are not necessarily real individuals whose discourse the participants recall. In addition, some fictional voices of the characters from the dilemmas are heard, as we have seen in Excerpt (1)

Excerpt (14) LAU1A: 'Work' dilemma; translated from French

```
1    Monique I think it's trivial to to to yeah
2            immediately test the employees like that
3            (Anabelle: yes absolutely) to say 'so
4            from the beginning we don't trust you and
5            we will check'
```

Here, Monique lets the doctor in charge speak (line 2) in a fictive dialogue with the person to be hired. However, she opposes two positions: her own ('I think it's trivial', line 2) and the one she attributes to the doctor in charge (lines 3–4). Moreover, she does so by making use of an 'implausible' verbalisation: it is hard to imagine a hospital administrator speaking in such a way. Thus, by creating this virtual voice, she constructs two perspectives: the one that she attributes to the administrator, and the one that comments on this attributed intention. However, the position attributed to the administrator is also the one that is drawn up within the discourse of her interlocutor. In fact, her discourse is opposed to the possible action of the indeterminate agent implied by the infinitive ('to test', 'faire passer', line 2), which she personifies with the help of the fictional discourse as 'the doctor in charge'. However the proposed action can be also attributed to her interlocutors who are on the verge of accepting systematic testing as part of the hiring process. Joël says: 'should see in which professional field' … because there are areas of risk so' (Excerpt 1: lines 50–53); Anabelle replies 'in this situation I would be asking more questions (I don't know/I am not)' (lines 63–64). Here again, we can see that many factors contribute to the construction of the discourse.

It appears that there are no clear boundaries between real and fictional characters, whether they are construed from the dilemmas or they are the participants' spontaneous creations.

Excerpt (15) LAU2B: 'The Couple' dilemma; translated from French

```
1    Paul    =(OK it's clear) the final objective is
2            still to (Liliane: hmm) ( to get to say
3            it), but I think that the break with with
4            with the secret is:: an act I don't mean
5            more dramatic but (.) at the level macro
6            uh personal it's it's clear that if
```

```
 7        there are a few cases like this uh it's
 8        the end of everything to do with trusting
 9        therapist, (Maud: hmmm) one cannot trust
10        anymore in one's lawyer if one tells him
11        'yes I actually killed that person' but
12        the lawyer is not going to repeat it (.)
13        so one can't anymore uh have any any:
14        trust, sincerity (? - hmmm) in all these
15        areas that are uh difficult, in that case
16        it's true that well I don't go to a
17        therapist and say 'look usually every
18        Friday I kill someone', it's really a
19        case even more [uh]
```

Here Paul invokes what Wibeck, Adelswärd and Linell (2004) call virtual voices. These 'virtual voices' also convey a complex interplay of positionings and attribution of positionings to the interlocutors. As we can see in this example, Paul construes a dyad that in principle is based on trust relationships: a lawyer or a therapist on the one hand and a client on the other. The line of argumentation that he develops rests on the perspective of this potential client whose confidence he invokes. This includes a strong identification with the client, constructed in Paul's discourse using, as we have seen, a play of pronouns, at first 'on' ('one') and then clearly 'je' ('I').

We have seen how the characters in the dilemmas become objects of the participants' potential identifications. We can observe here that this phenomenon is more pervasive, as subjects merge their voices with those of various others, whether real, typical or virtual, thus presenting a great diversity of points of view in their discussion. In their discourse, the participants mix points of view that they present as their own and as the positionings of others with which they can either identify or which they oppose. Therefore, through these fictional voices, participants may, with more or less clarity, invoke allies, present points of view that they do not hold (Wibeck et al., 2004) or attribute to others claims that they have not necessarily constructed.

5.7.2   The voice of common sense

These voices of real or fictional characters are not the only ones that inhabit focus group discussions. According to Bakhtin (1986) speakers find themselves in a permanent dialogue with the 'cultural sphere', with common sense, with all that is taken for granted and adopted by the entire cultural community and part of the discourses in circulation. The same holds true for institutional discourse, or for the rules that are assumed to be generally known and which frame our activities.

Such rather 'distant' discourse is put on stage in two main ways. One of them takes the form of an explicit reminder.

Excerpt (16) LAU3B: 'The Couple' dilemma; translated from French

```
1    Marcelle   well it's not uh: I think that there is-
2               somehow you have to see- pro professional
3               confidentiality of this doctor indicates
4               that he doesn't have the right to say
5               anything to the husband about his wife.
6               that's it. it's it's the deontological
7               code of medical ethics.
```

As in the previous examples, the reminder of the law introduces a third voice into the debate. Thus, Marcelle transforms the nature of her own discourse and its positioning; she talks simultaneously as a participant in the group and as a spokesperson for the institution.

More often than not, dialoguing with the cultural sphere takes place indirectly, without it being explicitly quoted. This may happen in generic discourse, the origin of which is necessarily discursive: participants cannot have a direct experience of the issue at stake, and their knowledge has been construed through the circulation of discourses. This is the case with Joël, in the example below.

Excerpt (17) LAU1A: 'Work' dilemma; translated from French

```
1    Joël    I I think I don't really think, because I
2            think it's rather- the risk for the
3            doctor is rather getting it than giving
4            it ((laughing)) if I can say to [catch
5            it]
```

Here Joël resorts to a 'distant discourse'. But it is interesting to note that he uses it as though he were the source (through the deployment of 'I think'). Hence, other voices emerge within a discourse, and these can be presented as if they originated in one single voice (Vion, 1998a; 1998b). This phenomenon can be likened to that of stereotypes or frozen phrases.

Excerpt (18) PAR1A: 'The Couple' dilemma; translated from French

```
1    Inès    ((very fast)) is it there that wouldn't
2            it be a case of withholding assistance
3            from a person in danger?
```

In this example we can note that the word 'case' acts as a clue signalling that the speaker calls upon another discourse, in this instance a legal discourse or a legal discourse as filtered by the media. This may be a case of what Bakhtin calls heteroglossia, a discourse that makes appeal to different styles or genres. Incidentally, this example reminds the act of naming (in this case 'withholding assistance' is anchored in past discourses, as we recall Bakhtin saying:

> The speaker is not the biblical Adam, dealing only with virgin and till unnamed objects, giving them names for the first time….In reality, and we repeat this, any utterance, in addition to its own theme, always responds (in the broad sense of the word) in one form or another to others' utterances that precede it. The speaker is not Adam, and therefore the subject of his speech itself inevitably becomes the arena where his opinions meet those of his partners (in a conversation or dispute about some everyday event) or other viewpoints, world views, trends, theories, and so forth (in the sphere of cultural communication). (Bakhtin, 1986, p. 93–94)

We could go further and refer to what Bres and Vérine (2002) call masked heterogeneity. By naming an experience in a certain way, we act as though we apprehend it only as an object, while disguising that what we are actually doing is leaning on the discourse of others. In a discourse that presents itself as the product of a single voice, that of the speaker, there may be other hidden sources, other enunciators that the speaker mobilises on his or her behalf.

Thus, speakers inscribe themselves in a double dialogism: first, the external dialogism of discussion, second the internal dialogism deployed in the utterance itself. This heterogeneity can take different forms such as quotations, represented discourses, fictional speakers and the expression of different points of view or perspectives. In none of these cases can the speaker be considered as a monolithic entity. It is through his/her voice that different voices speak and that the discussion is inhabited by a great range of characters and discourses.

5.8   Self-dialogism

So far we have made a distinction between the locutor who elaborates the utterance and the enunciators who correspond to the expression of the different points of view. We have also seen that within an utterance, the speakers can present their own voice, in which case either the locutor coincides with the enunciator, or each can portray the voice of another. In the end, the boundaries between one's own voice and the voice of the other are not so clear-cut and numerous discursive games deploy the complexity of the ways speakers present themselves. Moreover, we must add a final and essential facet that is constitutive of the subject's heterogeneity. Speakers comment, restrict, modalise or modulate their own discourses. They either distance themselves from their very discourse or adhere to it.

Let us go back to Excerpt (8). Anabelle's positioning with respect to the dilemma is two-sided. As she seems to lean towards approving the generalised testing of prospective employees, she punctuates her discourse by a certain amount of markers that modulate her position: she presents herself as locutor ('I would really say' in line 1, and 'I think' in lines 4 and 13). This presentation has the effect of marking her position as subjective (Kerbrat-Orecchioni, 1980) and therefore as a position to which not everyone necessarily adheres. The use of hedges ('I don't know' and 'it seems' in line 5) also narrows the scope of the validity of what she says. Thus she presents herself in two lights, adopting two different positions towards the meanings that she invokes. This is what Bakhtin refers to as `a dialogue within oneself':

> Finally, dialogic relationships are also possible toward one's own
> utterance as a whole, toward its separate parts and toward an individual
> word within it, if we somehow detach ourselves from them, speak with
> an inner reservation, if we observe a certain distance from them, as if
> limiting our own authorship or dividing it in two. (Bakhtin, 1984, p. 184)

Thus, subjects present themselves as multifaceted even in cases where they do not call upon the voices of others or when they do not present themselves as others.

However, this self-dialogism is not unrelated to other-dialogism. On the one hand, such a dialogue with oneself is also a dialogue with common sense. On the other hand this dialogue with one's self is inscribed within the interaction and is related to positionings of the other participants. Therefore, we can assume that if Anabelle produces so many markers that show a distance to what she is saying, it is, on the one hand, because she argues in favour of a response that is not 'politically correct' and on the other hand, because she differentiates herself from her two interlocutors. Moreover, we can note that in the same group, Monique who modulates her opinion very little in the 'Work' dilemma, presents more distancing markers in 'The Couple' dilemma.

Excerpt (19) LAU1A: 'The Couple' dilemma; translated from French

```
1    Moderator and then you were [also]
2    Monique   [so me] in the present [case]
3    Moderator [well yeah] ((muffled laugh))
4    Monique   well I find that it's it's certain that
5              the qualifications you have to put them
6              right ?, but uh in the present case in as
7              much as the doctor uh, as it has been
8              said here, has established a relation of
9              trust with Jean as well as with Pauline,
10             I think that: yeah the risks are too
11             great, as you say also two months could
12             pass, or more, to uh to uh hide this
13             diagnosis from from Jean.
```

We can also note that in Monique's discourse the allusion to others' discourse ('as it has been said' in lines 7–8, 'as you say' in line 11) functions as hedges. In this turn Monique is responding to the position the moderator assigns to her. We can note that modalisation concerns not only the subject's relationship to what she is saying, but also to the manner of responding to the positioning demanded or assigned by the interlocutor. Therefore, modalisation, which is in theory oriented towards self discourse can also be interpreted as a means of positioning with respect to others' discourse.

5.9   Conclusion

Participants in focus groups are frequently asked to debate, discuss or express their point of view on problems that are presented to them either as a dilemma or as an open topic. In this chapter, we have tried to show that the co-constructed and dialogical nature of participants' positionings cannot be conceived of as a manifestation of a simple relationship between the speaker and the problem with which he or she is presented. On the contrary, in responding to the problem speakers construct a multifaceted positioning: they answer from different points of view and they resort to different voices. This complexity can be summed up in the following way:

- Subjects position themselves explicitly in different ways with respect to a particular situation. They necessarily construct themselves as heterogenous and multivoiced subjects;
- They enter into an interaction with the characters invoked in the dilemmas. In so doing, they make explicit the fact that they take a stance from different positions;

- In their argumentation they contrast their perspectives to the discourses and the positions that they attribute to their interlocutors;
- They call on different voices, whether real, fictional or virtual, which allow them to evoke, adhere to or refuse different positionings;
- As locutors, they do not present a monolithic image, their own voice is also submitted to an internal dialogism constituted by restrictions, modulations and estrangements of various kinds.

Therefore, focus-group participants are positioned in a complex way. Since the 'same' contents have been constructed discursively in different manners, they do not have the 'same' discursive relevance. In and through these diverse constructions subjects also indicate the complexity of representations underpinning their discourses. Taking this heterogeneity into account is essential to the understanding of the processes that underpin social representations and, more generally, socially shared knowledge. It is not only a matter of asking who is speaking in a focus group. More importantly it is about how to identify dialogical characteristics at the heart of the construction of social representations and being truthful to their density and dynamism.

Notes

1   In this chapter we shall focus on another aspect of positioning. In Chapter 4, positioning is understood in the sense of orientation to role expectations, which can be considered one aspect or facet of the activity of the participants. Here we will focus on the way participants present themselves through their discourse, in the accomplishment of the discussion task.

2   This chapter does not aim to account for the dynamics of argumentation as such but rather of the dialogical nature of positioning.

3   This distinction is akin to the analysis of the notion of the speaker by Goffman in *Forms of Talk* (1981); our 'enunciator' corresponds roughly to Goffman's 'principal', and out 'locutor' to his 'author'.

4   In French the pronoun on is characterised by the diversity of its values: it can refer back to a defined whole, equivalent to nous (we), to something generic, equivalent to 'everyone' or 'anyone' and to an indefinite value, that can not be assigned to a particular entity and that could also be identified with the speaker.

6   Dialogue and the circulation of ideas

6.1   Introduction

We have characterised our approach to discourse as 'dialogical'. This approach has earlier made us do a close-up of the framings of communicative activities involved in focus groups (Chapter 4) and of positionings and voices in the discussions (Chapter 5). In this chapter, we concentrate more on the ways in which content is constructed and expressed: topics, topical trajectories, recurrent topics (or themes), analogies and distinctions, metaphors and other discursive devices used by focus-group participants. A thematic analysis will also look at dialogues as resources and opportunities for expressing socially shared knowledge. Thus, we will also approach aspects of social representations and cultural assumptions, which will then be further explored in Chapter 7.

The particular perspective to be adopted in this chapter implies that we take a look at how participants in focus groups generate – or activate – and circulate ideas and understandings. Our assumption is that the dynamics of a group discussion enables the participants to trade on others' understandings, to come up with more ideas and associations than is possible in, for example, individual interviews. Although interviewing individuals has occupied a central position in the methodological tool kit of psychology, the use of 'thought experiments' invoking groups has a respectable tradition too. For example, Fleck (1935) talked about the 'collective of thought' in a group of individuals having intellectual contact with one another, exchanging ideas and mutually influencing each other in the pursuit of the same goal. This can occasionally also occur in a situated interaction in a group assembled ad-hoc, as for example a focus group. Indeed, a conversation – as in a focus group – can be seen as a case of 'distributed cognition' (Linell et al., 2001), that is, the group as a whole works like a team in which individuals think together, or in other words, cognition is distributed across the different team members (and made public in and through their talk) but it is only in the group as a whole that the thoughts and their constituent ideas are accomplished.

Ideas emerge in the interaction between participants, as well as, of course, in the interaction within single selves ('internal dialogue/dialogism', Section 5.8). When participants discuss the issues-in-focus, they make use of metaphors, metonymies and other tropes, prototypical examples and stories, quotes – mostly hypothetical ones – from other ('virtual') participants, etc. They try to sort out their understandings and confusions, often using analogies and distinctions which serve to locate the phenomena under discussion in a world which contains other things that are often better understood than those which are now being explored. Arguments (e.g. analogies) give rise to counter-arguments (distinctions), which in turn make counter-counter-arguments relevant, agreements engender disagreements which in turn may give rise to new disagreements, etc.

Our analyses will enable us to explore the question of how meanings are constructed in situ. But we can also generate hypotheses about what semantic, conceptual and encyclopaedic resources participants recruit and draw upon, in order to make sense. These resources include word meanings and concepts (with their 'meaning potentials'; Norén and Linell, 2007) and bodies of knowledge ('social representations'), but also more concrete ideas – arguments, examples, wordings, etc. – that are brought in and reconstructed ('recontextualised', 'quoted').

6.2   The dialogue of ideas

Dialogues are opportunities for sense-making. This implies that we should not look upon focus groups as occasions in which we as researchers simply tap social representations that already exist beforehand in a fixed and ready-made form. In fact, many focus-group participants go through an initial stage of their sessions in which they claim, sometimes unanimously, that they do not know what to say about the issues-in-focus. This need not be just a ritualised opening; it may authentically reflect participants' initial predicament of uncertainty. Yet, in an overwhelming number of cases, the same participants later develop a rich discussion together. This seems to indicate the power of the dialogue dynamics to make people think together. In this chapter, we shall have a look at some cases of these 'dialogues of ideas'.

If we embrace a dialogical theory, it must imply that we look at talk both as interaction and as verbal discourse (or text). We can say that a dialogical analysis of (a piece of) discourse, such as a focus-group session or a corpus of such sessions, will focus on interaction at three different levels:

> The first is the interaction between speakers and interlocutors in the situated encounter. A conversation is not a series of juxtaposed individual contributions by autonomous speakers, but an intricate web of sense-makings, in which (in principle) each and every contribution is interdependent with previous and possible next contributions.
>
> Secondly, there is the interaction between thoughts, ideas and arguments in the discursive or textual web that is generated by participants, in accordance with the above first point.
>
> Thirdly, there is the 'interaction with sociocultural traditions', i.e. the interdependence between different discourses (ways and traditions of talking about the issue) and between the communicative genres involved.

According to the second point above that we will develop in this chapter, we must see the text itself as dynamic. Arguments are dialogically and interactionally constituted; hence, the interaction is not only between speaking and thinking selves but also between different contributions creating a dialogical web with association paths, and arguments with their elaborations and counter-arguments. Following Bakhtin, we recontextualise the notion of 'voices in the text' from participants' concrete utterances and enunciations to the expression and elaborations of ideas, positions and understandings. Even if participants try to build intersubjective understanding, their '[i]deas are in tension; they clash, judge and evaluate each other' (Marková, 2003a, p. 257). In other words, we look at how ideas and arguments – rather than speakers – are made to interact. At some level, we are interested in how ideas develop, irrespectively of who exactly produces the particular constituents of the joint argumentation.

The idea of the 'dialogue of ideas' is close to the notion of 'circulation of ideas' that has been current in French dialogist linguistics (François, 1993; Hudelot, 1994). It is important to emphasise that this perspective does not presuppose any set of fixed and ready-made ideas that just move around; rather, the ideas are continuously, or at least potentially, negotiated, modified and transformed, as they circulate in dialogue.

What we will propose in this chapter is a kind of rhetorical and interactional discourse analysis.[1] This approach does not only record what sorts of content are taken up, or get mentioned (as in conventional content analysis), but it also attends to which linguistic and discursive devices are used. It will ask under which contextual conditions, and with what rhetorical force and dialogical consequences, ideas and thoughts are constructed and used. This is of course also a particular kind of content analysis. However, we prefer to avoid the term 'content analysis', since this connotes a traditional kind of quantitative approach, in which key words are treated as decontextualised items and then coded in terms of (sometimes pre-determined) categories (e.g. Weber, 1990). We assume that one cannot decontextualise words and statements, because they belong to more comprehensive argumentation sequences. The meaning of a constituent contribution to dialogue and that of the whole sequence, of which it is part, are interdependent (Linell, 1998a, p. 87: 'act-activity interdependence'). Thus, while we do not intend our position as a wholesale rejection of conventional methods of content analysis, we do think that they are of limited value for finding out about socially shared knowledge. For example, as we pointed out in Chapter 3, our analysis does not build upon the basic assumption made in most conventional forms of content analysis, namely that each unit of content, each topic or theme can be (in principle) attributed to one single participant.

In the following sections, we will first deal with the analysis of free-floating discourse. We will then group the analytical products into two major categories, tentatively called discursive figures (roughly sections 6.4–8) and aspects of recurrent topics and social representations (roughly Section 6.9). The former are chiefly concerned with the communicative (rhetorical) devices participants use for developing matters of content, whereas the latter are more oriented to the actual content of the discourse. However, the boundaries between these two categories are quite fuzzy and should not be overstated.

Before we turn to the concrete analysis of manifest content of focus-group discourse, we need to define some of the terms that we will use in talking about the content. We shall use the terms 'topic' and 'theme', but also 'thema' (and, in Chapter 7, 'proto-thema'). The former terms are linked primarily with the concrete discourse itself, whereas the latter terms originate in the theory of science (Holton, 1975) and in the theory of social representations (Moscovici and Vignaux, 1994; Marková, 2003a). All these terms are assigned different meanings in different traditions, in grammar, literary theory and social-scientific discourse analysis. There is no need to go into an exhaustive discussion of these differences. Instead, we shall simply describe how we will use the terms:

- 'Topics' are things, subjects, states-of-affairs, ideas etc. that participants talk about for a while in a given situation. Thus, something becomes a 'topic' only if it is discursively pursued over a sequence, at the very least a short one (Linell, 1998a, p. 183). Participants have to stay on topic (the term 'topic' being derived from the Greek word 'topos' meaning 'place') for at least a local sequence, an episode or a sub-episode (see below); otherwise it would not be a topic, but only a thing mentioned in passing. Some topics are brought up only once or in passing in particular episodes, others recur more or less often (in our case: in several focus groups, or several times in the same group discussion). We are primarily interested in such recurrent topics, which we will call 'themes', which our next term.

- 'Themes' will here be taken to refer to topics that recur several times in a conversation, a focus group, a text, or a corpus of such discourses. Themes are simply recurrent topics. However, we often want to proceed further in the analysis, and group themes into big(ger) themes (or clusters of themes). The final step will be to relate these to underlying assumptions behind these, '(cultural) themata'. This is our next point in this list.

- 'Thema(ta)' is a term used about general cultural assumptions that (are posited by analysts to) underlie the discourse. However, they are more or less directly expressed in the discourse of the focus-group participants. (In Chapter 7, we shall also talk about 'proto-thema(ta)', which are assumptions that are not so overtly verbalised, or thematised, in the discourse.)

6.3 Topic analysis: from the flow of discourse to topics and themes

Faced with a focus-group transcript, where should one begin when one wants to make an overview of the content? As many commentators have remarked, a conventional content analysis reduces the data to abstract and decontextualised categories which can stand for quite different ideas in their various instances, something which the analyst will realise once she examines properly the contextual intricacies and the divergent sequentially dependent imports of the different instantiations. Hence, we noted in Section 6.2 that a conventional content analysis loses so many details of the talk that the dialogical nature of meaning-making becomes totally obscured.

Nonetheless, the analyst has to start somewhere. Since talk is organised in time, and topics are basically sequentially ordered, our suggestion is to start by trying to draw boundaries between topical episodes. That is, here we agree with all those discourse analysts who have argued that since topics as such (as defined above in Section 6.2) are difficult to operationalise in authentic free-floating discourse, one had better work with 'topical episodes', that is sequences of talk which are internally topically coherent, but which can be identified (at a reasonable level of reliability) by their boundaries, which demarcate them from adjacent episodes (Linell, 1998a, Chapter 10).[2] A topical episode is a continuous stretch of talk[3] which is made coherent by the participants pursuing – for a while – the same local activity or the same 'communicative project' (Luckmann, 1995; Linell, 1998a, p. 217ff.),[4] such as describing an object, telling a story or arguing a point, or finding out how much the interlocutor knows about the current topic. In other words, an episode is usually coherent, held together, on at least two accounts, in terms of the topic(s) (what is talked about) and in terms of the communicative project (why the topics are talked about).

In actual fact, however, what is often understood as the 'same' topic is not an inert object; rather it unfolds dynamically across topical aspects that shade into each other. In addition, topics do not simply follow one another as autonomous units in a sequence; rather, they develop out of interactions between prior, present and projected future topics, and the transitions are often shaded (or 'seamless'). As Korolija (1998) has demonstrated, while topical episodes are bounded action sequences, there are usually links across topical boundaries, and sometimes between topics and the surrounding situation.

The dynamic nature of topic development makes a complete and exhaustive dialogical analysis quite difficult, if not impossible. Therefore, in carrying out our analysis, we have to bracket some of the dialogical properties of the data. In practice, our analysis should begin by the attempt to identify episodes and label their topics. A topic is assigned to each local sequence consisting of the introduction plus uptake of an idea, an argument, a subtopic or topical aspect. The uptake comprises responses to the idea, and participants' joint negotiation of its meaning. In identifying a boundary between episodes, we exploit the fact that the closing of an episode is often characterised, apart from the absence of new semantic substance, by chains of minimal responses, pauses, laughter, the use of idioms and commonplaces, etc.

In practice, our analytic procedure will assign to each episode a label, alluding to its semantic content. Excluded from this coding are utterances or sequences that represent time-outs from the issue-in-focus, e.g. episodes evoked by the concrete surrounding situation, and episodes consisting of small talk or topic-less sequences. When different episodes deal with approximately the same content, they would be given the same, or a similar, label. At this most down-to-earth level, our labelling results in a rough – largely 'non-theoretical' but fairly exhaustive – list or catalogue of what focus-group participants talk about.[5] It would be desirable to show several examples of how the unitisation into topical episodes might be done. Due to space restrictions, we will confine ourselves to one example, which, in addition, has been cut down. It is an example with fairly long, single-speaker turns:

Excerpt (1) GEF1: Young Christian people discussing GMO. From the beginning of the session; translated from Swedish[6]

```
1   David    but after all this thing one reads about um (.)
2            gene manipulation now like that's journalistic
3            articles (Gaby and Hanna: mm) and um (.) then there
4            are always many people in the surroundings who
5            want to convey a lot of opinions, some kind of
6            opinion about gene-manipulated food. Then at the
7            end of the day it's easy to take a stance and
8            then one may not change that stance, like one's
9            stance, so very easily (Hanna: mm) (about 5 lines
10           omitted) so therefore it's a little dangerous
11           too if one forms an odd opinion
12  Hanna    mm coz it may have some odd basis too (David:
13           exactly) or something one has heard only half the
14           truth [like, one has listened mostly to somebody
15           to some arguments
16  David        [when once one has taken a stance it's not
17           so terribly easy to change it
18  Gaby     but I'd probably think this way that (.) it is
19           not so dangerous if it keeps- as long as it is
20           kept within the confines of ethics, but as you
21           say it's so different
22  David    but who is it that decides on the confines of
23           ethics?
24  Gaby     no, that's what I mean. Coz then one thinks that
25           this way that all people surely have some
26           barriers but (Eve: not now) if one has started
27           to research something then it's clear that one
28           goes on if one can and [that's what is horrible with
29  Hanna                           [yeah, in any case if one
30           thinks that this is something which is interesting
31           to find out how it functions and what happens
32           and how good it can get and so on. Then only
33           that can become, then perhaps one thinks like
34           it's more interesting than the purpose in the end
35  Eve      yeah, one loses track of the purpose perhaps
36           (Hanna: yeah) why does one do it
37  Hanna    even if that was not the intention from the
38           beginning
39  Eve      that's when the horrible thing starts I think
40           when you move across these boundaries
41  David    though after all there are always a lot of
42           other people in our society who think like
43           who slow down such a development (Eve: yes)
44           there are always conservative forces (.)
45           I think
46  Eve          [yeah but I-
```

```
47  Fred    [yeah if you say that there there's a
48          difference then between investigating the
49          genes and seeing what this combination of
50          genes may result in or so, y'know, if you
51          look at the DNA and look at which substances
52          they are, and then you can map out and look
53          at if you put these substances together in
54          this order then you get a a, well a better plant
55          that can cope with noxious animals in a better
56          way or or something like that, but then like
57          transplanting that into a tomato or something
58          like that and get a more robust tomato there
59          there's a difference between these things
60          after all ((continues for a few seconds more))
```

Our analysis is that a new episode starts with David's long turn on lines 1–11 (though the preceding sequence is not shown here). This episode may be labelled 'Rigidity of stances', but also 'Fear'. The next episode, dealing with 'Ethics', starts with lines 18–21; it is succeeded by another episode about 'Research vs. applications', starting with lines 46–47. It is clear that episodes could be named differently, and also that episode boundaries are not self-evident. Thus, when Gaby in lines 18–21 slips into talk about 'the confines of ethics', she uses elements of the previous talk about the fear of odd opinions ('not so dangerous' cf. line 10). Similarly, Fred in his last (shown) turn exploits the previous topical aspect of resistance to research. In other words, new episodes typically recontextualise topical aspects from prior episodes. Nevertheless, new episodes do focus on new topics or topical aspects. On the formal side, we can note that episode-initiating turns in this sequence often start with 'but' (lines 1, 18, 46). New episodes are typically initiated by somebody who was not the main speaker of the previous episode (Gaby initiates the second episode, Fred the third one). In many cases, the initiator also becomes the main speaker of the ensuing episode (David in episode 1, Fred in episode 3); one can therefore say that episodes and their topics are often 'owned' by particular individuals, even if they are of course developed in collaboration with the other participants.

The next analytic step, after unitising talk into topical episodes and labelling these, consists in going through the lists (and the corresponding transcripts) in looking for 'recurrent topics', or at least recurrent instances of similar topics. A recurrent topic may be termed a 'theme'. (Here, we allude to analogies with themes in e.g. music or film.) The question arises of course what one should mean by 'recurrent'. In practice, we have often set up what may appear as a rather low requirement (in our studies, which were based on 4–10 focus groups); a recurrent topic must occur in at least two different groups.

Recurrent topics are, as we will see, often associated with analogies, distinctions, metaphors, metonymies, and other discursive devices. If we find many manifestations of the same types, i.e. recurrent topics, examples and arguments, the analyst may posit themes and various topic-specific ways of thinking and talking (cf. topical trajectories in Section 6.4) about the issues-in-focus. Via several intermediate levels of 'thematic clusters', the analyst may arrive at what might be the 'big themes' (Jovchelovitch, 1995; 2000), the (analyst's) end-product of grouping themes into major categories, This can be done separately for each focus group, or culture-in-miniature, an empirical question being if the theme structure is the same for all focus groups (hence evidence of a wide-spread social representation) or different (evidence for variants of the same social representation, of different representations, or of the absence of anything like a social representation?). From the major thematic clusters, we can then proceed to seek to identify underlying assumptions. This we will take up in the final section of this chapter, and then more comprehensively in the discussion of themata in Chapter 7.

Themes are aspects of the collective discourse of the focus groups. It is true that sometimes, certain topics and themes are pursued mainly by single participants; they are 'owned' by them. But in general, we can not tie ideas and opinions to individuals. Myers (2004) has remarked that some focus-group researchers worry about 'the contamination of individual opinions' that takes place in the focus group, due to various aspects of the group dynamics. For us, this is not a major problem, but rather a pseudo-problem, since our interest is not in individual opinions but in socially shared knowledge. We follow Myers (ibid.), Bloor et al. (2001) and others in assuming that focus groups are better at 'explor[ing] norms and meanings held by the group, not individual responses' (Myers, 2004, p. 51). We would add that this is consonant with a dialogical theory of social representations.

6.4   Trying out arguments and understandings: analogies and distinctions

In focus groups, participants develop ideas and propose points on which they may agree or disagree. For example, in our GEF and GTD groups, participants discuss genetic modification of organisms and the application of gene therapy to human beings. In and through the discursive process, such abstract issues are rendered concrete and more precise. In the following, we shall see how participants try out examples, analogies, distinctions, metaphors etc. as 'candidate' (provisional) means for understanding the issues-in-focus. With the help of these discursive devices, participants make their often abstract and diffuse ideas and assumptions more concrete; this is what Billig (1987), in his analysis of argumentation, calls 'particularization'. Conversely, one can think of the examples, analogies, etc. as being tentatively proposed by the participants as typical of the abstract phenomenon (Billig's 'categorization'). We can also observe how, as Bakhtin, Billig and others maintain, 'the opposition of potential points of view is essential to interaction' (Myers, 1999, p. 574).

A common argumentative device is to propose that the phenomenon in focus, or some example thereof, is similar or analogical to some other thing, often something better known. Such 'analogies' have the basic form of X SIMILAR TO Y (X = phenomenon in focus, or an example thereof, SIMILAR TO is a semantic predicate that can be expressed as 'is like', 'reminds me of', 'is the same as', 'is similar to', etc.). Let us look at the following example first:

Excerpt (2) GTD4: 200ff., cf. Bakshi et al., 2000: 13; translated from Swedish. In the middle of a discussion of gene therapy, the focus group consists of parents of children at a secondary school

```
1    Brian   but how after all is this gene therapy different
2            from what we have been working with for a hundred
3            years?
4    Alex    you mean of course ordinary traditional
5            peasants' breeding?
6    Brian   yeah exactly [selection of
7    Alex                 [you take you take the most
8            magnificent bull and
9    Brian   exactly precisely (Alex: yes) that's of course
10           gene (.) manipulation that too, we
11           choose (Anne: mm then it's) breeding
12           [you take this cow and it-
13   Anne    [it's more *manual in a way*
14   Brian   yeah it is slow [I assume it has to be
15   Anne                    [indeed it is not, the other thing
16           it's y'know
17   Brian   but it's the same thing we are doing=
18   Anne    yes yeah (Kate: mm) and likewise this thing
19           too [and ba-
20   Brian       [tomatoes and animals and
21   Anne    yeah tomatoes and animals and=
22   Brian   =wheat and oats and [barley and
23   Anne                        [virus as a weapon (Cathy:
24           yeah) yeah
25   Alex    but isn't it after all so that when when you
26           breed it it's still some kind of natural selection
```

```
27            process still what you um (.) if you do gene
28            manipulation then then you CAN in some way
29            create something that is not [viable
30   Kate                                  [Belgian Blue
31   Alex     yeah it's such a boundary case, right?
```

In this episode, Brian and Alex propose an analogy between breeding ('ordinary traditional peasants' breeding', lines 4–5) and gene manipulation; referring to bovine breeding, they claim that 'that's of course gene manipulation too' (lines 9–10, cf. 'the same thing', line 17). However, other participants respond that there are crucial differences, which in our terms (cf. below) amounts to setting up a 'distinction': Anne says (laughingly) about traditional breeding that 'it's more manual in a way' (line 13). Brian holds on to the analogy (line 17), although he concedes that ordinary breeding is more 'slow' (line 14). Anne confirms that 'the other thing', i.e. gene manipulation, is not slow, thus consolidating her own position. Alex concludes that breeding, but not gene manipulation, is 'some kind of natural selection process' (line 26). Kate introduces a case which was much discussed in Sweden at the time: the bovine breed 'Belgian Blue' (line 30). The debate focused on the fact that the cows of this breed cannot give birth naturally. Interestingly, though 'Belgian Blue' is a result of 'natural' breeding, rather than genetic modification, it seems to be introduced here as a case of the latter, as an example of something unnatural ('not viable', line 29) which can be created through gene manipulation.

As we can see in Excerpt (2), another argumentative device, besides analogies, is to use 'distinctions' (contrasts, opposites) of the basic form of X DIFFERENT FROM Y (where the gloss DIFFERENT FROM can be formulated as 'is different from', 'is not the same as', etc.).

Let us look at another example, which is replete with analogies and distinctions:

Excerpt (3) GDT3: Members of an organisation for disabled people, cf. Bakshi et al., 2000: 25; translated from Swedish

```
1    Peter    okay, as I said where where do we begin?
2    Mark     well
              (Pause)
3    Mark     I think this is such a BIG subject it makes you
4             [like this
5    Peter    [yes it is
6    Mark     yes
              (Pause)
7    Mary     mm
8    Mark     no=
9    Peter    =yes but this thing about (Mark: yeah)
```

10		well fetal diagnostics then (Mark: yeah)
11		or I consider (1.5) it gives sort of
12		unanticipated possibilities then to to see (1.0)
13		to be able to see which diseases
14		the foetus can possibly suffer from but
15		those risks about it making a selection
16		they are terrible (1.5) so it is a VERY
17		DIFFICULT question
18	Mark	no I think you are already going into an
19		ethical cleansing operation so to speak
20		(Peter: mm) and and um (1.5) well in well
21		Nazism hh (Peter: yeah) quite frankly,
22		I think
23	Ellen	mm no it is [it is sad
24	Mark	[I mean I I–
25	Mary	yes I feel that just this it is like Hitler
26		manners (Mark: yes) but in a refined way=
27	Mark	=yeah (1.0) yeah yes yes (Peter: mm) disguised
28	Mary	yeah disguised sort of something like that
29		(Peter: yes) I feel and it is a very SENSITIVE
30		subject so you (1.5) and I believe that as the
31		parent of a child (Mark: mm) I think you feel
32		that um (1.0) it's very emotion- (1.5) it stirs
33		up a whole lot of feelings (Mark: yes)
34		within you like this that springs forth
35		(Peter: mm) and you (1.5) well I think this is
36		really hard to talk about (Mark: mm) because
37		you you have this.
38	Ellen	yes it's so close=
39	Mary	=it's so CLOSE to you (Mark: yeah)
40		and you know how much you love YOUR kids
41		and all that stuff
42	Mark	yes but then let me ask you, being a parent,
43		I think like this directly, I mean your child
44		children several of them? who has got that?
45	Mary	what did you say?
46	Mark	did you have one child?
47	Mary	um one child=
48	Mark	=yes (Mary: mm) but you don't want to be
49		without hi- her or him (Mary: no) I suppose
50		(Mary: no) no and I mean it's the same thing
51		with me and my wife then who are rheumatics
52		the two of us (Mary: mm) sure you feel like
53		this well if we have children there is
54		a very BIG CHANCE that this (Mary: mm)
55		or risk (Mary: mm mm mm mm) whatever you like
56		((giggle)) (Peter: mm) that they will be ill
57		then but (1.0) I I would rather have (1.0) I would

58		rather live than so to speak if I look back at my
59		twenty years as a rheumatic (Mary and Peter: mm)
60		if one were able to eliminate oneself so to
61		speak ((general laughter)) no but something
62		[like that
63	Peter	[yeah yeah sure
64	Ellen	mm
65	Mark	so (1.0) [I'd rather
66	Peter	[no it see- well what I consider to
67		be possibilities in this research or so,
68		are those they are beginning to manage to
69		remove the genes that are possibly defective
70		and replace them with healthy ones, and as
71		long as you can (1.0) rest- restrain yourself
72		and only remove those risk genes or whatever
73		they are called, and and replace and diminish
74		the risk for the child to GET a disease then
75		I think that it is great (1.0) but as I said
76		(Mark: yes) when you intervene and you decide
77		who are allowed to have children or which
78		children are allowed to be born
79	Ellen	which ones that [will be okay
80	Mark	[yes it yeah yeah
81	Peter	[which ones that will be okay,
82		yes then then it's frightening so that um
83	Mark	it sort of reminds you of breeding then I
84		think, doesn't it?
85	Ellen	it doesn't [feel well
86	Mark	[cows and animals and
87	Peter	[yeah and well
88	Mark	they remove everything that's defective
89		(Peter: mm) a dog that was born with three legs
90		he isn't allowed to live for long (Peter: no
91		and look) no but that's a bit like breeding
92	Andy	well that's the situation I [think
93	Mark	[yeah
94	Ellen	[yes
95	Mary	and then there is this thing about choosing
96		(Mark?: yes) who is (1.0) (Mark?: yes) who is
97		responsible, are you as a parent supposed to
98		drop your child (Ellen and Mark: mm) and then. (1.0)
99		I also think that this is a matter for society
100		too because if (Mark: Mm) if I as a parent take
101		that responsibility and decide that I want my
102		child even though it has a defect then society
103		will tell you that you made your own choice
104		(Ellen+Peter: mm) (Mark: yeah) you can't count
105		on any help from us, that's what I think is sort

```
106           of also (Peter: yeah) a danger (Peter: mm)
107           because it's it's ALREADY here (Peter: mm) that
108           way of thinking, this that (1.0) um well that you
109           (1.0) [you
110 Mark           [there shouldn't be any costs for it
111           sort of
112           (2.0)
```

This excerpt has been drawn from the very start of the focus group. After some initial difficulties in getting the discussion going, Peter brings up 'fetal diagnostics' as the first exemplar phenomenon (line 10). A distinction is hinted at; the technique gives new opportunities for diagnosing diseases, but it involves selection and risks ('but those risks...', line 15). The latter gives rise to an analogy with cleansing operations (line 19) and Nazism, both analogies being quite explicit ('cleansing so to speak', line 19; 'it is like Hitler', line 25). A new distinction is introduced; although fetal diagnostics is like 'Hitler manners', it is so in a 'refined' way (line 26), then reformulated as 'disguised' (line 27). That concludes the first subtopic, which was enacted through a local sequence or episode (lines 9–27) initiated by Peter but continued by two other main contributors (Mark, Mary).

From the turn beginning in line 28 onwards, a new local topic appears: 'sensitive' subjects 'stir up feelings' (lines 32–33), because these things are so 'close' (lines 38–39) to people. These turns, for example lines 38–39, involve a lot of mutual alignment and agreement, as does the whole sequence of episodes. This sequence has several associative links to the prior sub-episode; thus, 'disguised' (line 28) is taken directly from the prior turn, and 'hard to talk about' (line 36) goes back to the very emphatic 'a very difficult question' in lines 16–17. However, the sequence clearly expresses the parents' perspective, rather than that of those deciding on the use of fetal diagnostics. A parent would not want to 'be without' his child (lines 48–49), and those who are disabled (rheumatics are mentioned) would not want to 'eliminate [them]selves' (line 60).

Beginning with line 66, a new sub-episode is initiated by Peter who tries, it seems, to refer back to his argument on the difficult choice (lines 16–17). Now he introduces a distinction that comes up frequently in the GTD data; it is better to use gene therapy on living humans ('to remove risk genes', line 72) than to 'decide on who are allowed to have children or which children are allowed to be born' (lines 77–78). The latter is less acceptable, since it 'reminds you of breeding' (lines 83–84) animals ('a bit like breeding', line 91).

A fourth local topic is begun in the turn starting on line 95 (continuation not shown here); the question of who is responsible for choosing. If it is a matter for the parents, then it is also a matter for society. A clash of interests is hinted at, which becomes more explicit in other parts of the data; society leaves difficult decisions to parents, but is not prepared to back them up by taking on responsibility for the economical consequences (line 110).

As we can see, the four local episodes that build up this spate of focus-group talk contain several distinctions and analogies. We could identify cycles of such devices; using GTD for eliminating diseases might be good, but it is not good (Distinction no. 1) to choose selectively who are going to live, because such selections are like cleansing (Analogy no. 1) or Nazism/ Hitler manners (Analogy no. 2), although of a 'refined' or 'disguised' kind (Distinction no. 2).

As one might guess from these examples, an analogy is often part and parcel of (a partially) implicit argument of the following import: Y is good/ acceptable/accepted or bad/non-acceptable/rejected, and therefore X too should be accepted or not accepted, respectively. That is, the point of the analogies in our data is to evaluate GEF or GTD. Our examples include the following arguments (which of course usually build upon a non-demonstrable proof procedure in a strictly logical sense). The warrants for the arguments could be seen partly as underlying assumptions, partly as conclusions from the argumentative episode:

> Gene therapy on humans reminds us of Nazi society, elitist society, the production of perfect human beings, which are all arguably bad things, and, gene therapy is therefore, by implication, non-acceptable;

> Gene therapy is similar to other medical treatments (on adults), e.g. the use of penicillin, which are arguably good things, and therefore, gene therapy is acceptable;

> Genetic diagnostics is similar to other kinds of diagnostics, e.g. ultrasound, which is possibly good, and hence, genetic diagnostics is acceptable (?);

> Genetic engineering of food is akin to traditional plant-breeding (cross-breeding), breeding of animals, giving antibiotics in the food for animals, which might be good things, and hence, genetic engineering of food should, in most cases, be accepted;

> Gene technology is similar to other kinds of innovations or inventions, e.g. credit cards (sic!), which first gave rise to (unwarranted) fear or suspicion, but then proved to be good things, and hence, gene technology is acceptable.

When, by contrast, we are confronted with a distinction, the embedding, and sometimes implicit, argument is often the following: If Y is acceptable, since

X is different from Y, X, by contrast, should not be accepted. Of course, we also find the reverse case: if Y is not acceptable, and since X is different from Y, X should be accepted. Often, arguments make distinctions between X1 (one form of the phenomenon in focus) and X2 (another form of it). Examples from our corpus include:

- to choose who is going to live on the basis of sex, which is bad, is different from choosing according to presence of genes for diseases, which is therefore acceptable;

- to cure diseases or eliminate risks by taking away genes in living individuals, which is good, is different from aborting foetuses, which is (therefore) not acceptable;

- to use genetic engineering in the production of drugs used for medication, which is good, is different from the genetic engineering of food, which is (therefore) bad.

6.5   Analogy-distinction cycles and topical trajectories

Interestingly enough, analogies and distinctions often appear to be in dialogue with each other, as we demonstrated in Excerpt 3. Actors use analogies and distinctions in argumentative chains or (sequences of) 'analogy-distinction cycles'. Most often, an analogy is first proposed, whereupon a distinction is counter-posed (but the order can also be reversed). That is, the basic form is: X IS SIMILAR TO Y (in aspect Z) *but*, on the other hand, X IS DIFFERENT FROM Y (in aspect W).

Prototypical examples and analogies often come close to what might be regarded as metonymies and metaphors. By drawing examples from a family of metaphors, participants may point to a perspective present in the social representation; the phenomenon in focus is seen as similar to things in another field. We have already referred to numerous examples in the cases of GEF and GTD: Nazism, previous innovations (e.g. penicillin, credit cards, ultrasound), manufacturing of drugs, breeding of plants and animals, interbreeding, antibiotics for livestock, pesticides on crops, other dangerous new things, other cases with no real choice (opportunities to do good are constrained by economy, etc.). Analogies and metaphors are often drawn from science fiction dystopian scenarios, the superordinate category of which seems to be 'horrible or disastrous things' (see 6.7).

Our next example also involves some analogy-distinction cycles, in addition to other discursive devices:

Excerpt (4) GEF9: Greenpeace Members, cf. Wibeck, 2002; translated from Swedish

```
1    Ben      [but well also when it comes to food uh well for example
2             if you take these articles as a starting point if you
3             if you think for example about the (1.5) um (1.5)
4             modification or manipulation that has occurred with maybe
5             above all CROPS all (Diana: mm) well if you go back in
6             history like eight or ten thousand years you can you can
7             compare and see that each each grain of corn that you
8             planted generated about two grains of corn so to speak one of
9             which had to be replanted in order to yield a new plant
10            (Diana: mm) so well it was simply a one-to-one relationship
11            in principle so you received planted one and were able to
12            eat one (2.0)
13   Ben      so meanwhile then they have not by directly manipulating
14            the GENES for they kne(w)- had no knowledge about that,
15            but anyway by selecting the seeds that looked best and so on
16            during many thousands of years they have made them today
17            give fifty sixty and seventy times (.) the stake
18            (1.5)
19   Ben      [and and
20   Anne     [yes but that isn't only it isn't only
21   Ben      and this this I mean is a kind of genetic manipulation
22   Anne     (yeah but yes) though it isn't microscopic in the way
23            it is today and it has certainly led to some problems
24            but to a certain extent or to a certain maybe there isn't
25            a proper boundary but as long as you are in control of what
26            is taking place
27   Anne     but you AREN'T
28   Ben      no no that may be and that that is the problem I guess,
29            but the basic thought itself to simply get more out of less
30            (Anne: mm) that that seems to me a good thought but
31            on the other hand you often have a tendency not not to
32            see the disadvantages (Anne: mm) not to see what is on
33            the other side, because the farmer who sells this just says
34            'haa I got three grains of corn extra out of this' (Anne: mm)
35            he might not see that it has destroyed something else
36            somewhere that may destroy so much MORE than
37            [he could ever anticipate
38   Diana    [but well but isn't that somewhat different from genetic
39            manipulation cause I mean it's still they it is possible to
40            crossbreed them, I mean genetic manipulation then you
41            crossbreed things that don't actually fit [together then
42   Anne                                              [just the same
43   Fanny    it isn't NATURAL it would never (Diana: no well)
44            [work out in a natural way
45   Anne     [exactly exactly
46   Diana    so THAT'S what is a bit
47   Anne     and it's not that it sounds so good either (1.5) uh (1.5)
```

```
48              well we'll have more rice (Diana: mm) and there'll be less
49              starvation in the world (Diana: mm) and so on but it it
50              doesn't mean at all that (1.5) it it is the rich companies
51              or the rich successful companies that are gonna afford
52              this kind of research, they are going to be it it
53              do you see what I mean it it may not directly be for
54              the good of the poor or the starving COUNTRIES in that way
55              but it it it's more like US that already have (.)
56              a rather good production of food [yeah yeah
57 Diana                                        [a VERY GOOD production
58 Ben     mm mm
59 Anne    we don't actually NEED this (Diana: no no) sort of
60              do you see what I mean (Diana: yeah) they then maybe
61              in twenty years ten years maybe this can spread to Africa
62              but (Ben: mm) if those if those- if for example those
63              who say (Diana: mm) this soya it is less uh it is more
64              resistant to certain (Diana: mm) environmental toxins
65              and things like that (Diana: mm) or like. those herbicides
66              um that doesn't mean that it grows better in the Sahara or
67 Ben     no no certainly [certainly
68 Anne                    [you you you search for certain different
69              qualities and that isn't because it isn't a good deed
70 Diana   but it is more or less like this thing about they um
71              did this thing to tomatoes for example tomatoes they were
72              going to do something to them and then it didn't work out,
73              the tomato got very sensitive to blows and then they used
74              it for this typically mashed tomatoes and stuff like that
75              so they did it then, it was only to get sensitive tomatoes,
76              not that anyone wanted to profit from it but just for
77              them not to have to mash them try to make purée out of them
78 Anne    you mean like eliminating one part of the process then?
79 Diana   yeah
80 Fanny   but what I am thinking about, it's grapes (Diana: mm)
81              I've been thinking that there are those grapes
82              without seeds (Diana: mm) and they are not like that
83              from the beginning, that must be a genetically manipulated
84              product too
```

This excerpt comes from a group discussing genetically engineered food (GEF), and the participants have discussed the issue-in-focus for some time. In his first turns, Ben suggests an analogy between the systematic breeding of corn ('by selecting the seeds', line 15) and genetic engineering ('a kind of genetic manipulation', line 21), even though he suggests that today's manipulation is 'microscopic' (line 22), thereby opening up for a distinction. Thus, Ben himself seems to concede that today's genetic manipulation is invisible and possibly difficult to control (line 25), Anne, Diana and Fanny object to the first analogy, claiming that it is not valid (lines 38ff.). (Before this, Anne has made several attempts to protest; lines 20, 22, 27.) Instead, these participants speak for a distinction between genetic engineering and cross-breeding; the former is "not natural' (line 43). Accordingly, these participants fall back on a generalised contrast that is very dominant and massively represented in the GEF (and GTD) data, namely, what is "natural', or part of 'nature', as opposed to what is (unethical or unwarranted) interventions into nature. In connection with this, note also Ben's allusion to the absence of 'a proper boundary' (line 25), another very characteristic idea that we will return to (Section 6.10 below).

The next local sequence or episode, beginning with Anne's turn on lines 47ff, takes up a topic which is in fact touched off by an argument which was latent or implicit in Ben's first turn (lines 1ff). Discourses regularly involve multiple threads occurring simultaneously in one and the same sequence. Trajectories involve both relatively standard associative links as well as touch-off argumentation. In the latter case, new arguments are tangentially related to previous topics or arguments. Such links seem to be more accidental but they may still be part of the relevant social representations. In Excerpt 4, the topic of larger crops (line 17) gives rise to the 'less starvation' (lines 48–49) argument and the concern for the 'starving countries' (line 54). However, this immediately gives rise to a distinction; today, this is said to be a question less of such concerns, more of interests of 'rich' and 'successful companies' (lines 50–51). Therefore, we do not 'need' (line 59) these new genetically modified plants, and they do not help the people of 'Africa' (line 61), and it may be concluded that this is another point where they are different from the corn brands that have generated so much more food (cf. Ben's first turn). Similar arguments occur in other focus groups on GEF. We may therefore tentatively assume that there is a recurrent 'associative cline', a natural pathway along which arguments develop or are expanded (the sign > means 'develops into'): genetic manipulation increases the production of food > this is a remedy to starvation > (objection, contrast) this is used to increase the profit of the rich rather than help the starving peoples. Via the intermediate, bridging argument 'remedy to starvation', arguments recurrently slip from genetic manipulation to economy.

Returning to Excerpt (4), we witness another association emerging in Diana's turn beginning on line 70; genetically modified tomatoes are so 'sensitive' (i.e. they get easily bruised) that they can only be used for making mash or purée. By a somewhat indirect association, Anne suggests that it is a process where one part is 'eliminated' (line 78) (going directly from the raw materials to tomato mash?). Fanny then brings up the idea of 'grapes without seeds' (lines 81–82). It is not clear whether this is sparked off by the immediately prior discourse or something less local. Anyway, it seems to make up an argument for a similarity (analogy) between the breeding of something (seedless grapes) and genetic manipulation. As a whole, the meandering association paths of Excerpt (4) generate quite a number of ideas about GEF, and about its similarities and differences with regard to more well-known phenomena.

Excerpt (5) will provide another example of a recurrent association chain:

Excerpt (5) GTD1: 11–13; focus group with Master's students in communication studies; translated from Swedish

```
 1   Ida     but it would be quite horrible I think if it was
 2           seen as a right to give birth to healthy babies
 3           actually, coz then one gets a kind of such I
 4           dunno elitist society in some way. like OK, and
 5           in that case it would perhaps be that like you
 6           that like that if one had money then one would
 7           be allowed to take care of a sick child or else
 8           one would not have any choice but to abort it
 9           or something. it is super-horrible
10   Sanna   it would perhaps develop into STATUS high status
11           ((Disa and Ida laugh)) to have a sick child.
12   Disa    it only shows that one is sufficiently rich
```

The logic of Ida's turn 1 is not quite clear, but she seems to associate from one horrible thing – that it would be a human right to have only children who are healthy– to another. i.e. that only rich people can afford to have disabled children. There is a link proposed between being rich and having a disabled child, and this type of association recurs in several groups. It seems to be part of a common discourse on disabilities and society.

Excerpt (5) also exemplifies parts of a fairly common associative cline of the following kind: gene therapy applied to humans > breeding of 'better' human beings > practices associated with Nazism and Hitler (although the last step is not taken up here, but cf. Excerpt (3), lines 18–26).

Analogy-distinction cycles contribute to building up discourse-semantic 'trajectories', through which participants complement, extend or contradict what has been said so far. Patterns of counter-arguments point to contradictions, stories and counter-stories about the issue-in-focus, within the group, which might in turn reveal dilemmas or inconsistencies within the focus-group discussion. This would be in line with Bakhtin's thinking; 'for him, dialogicality meant a contest of points of views, of opposing evaluations and accents. For dialogue to take place, a dialogic tension, created by such oppositions, was indispensible' (Marková, 1997, p. 32).

As topical or argumentative trajectories are often recurrent across focus groups, they seem to indicate associative relations, or paths, that are typical of not only particular discussion events but of underlying social representations as well. Or to put it differently, analogy-distinction cycles point to the interplay of arguments and counter-arguments in the sense-making practices, and therefore possibly also in the constitution of social representations. Later (Section 6.7), we shall also point to the role of metaphors and prototypical examples. These communicative tropes may be said to illustrate the notion of anchoring, which is often used in social-representations theory, that is, the 'anchoring' of new or strange ideas in familiar contexts. In other words, this amounts to 'familiarising the unfamiliar' (Bauer and Gaskell, 1999). The use of analogies, distinctions and analogy-distinction cycles serve to cognitively integrate the phenomenon in focus within familiar classifications, types and names. Focus groups play with exemplar situations, possible worlds and alternative horizons of understanding and interpretation. When several cycles have been brought to completion, a number of ideas have been established and recognised as something one 'might think' about issue-in-focus.

6.6   Arguments: stories in the service of arguing a point

Focus groups are arenas for displaying ideas and opinions. However, such a display can be accomplished in many ways, on a scale from pronouncing firm opinions to trying out understandings, arguments and stances by tentatively formulating and at the same time modifying them, as in the episodes given above. Another, slightly different, way of doing this is by means of more lengthy accounts, often presented chiefly by one speaker. Such single-speaker turns are of course still 'dialogical' at many levels (Chapter 5).

A discursive argument often comes with the tripartite structure identified by Antaki and Wetherell (1999); the speaker (alone or in collaboration with interlocutors) first formulates a thesis, then moves on to modifying (mitigating), elaborating and thus complicating this by considering objections, and finally she returns to the thesis in a reprise. One example is (6):

Excerpt (6) ROM5: 39, cf. Levin 2003: 158; translated from Swedish. From a study of the understandings among employees of a major work-place change in a military garrison. This excerpt is from a group of union members

```
1   Frida   but this has not been so awfully simple coz it has
2           made many feel unwell and feel that we won't do
3           any more all of a sudden. Now there are a lot of new people
4           coming in and then what's old isn't worth anything
```

```
 5      and in terms of wages too it has become this way that
 6      it's been these new guys who've overtaken those
 7      who've been⁷, and it it has not um turned out
 8      very well. This we have brought up (Philip: mm)
 9      with the management and they have tried to straighten it
10      out but but-. It's always possible to be wise after
11      the event but one could perhaps have turned it around
12      and said, told us at a briefing that that what you do
13      you are good at that and you are doing this very well,
14      right?, but now we need this or that one for
15      this job, right?, then maybe they had looked at it in
16      a different manner. Now there are many who feel that that
17      they're not worth anything, and it it's a bit hard to
18      do away with that then, y'know. So it-
```

Here, Frida is complaining about the way the management has treated the old employees, who have now seen new people coming in, and getting better payment at that. Her point is that people feel 'they aren't worth anything'. This point is stated twice in the beginning (lines 2, 4), and then once more towards the end, in the reprise on lines 16–17. In between, the point is supported with a short account of what happened, and an argument is advanced that the management could have acted differently. The argumentative technique used is quite common in conversational argumentation and involves the advancement of a thesis which is formulated several times, or rather (at least) twice, in the entry to and exit from a lengthy turn. In between, there are modifications which anticipate possible objections, and make the thesis come out as well justified, or alternatively as somewhat tentative in nature (in (6), Frida concedes that she is being 'wise after the event', line 11). This sequence type often occurs in focus groups, as a method of trying out justifications for a stance (rather than trying out the understandings as such, as in Excerpts (1, 2)), both stating and partly withdrawing a thesis. There is a dialogue of ideas, between the thesis, the mitigations and complications, and finally the reprise.

Excerpt (6) involves Frida telling some rudimentary parts of a story. Such a story is not told for its own sake; rather, it serves to bolster an argument in the discussion of the issue-in-focus. Moreover, these stories are often generalised stories, sometimes involving hypothetical features. For example, Frida accounts for what some people could have said (lines 13–14), rather than what specific people have actually said or done at a particular occasion. We had another example in Excerpt (4), when Ben used a constructed quote from a fictive (stereotyped) farmer (line 34). Stories thus become prototypical or exemplary stories used for specific argumentative purposes.

But there are also cases when speakers use specific, personal stories to argue a point. Such stories may also contain quotes, often in the form of directly reported speech. Myers (1999, p. 584) has suggested that direct (reported) speech serves to assign authority to the figures of the story (often the speaker herself). Excerpt (7) is taken from the group composed of relatives of disabled persons, who discuss gene therapy. In this episode they argue about the reactions to the event when somebody gives birth to a disabled child:

Excerpt (7) GTD3: 204ff, Bakshi et al., 2000: 31–32; translated from Swedish

```
1    Maria    I was present very much at these educations then which-
2             for midwives how they are to cope with people among other
3             things it it's also a thing I think, this thing when when
4             one gets a child with a disability, there the staff stand
5             at a loss (Markus: yes oh dear) more or less, don't say
6             congratulations to the life (Elsa: no) (.) to the child
7             .(Markus: no) or anything but precisely [oh dear
8    Elsa                                              [they are really
9             handicapped
10   Markus                                          [oh dear what are
11            we to do NOW then, [yes exactly
12   Maria                      [pooh how TERRIBLE this is
13            [more or less, y'know
14   Elsa     [what do we [do now?
15   Peter                [poor you
16   Maria    poor me (Peter: mm) and and then then directly you put
17            this on the parent directly (Elsa: mm) oh dear (Arvid: mm)
18            this is [very bad
19   Elsa             [one doesn't look to the child but one looks to
20            the disability (Maria: mm mm)
21   Arvid    yes we saw this y'know when we got our second lad (Elsa:
22            *yes*) it was visible from (Maria: mm) the staff directly
23            [they became (.)
24   Elsa     [directly at the deliv[ery
25   Arvid                          [they became silent, like [nobody
26            said anything
27   Maria                                                    [mm mm
28   Maria    [no
29   Elsa     [very strange all of this [it was
```

In this episode, with a lot of collaboratively produced utterances, explicit alignments and overlapping talk, two people – Arvid and Elsa, a married couple – tell about the delivery staff's reaction when they got a disabled child (especially lines 19–24). This co-narrated story is occasioned, however, by other talk about the topic. This is initiated by Maria (lines 4–7), when she talks about this kind of situation, although in a generalising way, by means of a hypothetical, generalised narrative (lines 3–20), co-authored by no fewer than four speakers.

Notice how this collaborative argument is replete with hypothetical quotes, centering on expressions like 'oh dear' (lines 7, 10, 17), 'poor you/me' (lines 15, 16) and 'what are we to do now' (lines 10–11, 14). Note, incidentally, Elsa's point that the staff in the hypothetical narrative behave as being handicapped (lines 8–9), an ironical turn of a situation involving the birth of a disabled child.[8] However, the argument around people's inability to cope with the event of somebody's having a disabled child is then strengthened when two of the participants, including Elsa, relate an actual, personal experience of the same kind (lines 21–29).

6.7   Metaphors, metonymies, prototypical examples and other discursive figures

The analogies discussed earlier are rather like similes (X IS SIMILAR TO Y). Accordingly, they are related but not equivalent to metaphors. Metaphors, on the other hand, are very common discursive figures used in most kinds of discourse and socially shared knowledge (Lakoff and Johnson, 1980). For example, Musolff (2004), in a study of political discourse about Europe and the EU in Britain and Germany, was able to show how politicians and journalists formulate a great deal of their apperceptions and visions in terms of recurrent metaphor families, such as 'Europe is a family', 'Europe is a house', 'Europe is a body (which can get sick etc.)' and the European development is 'a journey (by train, ship etc.)'. Other studies show that other domains of socially shared knowledge are likewise permeated by metaphorical language and thought.

However, the issues discussed in our focus groups did not seem to invite much (domain-specific) metaphorical language. Rather, participants used analogies and distinctions to explore issues of which they had no clear pre-formed ideas (see above). But metaphors were of course not entirely absent. For example, the ROM groups often explained the frequent reorganisations of the military in terms of rapid movements of which nobody seemed to be in control of and which often developed in (vicious) circles. The employees were often portrayed as being peripheral, without any influence or control:

Excerpt (8) ROM2: Levin, 2003: 155; translated from Swedish

```
1   Magnus   there comes so much from above, it's a bit of
2            this LP record effect if I put it like that,
3            then you find yourself in a certain end of the
4            LP record then it goes round fastest, and it'll
5            always be fastest most far out, and that's
6            where we find ourselves
```

Another class of discursive resources used in argumentation is 'examples'. Wästerfors and Holšanová (2005, p. 519), who base their analysis on a focus-group interview, point to the fact that examples are a classical rhetoric device ('exemplum'), and they summarise their own argument in the following terms:

> [Examples] may serve as objectifications of an argument, they may mobilize associations, display attitudes, or indicate 'types' of persons or items. Some examples are virtual; they exemplify what could happen, or what never happened. Speakers may question another's argument by referring to counterexamples, or request examples and thereby 'disarm' an opponent.

In our focus groups too, participants often came up with examples when they discussed a particular issue, such as GEF. Some of these examples were used recurrently in the groups, and came to stand as icons or metonymies for particular phenomena. For instance, the GEF groups often used genetically modified tomatoes as a general and recurrent example of genetically engineered food. They also repeatedly retrieved the example of the potato with the fish gene, which was assumed to be resistant to low temperatures. As regards gene technology applied to animals, not surprisingly, the first cloned sheep 'Dolly' was often mentioned. Another example in the realm of animal breeding was the bovine breed 'Belgian Blue', mentioned in connection with Excerpt (2). In the GTD groups, fetal diagnostics is a particularly common example, usually discussed as a premise for a potential abortion. The Chinese practice of aborting female foetuses was held up as a dystopian scenario for other countries as well. Such examples are used as prototypes (stereotypes) or icons, which stand for a good deal of the social representation. In somewhat similar ways, Kitzinger (2004) talks about templates, i.e. concrete examples used for comparison. For example, syphilis and the plague were used as templates for understanding AIDS. In terms of social representations theory, these phenomena are often discussed in terms of 'objectification' (Seca, 2001, p. 62–65).

Other examples were of course less frequent, and sometimes more specific. But examples often showed recurrent features. In the case of GEF and GTD, many example were of a dystopian type: such scenarios and fantasies included eugenics, Nazism, Hitler-type society, and others. In one single group, we find, e.g., invasions of South-American killer bees and carnivorous plants, tomatoes spreading like weeds, industrial breeding of human beings to get spare parts, cloning soldiers (similarly, in GEF groups: cloning Hitler copies). Such clusters of examples homed in on (what participants suggested as) risks and fears. It is as if participants' discourse exhibits frequent movements between dystopian examples using risk and danger as points of orientation, as a kind of 'landmarks' in their argumentative discourse. This is also a 'dialogical' property of the discourse.

In the WPC study of members of a large industrial company discussing workplace and organisational changes, it was found that group members recurrently used various metaphors for their organisation, including pyramid, network, chain, octopus, and others. Sometimes, these were transformed into concrete images in that members made drawings on a whiteboard or a piece of paper. This applied specifically to the image of a pyramid, as in the following excerpt:

Excerpt (9) WCP4: Åkerblom, 2003: 69. The symbol ▼ indicates a gesture pointing to the drawing on the piece of paper

```
 1   Ian     yes (.) alright (.) no but isn't it like this that
 2           (.) y'know if one is sitting in this PYRAMID ((draws
 3           a picture on the paper)) um (.) then it's very seldom
 4           that something gets noticed down HERE ▼ (.) then it
 5           has to be VERY much overarching (Elias: mm) on the
 6           other hand (.) HERE ▼ and up there at the top it's
 7           always blowing (Elias: mm) and there it will perhaps
 8           blow a bit more often (Elias: mm) but down THERE ▼ (.)
 9           no for ME it's business as usual most of them will
10           say down here
11   Elias   okay (.) now we have some other letters they say
12   Ian     yeah
13   Ivan    no (.) but if you are lucky down there then you
14           have groups of six (.) eight then people who sit
15           sit working together
16   Elias   yes
17   Ivan    and there you NEED not change things coz it's when
18           you get higher up (.) y'know down THERE ▼ (.) those
19           manage to talk with one another (Ian: yes) without
20           having an organisation regulating HOW they should
21           talk with one another
22   Ian     yes (.) exactly
23   Ivan    but it's AFTER that (.) when you have to coordinate
24           all these groups that you need some systematicity in
25           how to break down work among yourselves and such like
```

The metaphor of the pyramid is a resource available in the management literature, to which participants sometimes refer. Here, they collectively use it, in quite a concrete way, as they have drawn it up on a piece of paper. The artefact is useful particularly when participants point to the contrast between those at the top (line 6) and those at the base of the pyramid (lines 4, 8, 18).

In addition to metaphors, participants in focus groups use proverbial state-ments, idioms and other expressions that formulate cultural experiences in a stereotypical way. For example, in the WPC study just referred to, a recurrent reference was to 'the survival of the fittest'; the world of business and industry is indirectly characterised by recourse to Darwinian selection. Idioms and proverbs seem to be a way for people to anchor their experiences or opinions of the issues-in-focus in more wide-spread parts of their social knowledge.

6.8   Quotes and hypothetical quotes

One category of discursive devices that we briefly touched upon above (Section 6.6) consists of explicit and implicit references to other people's utterances and thoughts. This is of course a typically Bakhtinian idea; speakers' discourse is multivoiced. In the terms of Chapter 5, the speaker has an internal dialogue with herself, establishing identities and voicing stances and attitudes other than those which her own thesis would presuppose or entail. Accordingly, quotes are used to characterise persons and positions. They are a major rhetorical device in focus groups and public debates and more generally in argumentation (Myers, 2004; Holšanová, 2006). Such contributions can be analysed in terms of quoted or masked other-discourse. These 'quotes' are most of the time 'hypothetical' in that they relate other (real or imagined) participants who are just 'virtual participants', i.e. they are not physically present (Adelswärd et al., 2002). Such quotes do not relate what other people have actually said at particular occasions, rather they show – according to the present speaker – what these other people could have said, or would typically say. Such 'quotes' are 'demonstrations' or depictions of other people's stances (Clark and Gerrig, 1990).

Quoting other people is a resource for argumentation. Quotes can be a way of adducing support from other sources and putative authorities. But it can also be a way of pointing to differences of opinion; attributing specific views, often stereotypical ones, to others and letting these others advocate positions one does not (necessarily) agree with (playing the devil's advocate) provide opportunities for attacking these views. Thus, presenting views as being not one's own can serve at least two goals; on the one hand, it is a way of trying out views without committing oneself, and on the other, speakers can implicate what their own preferred views might be by attacking these others' views.

As already noted, quotes are often hypothetical or 'constructed' in the sense that they were probably not uttered in that form by the others (Tannen, 1989). In addition, they are often ascribed to constructed collectivities, such as 'scientists', 'the media', etc., as if these putative communities could express their views with one voice. Going back to our GEF studies, 'the researchers' was used as a membership categorisation device (Myers, 2004, p. 35), and this constructed collective was often ascribed stereotypical category-bound activities and opinions (Silverman, 1998: 'category-bound activities'). Here is a contribution from a focus group with farmers:

Excerpt (10) GEF4: Farmers; translated from Swedish

```
1    Frank    no but if we were a bit prejudiced about this,
2             then it is that these researchers have got
3             their field which they research, and what
4             happens outside of their door they completely
5             ignore. they are only looking straight ahead
6             that 'this is what one ought to do', putting
7             together a new product, and 'this will be
8             super, won't it', and what happens to it
9             afterwards I think they ignore
```

What Frank does here is to concede initially that he will be stereotyping ('if we were a bit prejudiced', line 1), and he then turns to characterising 'these researchers' as a collective as short-sighted, just being fascinated with their research ideas and not caring about long-term consequences (lines 4, 5, 9). He uses the discursive device of attributing to this constructed collective (or to any member of it) some prototypical utterances, pronounced with a special voice quality and marked in the excerpt with quotation marks (lines 6–8). Members of several of our GEF groups similarly portrayed 'researchers' as competitive, with no other desire but to do research, earning their living on developing new technologies, having no sense of the whole (of long-term consequences), forming secret communities, while, at the same time, being cautious and in need of self-preservation. Another classical stereotype of the 'researcher' appears in the following short excerpt:

Excerpt (11) GEF5: Biology students; translated from Swedish

```
1    Björn    well that is I s'pose the stereotype of the
2             researcher then (Annika: yes but) the odd
3             researcher of German descent who is sitting
4             locked up in his laboratory doing dreadful
5             experiments which aim at his taking over
6             the world some time in the future
```

Again, the participant concedes that he is going to come up with a 'stereotype' (line 1). He then clearly draws upon the idea of Frankenstein, a dystopian figure who appeared several times in our GEF groups. This category of researcher is associated with typical 'category-bound' activities, here exemplified by being 'locked up in his laboratory' 'doing dreadful experiments' etc.

Stereotyping other categories of stake-holders was common in our data. For example, 'the media' were seen as biasing and manipulating opinions. 'Consumers and individual people' are said always to buy what is cheapest, to get frustrated by the profusion of information, and to be afraid of new technologies. In other words, anonymous collectives are treated as homogeneous categories, as if they would or could speak with one voice.[9]

We are here faced with the discursive construction of actors and communities of actors; categories of actors are constructed in (and behind) the texts as operating in society, as 'bearers of representative views' (Myers, 2004, p. 130), and as allegedly representing interests in the debate or on the market. In the GEF and GTD data, these were politicians, researchers, journalists, commercials, consumers and 'the individual human being' (or 'the man in the street'). It does not seem far-fetched to assume that many of these actor categories will appear in people's discourse on entirely different societal issues.

6.9 From themes to global patterns and underlying assumptions

Ultimately, when focus groups are used to explore socially shared knowledge, and in particular social representations, one would want to summarise the major patterns exhibited in each focus group and also to generalise across focus groups in terms of their similarities and differences. This involves finding global patterns in the focus-group discourse (texts), and, by the same token, setting up hypotheses about possibly underlying social representations that participants in the different groups use as meaning-making resources.

We have already (Section 6.4) suggested how to move from (local) topics via themes (recurrent topics) to (issue-specific) thematic clusters (or big themes). In our GEF case, such clusters often built on dystopian ideas (see Section 6.7): side-effects in the long run, species becoming resistant to antibiotics, etc, cloning Hitlers, people getting fed up and accepting anything. These clusters in turn might form recurrent abstract arguments, i.e. ways of thinking underlying substantial portions of the discourse. We shall mention here some of these that characterised our GEF and GTD groups.

First, there was a common idea or presupposition that a boundary should be drawn somewhere between applications of biotechnology that could or should be accepted, and those which could or should not. Sometimes, this was simply formulated as a 'commonplace' of the type 'One must draw the boundary somewhere'. At other times, participants remarked on the absence of a 'proper boundary' (see Excerpt (4), line 25). In general, the focus groups kept coming back to the issue of where more exactly the boundary should be drawn. Excerpt (12) shows a case where this is made explicit:

Excerpt (12) GTD2: 2ff.; Bakshi et al., 2000: 27; translated from Swedish. From the beginning of a session with nurses in neonatal wards; Yvonne is referring to a journal article which had been distributed to participants beforehand

```
 1   Yvonne   yes I read it this morning (Anita: yes) (.) so
 2            that I would have it fresh in memory (.) but I
 3            think there are y'know like two sides of this
 4            thing, that you get rejected because of your
 5            SEX (Anita: mm) that's like that's y'know wr-
 6            (.) WRONG then (Anita: mm) but then it is the
 7            other side (.) be rejected that's as you say
 8            one can see certain grave disabilities¹⁰, diseases
 9            and such (Louise: no but) the difficulty is
10            then that I have to choose then to have (.)
11            not have the strength of taking care of such
12            a child for example (Anita: mm). then I may
13            think that then it's okay so to speak but yes
14            is not ok- it's not okay if if they take you away
15            ((i.e. 'kill')) only because you're a girl (Anita:no)
16            but how could you be able to REGULATE that?=
17   Anita    =but where would you draw the boundary?
```

Here, Yvonne accounts for a number of pros and cons with regard to fetal diagnostics using gene technology. The implicit argument is that it is necessary to draw a boundary somewhere between permissible and non-permissible applications. Her conversational partner Anita makes this explicit (line 17).

In Excerpt (13), a GTD group has talked themselves into a discussion of the blurring of boundaries between species that might result, if we start doing transgenic transfers, and then transplanting spare parts (e.g. cardiac valves) from pigs to humans. Here, Andrew is talking about these pigs which have been bred in order to become producers of spare parts:

Excerpt (13) GTD4: Parents of secondary school children; translated from Swedish

```
 1   Andrew   [though I bet those pi- those pi- that which
 2            is left behind from those pigs will never
 3            appear on any food market coz it would've
 4            been unethical y'know coz then I'd have
 5            eaten a piece from the same thing as
 6            [is in a human being
 7   Anna     [as I have in *my heart*
```

```
8   Andrew   then you'll become a [cannibal
9   Benny                          [there the cannibal
10           problem will come in
11  Kate     [cannibalism, yeah exactly
12  Andrew   [*yes well then it's difficult*
13  Benny    [*yeah then it's difficult*
14  Anna     ((laughs))
15  Andrew   yeah no that's impossible
16  Benny    no it's true of course
17  Kate     yes but it becomes difficult [to draw
18           boundaries it becomes
19  Anna                                 [yeah yeah
20  Andrew                               [yeah yes
21           like I said then you are back again, how
22           *much does one have to change in a human being
23           before it becomes a pig*
```

It is clearly a moral problem (cf. line 4: 'unethical') that this group is discussing, although they do it in fairly drastic terms which gives rise to laughter on the part of several participants (lines 7, 12, 13, 14, 22–23). The previous talk on cardiac valves makes the comment on having things 'in my heart' (line 7) possible and relevant. This utterance arguably adds to the morally sensitive nature of the topic. Let us note, incidentally, the amount of simultaneous talk, where several participants say almost the same things. We are faced with people thinking together, and thinking along quite similar lines. The group concludes that the development becomes 'difficult' (a characterisation used by three different speakers in lines 12, 13, 17) or even 'impossible' (line 15). This conclusion is formulated by Kate in terms of 'drawing boundaries' (line 18).

The frequent discussions on boundary drawing in our different focus groups often raise the issue of who should determine where the boundary should be drawn, as in Excerpt (14):

Excerpt (14) GEF3: Dieticians; translated from Swedish

```
1   Gerda    but it's clear, sometimes if one would think one
2            step ahead then one wonders a bit about this
3            who is it that gives US the right to enter this
4            and change a lot of things? that everyone should
5            look alike and such, and like you said, what will
6            happen then? can one do this to the humans too
7            and who who is it that decides on that? where
8            does the BOUNDARY go?
```

In relation to the boundary-drawing issue, one could identify several hierarchies (or scales) of acceptability in the case of GEF: (here, > means 'is better than' (as objects for biotechnological intervention)): medication > food, (application to) plants > animals > humans (except for some subjects who revert the order: humans > animals), processed products (e.g. tomato paste, margarine) > natural objects (fruits, vegetables) > animals, and in the case of GTD: eliminating genes in living individuals > diagnosing embryos or foetuses (and decide on the life and death of the unborn). Underlying several hierarchies is the idea that cases where the individual decides on applications to him/herself are more acceptable than cases where others decide on behalf of individuals (born or not yet born).

Another case of a common underlying assumption would be Marková's (2000, p. 447; 2003a, p. 185) contention that the distinction between edible and non-edible things is universal. What is specific about different cultures is that they would draw the boundaries around edibility at different places. Yet another example is that of trust, as it was discussed in Chapter 3, with regard to the dilemma of 'The Couple'; participants in the focus groups were in agreement that relations of interpersonal trust were indeed at stake, but they had divergent opinions on how this should be interpreted in the current dilemma. In general, as Marková (2003a) argues, people 'think in relations', but the relations are differentially specified across cultures (Chapter 7).

Yet another underlying assumption in the GEF and GTD groups is that 'nature' is basically good and that, therefore, going against (intervening in) nature is basically wrong.[11] The issue which is discussed concerns how exactly 'nature' ('natural') should be defined.

Excerpt (15) GTD4: 360; translated from Swedish

```
1   Andrew   [yes but this this thing that we go inside and
2            poke about in the core of creation playing
3            God (.) or whatever are (.) master-builders
4            when one is inside poking at the genes (Anna:
5            yeah) that's y'know like mighty [that way
```

The expression 'playing God' is common in our data, and especially in the GTD groups. In another passage from the same group, a woman points to the moral aspect of touching 'the meaning of life', and later, the group returns to the discourse of being 'close to the sacred things', 'poking at things that we should not'. The mundane expression 'poke about/at' (Swedish 'pilla i') (Excerpt 15) suggests that the people referred to are about to do something that is both inadmissible and careless.

Other recurrent ideas in our GEF and GTD groups include:

- that economy always gets the upper hand (despite good and noble intentions);

- that people get accustomed to dubious phenomena (such as GEF and GTD) and therefore become increasingly tolerant;

- that gene technology is normally invisible (in analogy with other new and dubious technologies, such as in the domestication of radioactivity and nuclear power), and this invisibility makes it easier for researchers and commercial forces to let the technologies 'sneak in' gradually and not openly, and then to have them accepted;

- that when information or knowledge accumulates, it cannot be controlled and will sooner or later be abused.

As regards major thematic clusters, many of the GEF topics and themes were related to two core issues: 'What is right or wrong?' and 'How do we know?' (Wibeck, 2002). In the GTD groups, the corresponding major issue seemed to be 'Who has the right to decide?' On this point, however, one must concede that this last-mentioned issue may have been induced by the moderator and the stimulus materials. In this regard, the 'How do we know' question was more independently generated. The GEF groups differed as regards the absence or presence of a meta-perspective; some, but not all, groups spent a great deal of time discussing whether we have knowledge that is reasonably certain and reliable, and in that case, from where we get it, and who is responsible for information and disinformation on the issues involved. All these issues seem to touch upon the notion of trust, which we will deal with in Chapter 7.

Some of these points are undoubtedly specific to the issues-in-focus of GEF and GTD as handled in our groups. Others might find their counterparts in focus groups (and other texts) on other issues, or in the exploration of other social representations.

We can see that thematic clusters seem to form 'big themes' and to reflect underlying assumptions of considerable, even great (or universal?) generality. (Recall that one might think of underlying assumptions as abstract cognitive structures, while 'big themes' are more of summaries of many related and recurrent manifest themes.) However, it is more typical that these assumptions are not verbalised as such at all (although they can be deduced from the talk). In Chapter 7, we shall develop the discussion of these cultural assumptions in terms of 'proto-themata' and themata, a distinction based on whether the assumptions are only implicitly present or more explicitly expressed (thematised).[12]

6.10 Conclusion

Let us conclude by recalling some of the assumptions behind our discussion in this chapter and throughout this book. Focus-group discussions are not a neutral record of something pre-given and stable; rather, they contribute to creating and re-creating socially shared knowledge. Social representations are dynamic and not static; they are produced and reproduced in thinking and communication, have an unequal social distribution, are replete with heterogeneities and polyvocality, but they also tend to build upon some more or less common cultural assumptions.

We have analysed the content of focus-group discussions in terms of a dynamic analysis that focuses on topics, topical trajectories and themes (i.e. recurrent topics), and their discursive management. Themes can be grouped into 'big themes', to be further analysed in terms of what underlying assumptions they presuppose. These deep-seated cultural assumptions, which will be analysed in terms of 'themata' in Chapter 7, are implicit premisses that we think and talk 'from' rather than 'about' (Ragnar Rommetveit, personal communication). This also implies that the identification of themes is relatively data-driven – themes are recurrent aspects of topics manifest in specific corpuses of discourse – but the assumption of the abstract themata involves more of theoretical interpretation.

In many mundane situations, the process of topic progression is largely unplanned and unrehearsed, and this also applies to (some types of) focus groups. But our empirical experiences also show that recurrent ideas and arguments tend to be voiced across different groups, and this is an important reason for talking about socially shared (or partially shared) assumptions about the phenomena talked about.

Finally, let us concede that categorising topics into themes (recurrent topics) and 'reducing' these themes into bigger themes does not come out as a particularly 'dialogical' form of (discourse or text) analysis. Instead, such systematising practices may seem quite monological in nature. Indeed, most coding analyses of discourse have to bracket a major part of the dialogical properties of the data (Marková and Linell, 1996). It is therefore important once again to recall that the argumentation in focus groups, or in any dialogue, is interactional in character. Socially shared knowledge is not an entirely coherent and consistent, monolithic body of knowledge. Instead, participants' understandings and opinions contain heterogeneities, complexities, ambiguities, ambivalences and scepticisms, vaguenesses, contradictions, tensions, discontinuities, indeterminacies, etc. (Marková, 2000, p. 442). These dialogical properties have been a major issue in Chapter 5 and also in this chapter.

Notes

This chapter was written in collaboration with Victoria Wibeck.

1   Our analysis has earlier (Linell, 2001, cf. also Wibeck, 2002) been dubbed 'dialogical text analysis', although a better name might be 'dialogical discourse analysis'. Although the analysis will here be applied to focus-group discourse, there is, of course, no exclusive restriction to focus-group discourse or even to spoken data. Similar ideas have been propounded by Billig (1987; 1993) and Myers (2004). Cf. also Fairclough's (1992) text-oriented discourse analysis (TODA). Other sources of inspiration can be found in modern rhetoric, e.g. Perelman (1997), Grize (1990) and Korén and Amossy (2002) and in empirical argumentation analysis (e.g. Jackson, 1992, and other contributions to van Eemeren et al., 1987; 1992).

Note that many kinds of textual analysis, including perhaps ordinary rhetorical analysis and argumentation analysis, cannot be unproblematically applied to such largely unrehearsed discourse as focus-group talk, since they have mostly been developed for the analysis of planned and edited discourse, that is, typically written texts or well-prepared speeches.

2   If we compare our terminology (cf. Linell, 1998a) to that of conversation analysis (CA), our terms 'episode, sub-episode, topic, and communicative project' would correspond roughly to the CA terms 'sequence, subsequence, topic, and activity'. Also note that in CA treatments, 'activity' usually refers to something much more local than we do with our term 'communicative activity' (Chapter 4).

3   That is, the sequence is not interrupted by other communicative projects, except for so-called side sequences and insertion sequences (Svennevig, 1999, p. 259).

4   As the notion of 'communicative project' has been understood, the term can refer to joint projects of varying size, which are nested within each other, etc. (Linell, 1998a). Here, we are concerned with 'middle-sized' projects, which are pursued over a (local) sequence in talk.

5   Apart from the fact that the analysis brackets some aspects of dialogicality (see above), there are some methodological (and theoretical) problems in determining *exactly* how these units of analysis, i.e. episodes or subepisodes should be identified and coded. But there is usually a sufficient inter-coder agreement, and for us, the problem is not critical since we are not concerned with a strict coding-and-counting approach.

6   In the examples of this chapter, and elsewhere in this book, we have given listener support items ('backchannel items') within parentheses in the current speaker's turn, thus not treating these items as full-fledged contributions to discourse.

7   The speaker evidently means 'been here before'.

8   The speakers use the Swedish words 'handikapp', literally: 'handicap', and 'handikappad' 'handicapped', throughout the episode (lines 4, 8, 17).

9   Another kind of use of virtual participants is at hand, when group members were directly affected by the the issues-in-focus and discuss in terms of 'we' versus 'they' ('us' versus 'them').

10   The Swedish word used here is 'handikapp', i.e. 'handicap'.

11   It is interesting that while this thema was ubiquitous in our focus groups, it is far from universal. Earlier epoques in the Western history of ideas have assumed that nature is evil or savage, and should be domesticated. Another idea is that nature is neither good nor bad, but that man is entitled to make the best of it.

12   Cultural assumptions in our sense are akin to what Holton (1975) and Moscovici and Vignaux (1994) have termed cultural 'themata' (Chapter 8) and to what rhetorical theorists (Perelman, 1997; Sarfati, 2002) have called 'doxa' (or more broadly: topoi) (also Bakhtin, 1979/1986).

7 Themata in dialogue: taking social knowledge as shared

7.1 Introduction

In Chapter 6 we have performed analysis of the 'dialogue of ideas' in focus groups. We have started from topical episodes, arriving at underlying – or we could say deep-seated – presuppositions of participants' talk and thoughts. In this chapter we shall ask further questions about these presuppositions. To what extent do they underlie dialogue in focus groups? Are they in some form involved in the structuring of our socially shared knowledge? More specifically, in what ways do they contribute to generating and transforming social representations? In order to start formulating responses to these questions, we shall introduce the following concepts: relational categories, proto-themata and themata. But before we do that, we must take a step back and provide some underlying ideas enabling us to introduce these concepts.

Throughout this book we have emphasised that forms of socially shared knowledge, like lexical meanings, opinions, interactions, and so on, are all dynamic; they are embedded in webs of other forms of knowing and we cannot describe them fully in any fixed terms. Many of these forms of knowing and meanings circulate in public discourses at large. They are part of everyday communicative activities, e.g. of implicitly shared routines of interaction, contents of social representations like those of nature, AIDS, trust, and so on. The focus-group participants bring them into their discussions, sometimes implicitly, sometimes explicitly. Other forms of socially shared knowledge and meanings are construed directly (of course, from previous forms of knowledge) in focus groups through gaining information, arguing, reflecting upon unquestioned meanings, evaluating pros and cons of particular positions, and otherwise. So we can say that at one pole of the spectrum of these forms there is a commonly shared and relatively stable knowledge, and on the other end we find knowledge that is created and recreated in and through focus-group discussions. All this shows that forms of social knowledge are multifaceted and heterogeneous.

While it is quite natural that these kinds of knowledge are generated in numerous ways, it would be impossible in this chapter to account for such diversities in anything but a scanty and brief manner. Hence, we can do here no more but consider one way only, in which socially shared knowledge is generated or activated. Specifically, we shall turn attention to relational categories, proto-themata and themata, and the ways they activate formation and transformation of concepts with 'more complex contents', topics and themes (on the difference between themes and themata see Section 7.2.4 below). We shall explain our theoretical position while proceeding through several stages. In doing that, we shall partly follow ideas of Geoffrey Holton (1975; 1978)[1], the philosopher of science, and more closely those of Serge Moscovici (Moscovici, 1992; Moscovici and Vignaux, 1994/2000), regarding themata. However, while building on these ideas, we will introduce some further conceptual specifications in order to develop our dialogical approach, linking relational categories, proto-themata and themata with certain aspects of socially shared knowledge.

7.2   From relational categories to concepts with 'more complex content'

7.2.1   Relational categories

There is one important observation about human thought and language which all wide-ranging semantic theories that have developed during the last five decades or so, have taken on board. All these theories presuppose or acknowledge that lexical meanings have something to do with the essential capacity of living organisms in general and with that of the human mind specifically: making distinctions and thinking in oppositions. This capacity is so basic that no organism could survive without being able to distinguish, in one way or another, between danger/safety, food/poison, and so on. Animal species make distinctions on the basis of their fixed biological instincts. Human beings do not have fixed instincts but instead, they have flexible capacities of symbolic and communicative thoughts and images. They make judgments about what is good or bad and they evaluate conduct as moral or immoral, trustworthy or otherwise, and so on. Diverse cultures and societies use the capacity of making distinctions and thinking in oppositions in their specific ways. This capacity and its cultural specificity has been presupposed and empirically proven; it has been theoretically justified in cognitive studies, linguistics, philosophy of science and anthropological explorations all over the world; and it has been found in everyday talk-in-interaction and common-sense thinking. For Western philosophers ranging from Aristotle through to Kant and Russell, this capacity opened up theoretical routes for ideas about thinking in categories, the formulation of typologies, and proposing theories of meaning (Marková, 2003a).

Not surprisingly, therefore, human and social sciences have reflected upon, and pronounced ideas about thinking and talking in oppositions, in numerous ways. For example, in semantic theories they have been conceived in terms of mutually exclusive 'binary oppositions', 'formal logical oppositions', 'semantic oppositions', 'semantic features', and so on. Some semantic theories treat categories of oppositional nature as innate or relatively rigid and stable (e.g. Bierwisch, 1970). Other linguists and semanticists, rejecting such a formal position, have argued that any claims about oppositions are necessarily bound to contexts and language use (e.g. Cruse, 1986; Croft and Cruse, 2004).

Making distinctions and thinking in oppositions is crucial to our dialogical approach. However, within dialogism we insist on one fundamental feature of oppositional thinking. We postulate oppositions NOT as mutually exclusive, that is, as 'either' – 'or' but as mutually interdependent, one making sense only in terms of the other, like figure and ground, i.e. as relations. For example, rather than presupposing that something is either 'cold' or 'hot', we consider 'cold' in relation to its counterpart: 'cold' in relation to 'warm', or in relation to 'friendly', or in relation to 'benevolent', and so on. While this point is quite trivial and non-controversial, its epistemological and theoretical implications can become controversial because it is precisely this perspective that abandons thinking in static categories and decontextualised meanings. Moreover, we hypothesise that relational categories, whether hot/cold, or moral/immoral, etc. are not pre-established categories resulting from cognitive processing in the brain of the individual, but that they are all dialogically established in and through communication and socially shared knowledge during history and culture.

Relational categories are such an essential and wide-spread feature of human thinking and talking that they often remain implicit, taken-for-granted and therefore are not spelled out explicitly. They are part of the un-reflected upon systems of socially shared knowledge or of knowledge taken-as-shared. We can say about relational categories that they form our cultural assumptions 'from' which, rather than 'about' which, we think and talk (Chapter 6). If we talk 'from' the position of something, it usually means that we do not need to spell it out explicitly. In other words, speaking 'from' the position of something implies that we take that something for granted. Moreover, the assumption of taken-for-grantedness may be so strong that we even do not consider the possibility that our interlocutors might not hold the same position as we do.

7.2.2   Proto-themata

In everyday thinking and talking we use some relational categories more frequently than others and some of them are more relevant to our concerns than others. For example, danger/safety, health/illness, moral/immoral are likely, at least in many contemporary societies, to be more relevant and charged with problems in public discourses than, say, white/black, cold/warm, etc. [2] Some relational categories, like male/female or equality/inequality, are of a very long duration while others may be just passing relations, e.g. fashions, food habits or health guides. The latter may come and disappear, return after a while or take on new guises.

Hence, our next question is whether debates and thinking about social, political, economic or other phenomena of public concern, like democracy or AIDS, could be underlain by some more basic relational categories, which conceivably would be of long duration and deeply embedded in the dialogical nature of the human mind. For example, could we, in the study of social representations, determine relational categories from which we think and talk when we debate problems of AIDS, totalitarianism and so on?

On the one hand it would appear that collective actions, public debates, dialogues and thoughts could be determined only by contemporary or even immediate social or political concerns. On the other hand, social and human scientists (e.g. Billington, 1966; Moghaddam and Harré, 1996; Hosking, 2004) have shown that such collective activities are often deeply rooted in history and in unquestioned forms of socially shared knowledge. This issue therefore can become very significant if we want to understand more fully the dialogue and forms of socially shared knowledge in focus groups. If we could identify such relational categories of the basic nature that activate more complex forms of socially shared knowledge, this would in turn enable us to explore the dynamic structures of social representations, as well as to understand reasons for the prevalence of specific opinions, beliefs, collective actions and so on.

Our first step will be to introduce the concept of proto-themata. By proto-themata we shall mean very basic relational categories. They often, though not necessarily, pertain to the Ego-Alter. They are of a very long duration, are relevant either personally and/or collectively (e.g. male/female, good/bad, equal/unequal), or can have an epistemic significance (e.g. stability/change, old/new). They could be of biological, cultural, historical or even more contemporary origins. These very basic relational categories are communicative. They may not be directly and fully brought into language, although the potential of bringing them into language is always present and, they may come up in a dialogue indirectly, through participants' topicalising other issues. This is why proto-themata as underlying cultural presuppositions in common-sense thinking, have a particular relevance in the theory of social representations.

While there is no dogma about which relational categories in mundane talk and thinking should be more relevant to interlocutors' concerns than others, we can presuppose – and observe – that it is above all relational categories that involve Ego-Alter interactions that frequently occupy public discourses, activate conflicts and their resolutions and lead to collective actions. Debates about citizenship, totalitarianism, political distrust, medical confidentiality, democracy, AIDS, etc. are usually more passionate than those that are more relatively 'neutral'.

Our choice to refer to significant underlying relational categories as proto-themata (rather than themata) is given by the fact that they are the most elementary source ideas. They are meaning potentialities in waiting: once the situation obtains, they will start generating concrete contents in specific conditions and activate the formation of more complex forms of socially shared knowledge. For example, we can suppose that the relational category male/female established itself first phylogenetically with respect to biological reproduction. In human species, in and through cognition and communication, it became a proto-thema with meaning potentialities to be further developed in a variety of directions. For example, this proto-thema obtained specific meanings in relation to beauty, the management of household, work outside the home, responsibilities in family and so on. In other words, in certain socio-historical conditions the proto-thema male/female becomes a thema, it becomes thematised. This is why we make a distinction between a proto-thema as having a meaning potentiality and reserve the notion of thema for the next stage of our analysis, which is concerned with actual meanings of these dyadic relations in specific conditions.

It would be impossible to state which dyadic relational categories should be named proto-themata and which not. Researchers have different choices and reasons for characterising this or that relational category as a proto-thema. As guidance, proto-themata are taken-as-shared or taken-for-granted cultural presuppositions from which we think at a particular period of time.

7.2.3   Themata

Our concern here is everyday socially shared knowledge and to that extent its underlying cultural presuppositions. While proto-themata are socially shared cultural presuppositions from which we think and talk, when they become explicitly formulated and negotiated in discourse, they transform into themata. This means that interlocutors no longer think and speak 'from' them but 'about' them. This happens when proto-themata, for one reason or other, enter into interlocutors' awareness because they become problematic. This could take place over time or quite suddenly.

There could be political, ideological, scientific or other reasons that start creating tension or conflict and bring a proto-thema, e.g. 'morality/immorality', into the centre of collective attention and communication. With its content no longer taken for granted, a proto-thema enters awareness, creates communicative tension, and starts generating new contents and new relations in networks of other concepts. In other words, it begins to facilitate the transformation of existing meanings and produce new forms of socially shared knowledge. In general, we can say that proto-themata turn into themata when, for one reason or other, they rise from an unreflected common-sense thinking to the level of active consciousness. They become themata in and through communication. Communicative processes, through which these changes in meanings are usually achieved, carry symbols and images, which not only circulate in public discourses, but also organise and generate discourses, shape common thinking, language and behaviour and provide grounds for the formation of new social representations.

Let us continue with our discussion of the relational category male/female, which has served to Moscovici and Vignaux (1994/2000) as an example for developing their ideas about themata. While it supposedly emerged first as a biological relational category, we know from the study of history, anthropology, psychology, and other human and social sciences that through commonly shared experience, social practices and communication, male/female has become an essential feature of myths, symbolic rituals, power relations and interactions of various kinds. It became thematised in infinite private and public discourses throughout the history of mankind. We can also observe that due to socio-cultural circumstances, e.g. the division of labour, the roles that have resulted from biological differences between male and female, this thema has become filled with particular kinds of contents in specific cultures and regions of the world.

The turn of a proto-thema into a thema is accompanied by various kinds of social and ideological tensions and conflicts in and through thematisation, which is explicitly and/or implicitly brought into language and communication. For example, the thema male/female generates and becomes involved in different forms of socially shared knowledge. It takes part in creating social representations in which male/female plays an important role, e.g. equality and inequality between sexes, beauty, power relations and so on. Sure, when established, the thema, so transformed and legitimised, may become stabilised and it may lose temporary significance; it may fall again into implicitness and oblivion, until another change of socio-cultural conditions re-awakens it once again.

Moscovici and Vignaux (1994/2000, p. 179) point out that thinking in themata 'generally takes the form of notions anchored in systems of oppositions (i.e. terms which are contrasted in order to be related) relative to the body, to being, to action in society and the world more generally; every language bears witness to this'. These authors conceive of such communicative themata in terms of the 'source ideas' or 'generic images' of 'more complex contents' of lexical meanings and conceptual structures. Conceptual and communicative themata generate different kinds of discourses, cultural positions and social representations, like:

> (...) 'feminism' versus 'male chauvinism', 'the woman at home'
> versus 'the woman at work' etc). Thus, comparing discourses bearing
> socio-ethical conflicts, we can find again those topics comparable to
> the properties assigned to the 'other' and legitimating opposition. (ibid.
> p. 179)

Themata constitute aspects of various forms of socially shared knowledge, e.g. of common-sense thinking and social representations, and they are usually thematised and problematised together with other proto-themata and themata with which they are communicatively associated. For example, male/female might be thematised together with, or in relation to, moral/immoral, equal/unequal, right/duty, and so on.

It does not mean, of course, that all proto-themata and themata rise to the same level of assumed importance and relevance in discursive and other kinds of activity. Some may be settled quickly and fall into oblivion. Others endure generations and continue engagement in thematisation of difficult discourses over aeons of time.

7.2.4   Themata and themes

The use of terms 'proto-thema(ta)' and 'thema(ta)' on the one hand and 'theme(s) and 'topic(s)'on the other hand, in this book, could become somewhat confusing. Therefore, in this section we shall attempt to explain differences and relations between these two sets of concepts.

Let us recapitulate: In this chapter we have characterised proto-themata and themata as relational categories that are embedded in the human thought and language. Transmitted through common-sense thinking from generation to generation, people implicitly understand and use proto-themata like male/female, good/bad, equal/unequal, and so on. If they are deeply embedded in human thought and presupposed in talk, such proto-themata may not even be directly expressed in language. Yet, they nevertheless are in language. They are presupposed but not thematised as such; we can say that they sleep – or are in a state of potentialities. However, changes in social, political or economic conditions may awaken them and call them to the public attention. What was a sleeping proto-thema, i.e. a presupposition that had not been previously discussed, has now become problematised and thematised. In our example above, male/female has become a thema, i.e. a relational category about which one speaks; in and through communication its content is activated.

Let us consider another example, this time from the epidemic of AIDS. The epidemic has brought up a number of conflict-raising questions in public discussions, institutions and in the media. Is sexual promiscuity moral? Is it moral not to tell your sexual partner that you are HIV infected? Is it immoral to recommend wearing condoms as a protection against HIV infection? Has the notion of morality become old-fashioned? What indeed is morality? During the epidemic many of these issues have been discussed and argued in very concrete situations, for example: how should the medical profession cope with irresponsibility of some patients? In other words, the thema moral/immoral has become a passionate feature of discussions; it creates communicative tension and actives the emergence of new contents.

So, how is a thema related to a topic or to a theme? Let us take our last question in the previous paragraph. 'How should the medical profession cope with irresponsibility of some patients?' 'Irresponsibility of some patients' is not a thema (it is not a dyadic relational category) but it could be a topic or a theme, or an aspect of a topic or a theme, of discussions, media programmes, even an issue for political parties. A discussion of such a topic (or a theme) could activate discussion, i.e. thematisation of some other themata, say, moral/immoral, trust/distrust, in addition to other issues like rights of patients, duties of doctors, problems in the National Health

Service, and so on. As we pointed out in Chapter 6, something becomes a topic if it is discursively pursued over a sequence, or an episode. And if a topic becomes recurrent in a discussion, in a focus group or in a text, we can then call it a theme, or a 'big theme'. A topic or a theme, therefore, is something that is being discussed in a single focus group or in several focus groups and what the researcher pursues through analytical means as we have seen in Chapter 6.

So the relation between themata and topics (themes) may now become apparent: Themata, i.e. dyadic relational categories (e.g. male/female, moral/immoral), by becoming sources of communicative tensions and public concerns, create and enter topics (or themes) of discussions. They generate different kinds of discourses, and 'comparing discourses bearing socio-ethical conflicts, we can find again those topics comparable to the properties assigned to the 'other' and legitimating opposition' (see above, Moscovici and Vignaux, 1994/2000, p. 179).

By analysing concrete topics (or themes), say in focus groups, the researcher can analytically discover how themata are organised and in what ways they take part in such topics and themes and more generally, in the formation of social representations and other forms of socially shared knowledge.

It may have now become clear why we think that in the theory of social representations it is important to discuss proto-themata and themata. We hypothesise that they generate and activate the formation of social representations. Our previous research (e.g. Marková et al., 1998) has shown that social representations of democracy involve themata like free/not free, justice/injustice and equality/inequality, among others. Yet citizens in different socio-political systems thematise them in specific ways, according to local and political conditions and historical circumstances. Hence, democracy in Mexico means to citizens something else than to citizens in Scotland. While we have found that in a traditional democracy like Scotland, freedom was thematised in terms of individual and collective responsibility and public education, in the Czech Republic our participants thematised freedom in terms of market, privatisation and new economic institutions (Marková et al., 2001).

We can say more generally that relational categories, proto-themata and themata lead us on the route in studying dialogue and forms of socially shared knowledge (e.g medical confidentiality, AIDS, democracy). In the second part of this chapter we shall consider in what ways the thema (trust/distrust) can become a theme (medical confidentiality).

7.2.5   How do we study themata and more 'complex lexical items' in focus groups?

Basically, we may proceed in two directions. In the first case the researcher may already have an expectation of an underlying thema. For example, in the case of trust/distrust or moral/immoral the researcher may form such an expectation on the basis of own or others' previous studies or the researcher can get an idea from the media or other sources. In any case, before starting research, the researcher already may have a hunch that a particular thema underlies the form of socially shared knowledge in question.

Alternatively, the researcher may not have any specific hypothesis about a thema. Instead, he/she may study social representations of AIDS, lay knowledge and the understanding of AIDS or sexual practices in his/her milieu. However, through such studies he/she discovers that discourses are guided by particular value judgments, by evaluations as to what constitutes good and reproachable behaviour, and so on. From the ways focus groups thematise various events, make judgements and evaluations, the researcher finds out about the ways in which good/bad and moral/immoral have been thematised and rethematised. In sum, the researcher may either present a thema to a focus group and study how it is negotiated, argued about and contested or discover a thema through the discussions of focus groups of a related toic.

7.3   Themata underlying social representations of AIDS

When in the 1980s a 'new' killer disease, AIDS, spread rapidly throughout the world, it became quickly associated, in socially shared knowledge, with immorality, 'misbehaviour', sin and punishment, in analogy with sexually transmitted diseases (e.g. syphilis) known from before (Brandt, 1988). In addition, issues like whether the doctor should or should not keep medical confidentiality in relation to those infected by the HIV, and whether those with the HIV should disclose their infection, have been widely discussed. In making judgements about good or bad behaviour, about morality and immorality, about whether something or someone could be trusted or not – we are touching some very basic relational categories, i.e. proto-themata, that were discussed and problematised during the AIDS epidemic in very specific ways, and so, in view of the perspective taken in this chapter, we can say that they became themata.

The relationship between sin, punishment and illness has been well established in forms of socially shared knowledge throughout the history of humanity. Beliefs that violation of social taboos result in illness have existed for centuries. Illness has been a social marker of the boundaries of behaviour that has not been publicly acceptable. Research findings at that time, as well as analyses of the media and public discourses in relation to social representations of AIDS have revealed specific underlying relational categories that, during the epidemic, have been thematised and rethematised. For example, during the nineteen eighties, we could find in the United Kingdom numerous references to morality/immorality in newspapers and magazines, like 'Morality back in fashion' or 'Churchmen attack war on AIDS as immoral' (Marková and Wilkie, 1987).

Another proto-thema that became thematised was trust/distrust. As we discussed this in Chapter 1, according to Georg Simmel (1950), the orientation towards others is based on a-priori trust. Without trust, Simmel argues, the society could hardly become established. It follows that such a basic proto-thema as trust/distrust is not negotiable because it is one of the pillars of society. The question of what is and what is not negotiable touches on deepest presuppositions of forms of socially shared knowledge. In discussing thematisation of discourses concerning man/woman, Moscovici and Vignaux insist that

> What is important in the analyses of these discourses, which intuitively each time one collects as representatives of movements of opinion or social positions, is really to bring to light the negotiations at work here, linguistically, on the frontier between the 'negotiable' and the 'not negotiable', between what functions as stable belief or as developing social cognition. (Moscovici and Vignaux, 1994/2000, p. 179)

The question of what could and what could not be negotiated became a subject of discussion during the AIDS epidemic. In particular, trust/distrust became a subject of negotiation and negotiability in various ways and in different contexts. For example, given the risk of HIV infection, can the individual trust his/her sexual partner? Can the patient trust blood products that he/she needs for the treatment of illness, e.g. haemophilia? Is blood transfusion safe? Can the patient with the HIV trust that the doctor will not reveal to anybody his/her infection? Under such circumstances a variety of paradoxical discourses took place.

Our research at the time has shown that while according to the media discourses and public education campaigns, wearing a condom was supposed to form a basis of trust and of diminishing the risk of HIV, it could, in quite a contradictory way serve as a basis of distrust. The male patient with haemophilia thought that if a girl had her own contraceptive protection, she would question why he wanted to use a condom (Marková et al., 1990). It signified to her the possibility of HIV and therefore, not wearing a protection, paradoxically, the woman viewed as a matter of trusting her partner!

The question of trust/distrust with respect to HIV/AIDS had important implications for the individual's interpersonal relations as well as for his/her activities as a patient, spouse, professional and otherwise. For example, and as we have shown in the excerpt in Chapter 3, the participants in a focus group can thematise and negotiate trust with respect to married couples in different ways, referring to trust not only as a basis for interpersonal relations but also as an institutional basis of marriage.

7.4   From trust/distrust (proto-thema, thema) to medical confidentiality (topic)

Let us now consider some ideas that are related to thematisation of trust/distrust during the AIDS epidemic. In the first instance, we can think about trust/distrust as a proto-thema in the sense of Simmel: a-priori trust as 'holding society together'. The potential meaning of this relational category can become actualised when trust/distrust is problematised, and turns into a thema. As a thema it can be thematised in a variety of directions, e.g. who can one trust? How does one recognise a trustworthy person? What is the meaning of trust within a couple? Is trust and morality the same?

Thematisation of trust/distrust can contribute to topics (or themes) of discussion in focus groups, the media, political parties or other institutions. In our data we have found that it contributed to the discussion of the topic (and theme) of medical confidentiality.

7.4.1   Medical confidentiality as a bond between doctor and patient

Medical confidentiality as a form of specific kind of trusting relationship between doctor and patient was adopted in Europe approximately 2000 years ago and has become known as the Hippocratic Oath. This Oath proscribes the doctor from divulging any information about the patient's diagnosis or any information that the patient may give to the doctor on trust. Medical confidentiality has become an unquestioned part of the code of medical ethics and as such it has turned to become an aspect of socially shared knowledge.

At the time of HIV/AIDS epidemic in the nineteen eighties when it became obvious that a person infected by HIV could pass, either by negligence or intentionally, an HIV to another person, medical confidentiality became discussed and scrutinised in everyday conversation as well as professional discourse, e.g. in legal institutions. Has it become obsolete? How should the doctor deal with the problem that his/her patient is infected and can spread the virus? How can society be protected if an individual can infect others through neglect or even wilfully? Should HIV infection become notifiable like other infectious diseases? How does the general public think about this problem? Many similar questions were raised at the time.

In order to explore some of these questions, and specifically, negotiability of medical confidentiality with respect to HIV/AIDS, we have used, in a series of studies based on focus groups, the dilemma that has already been presented in Chapter 3 (Collins and Marková, 2004; Orfali, 2004):

> You are Chief Medical Advisors in the Ministry of Health. Your primary task at present is to contain the spread of HIV/AIDS. People with HIV and AIDS are protected by medical confidentiality. This means that the doctor must not tell either his/her professional colleagues or the patient's spouse or anybody else that the patient has HIV. However, if the patient does not behave responsibly he or she can infect other people. As a group of advisors you are responsible for the health of the public. What advice would you give to the Minister in resolving this dilemma?

We assumed that although the dilemma focuses on medical confidentiality, the participants would also bring into discussion other topics. For example, in this case it could be the relation between the individual and society, questions concerning responsibilities, rights, trust/distrust, and so on. The discussed topics may show the progression in talk, some themes could be developed while others could be reformulated and still others might disappear. In addition, the discussed topics could be underlain by other proto-themata and themata, e.g. trust/distrust, self/others, moral/immoral, etc. and they could be related to specific suggestions for social actions, whether individual or collective ones. Clearly, the researcher's concern with the socially shared knowledge of medical confidentiality would be based on a number of specific problems, for instance:

- How do the participants of the focus group reformulate the notion of medical confidentiality?

- What do participants consider as a problem and how do they thematise it?

- Which other issues intertwine with the notion of medical confidentiality?

We can hypothesise several ways in which participants might formulate the question of medical confidentiality. If, for instance, the participants in a focus group state at the beginning of their discussion that medical confidentiality is not negotiable, then, obviously the subsequent talk will be structured differently, than if they think that confidentiality is negotiable. Let us consider some examples from our data related to these possibilities:

7.4.2   Medical confidentiality is not negotiable

Our data[3] from several European countries (Collins and Marková, 2004; Orfali, 2004), using the above dilemma have shown that if medical confidentiality is not negotiable, then, either it is not discussed at all or, if it is, discussion includes justification of its non-negotiable status. The participants make instead suggestions for taking specific actions, e.g. the individual has responsibility for him- or herself to avoid infection or to make preventive steps, or there should be public and patient's education concerning HIV/AIDS, and so on. Of course, negotiability and non-negotiability of medical confidentiality in a focus group does not depend only on some relatively permanent views that the participants might hold, but also on how the dilemma is framed, how its relation to other topics and to other themata is interpreted (Chapter 5).

In the present case, non-negotiability of medical confidentiality is sometimes marked linguistically and discursively, e.g. by repetition, 'The thing is that you are bound, you are bound … by confidentiality', rhetorically 'Can you advise doctor to tell everybody that he has AIDS?', and otherwise. Consider the following example:

Excerpt (1) 'HIV/AIDS' dilemma: Marková, Moodie and Collins, 2000[4]

```
1    John      so- we- we have to work out what advice
2              we'd give to the minister
3    Moderator uhhh
4    Carol     well I don't think you can:
5              (.)
6    Martha    go around telling everyone
7    John      you can't you can't- [(.) you know y- (if)
8              y-
9    Carol                          [break the(ir)
10             confidentiality (.) °or anything°
11   John      no (.) I think you have to (1.1) you
12             know(the) the whole medical system relies on
13             hh cos the
14             thing is (it's) .hhh if you start telling
15             people (tuts) if- if- you know (.) if someone
```

```
16              comes to you
17              for- for- an- an Aids test or an HIV test an:
18              and then you go okay right that's it we're
19              gonna have to tell everyone now
```

This excerpt shows that the participants in the focus group are in agreement that medical confidentiality cannot be broken. But we can also consider some linguistic and discursive details of the participants' implicit showing of agreement, i.e. taking knowledge as shared. One way in which we can consider their taking knowledge as shared can be revealed through marking it by the collaborative construction of utterances. The term 'collaborative utterance' describes the means by which two or more participants in a conversation collaborate in the production of a single utterance (Collins and Marková, 2004).[5] This means that one participant starts saying something and the other participant completes the utterance. In everyday language, utterances are collaboratively constructed for a variety of reasons, only one of them being to indicate mutually shared knowledge. Although the completion of an utterance by two or more interlocutors can have different discursive results and implications, in the present section we shall analyse only those cases where the participants successfully assume that they share knowledge that medical confidentiality is not negotiable. Alternative cases will be treated later as we go along.

In the Excerpt (1) we can notice two interlinked collaborative utterances indicating that the participants, first, assume that they share knowledge and second, that they actually confirm it in their dialogue. Both interlinked collaborative utterances indicate that medical confidentiality is not negotiable. There are two pairs of such jointly constructed utterances. The first pair of collaborative utterances refers to lines 4–6 of the above transcript,

```
4   Carol    well I don't think you can:
5            (.)
6   Martha   go around telling everyone
```

and the second refers to lines 7–10:

```
7   John     you can't you can't- [(.) you know y- (if)
8            y-
9   Carol                         [break the(ir)
10           confidentiality (.) °or anything°
```

In the first case, as the transcript shows, there is no overlap between the two utterances: one participant starts and the other completes the utterance in mutual agreement. In line 4 the participant marks his position ('I don't think') by his prosody putting the emphasis on 'I'. The syntactic continuity that is expressed by the participant in line 6 shows that her contribution to the joint utterance represents something like a shared response to the problem. In relation to the second jointly constructed utterance by John and Carol there is an overlap between the two contributions. We need to see this second case of the joint construction as a continuation of the dialogue that has already established the socially shared knowledge. John does not emphasise his own position by 'I' but we can suggest that this is no longer necessary because the shared knowledge has been now agreed, through the collaborative completion.

The joint construction of utterances in focus groups can not only confirm that knowledge is socially shared but it may, in addition, strengthen and re-affirm the participants' position that trust between doctor and patient is not negotiable. Moreover, the awareness and confirmation that this knowledge is shared enables the participants to search for an alternative solution to the problem as the following two examples show:

Excerpt (2) 'HIV/AIDS' dilemma: Marková, Moodie and Collins, 2000

```
1    Joan     yeah an what's: (.) what's gonna happen
2             is it's- it's- it's so important that people
3             that've got
4             HIV actually-
5             ((hands come up off the desk, as if
6             trying to form what she's looking to say))
7    Sally    are aware of it=
8    Joan      =(loudly) get diagnosed and get treatment
9             so: (.) you know you can: prolong their quality
10            of life for as
11            long as possible .hhmm where- an if
12            people are actually scared of the consequences
13            of coming for (the) test
```

In this excerpt the participant Joan starts saying that 'it's so important that people that've got HIV actually' (lines 2–4). As the transcript describes it, Joan says this with accompanying hand movements 'as if trying to form what she's looking to say' (lines 5–6). This seems to provide an opportunity for the other speaker, Sally, to continue saying something that apparently is taken as shared knowledge, like 'are aware of it' (line 7). Syntactically and pragmatically, the utterance is already possibly complete but Joan then re-completes this jointly constructed utterance by strengthening her position by saying 'get diagnosed and get treatment' (line 8). This second completion upgrades both Joan's own contribution and the one made by Sally. Joan speaks louder, and employs active verb forms, in which 'get' is emphatic and repeated. We can see that the participants build on what has been said already; they move the talk forward and suggest what actions should be taken since medical confidentiality is not negotiable. The proposed solution for people with HIV is to be diagnosed and get treated.

Excerpt (3) 'HIV/AIDS' dilemma: Marková, Moodie and Collins, 2000

```
1    Joan        anyway so: (.) so we-we wouldn't
2                recommend that the doctor (.) erm
3    Moderator   (.) anyway
4    Sally       went round telling everyone
5    Joan        went round telling [everyone .hhh
6    Moderator                      [definitely not
7    Sally       ( )
8    Joan        but what about (.) the idea of making
9                it (.) illegal
10   Sally       illegal to s:-
11               (nodding)
12   Joan        to knowingly [infect
13   Sally                    [knowingly infect
14   Moderator   mm
15   Sally       someone without their:
16   Joan        without their consent
17   Moderator   for sure
18   Sally       uh heh heh yeh do you wanna die!
19   Joan        uh hhuh .hh
20               hhhuh huh huh
```

This excerpt shows that at the beginning the participants reject the possibility that medical confidentiality could be broken. They even exaggerate and ironise the case: they will not advise the doctor to go round and tell everybody about the patient's infection. Here again we can suggest that Joan and Sally express shared knowledge at the beginning of this extract by constructing an utterance jointly. Their agreement is then re-stated by Joan. Having agreed on non-negotiability of medical confidentiality the participants come to propose an alternative, and interestingly, their proposal also brings out a collaborative sequence. The alternative proposal suggests 'the idea of making it illegal' (lines 8–9) and they jointly construct the sequence to 'knowingly infect someone without their consent' (lines 12–16). The outcome of course is silly, it was not foreseen, but humorously produced either unwittingly or, one can suggest, even intentionally.

In conclusion, if the participants in focus groups take knowledge as shared and confirm that, they usually re-formulate the dilemma and try to find out acceptable solutions. In the present case, in taking medical confidentiality as not negotiable, they discuss possible alternative actions, i.e. getting diagnosis and treatment. The participants in our focus groups also proposed other possibilities, like the suggestion of changing the law and making 'knowingly infect' illegal, they recommended counselling, and otherwise. In other focus groups (not discussed here) the participants suggested education, they discussed questions who should be educated, they raised whether the public, the doctor, the patient or the spouse, what were the best ways of educating people, and so on.

We can propose that if the topic of medical confidentiality is not negotiable, it is based on the fundamental appeal to the thema of trust on which doctor-patient relation and interaction is presumably based. This could also mean that in this case the discussion of the topic of medical confidentiality is underlain more by the thema trust/distrust than by other themata. For example, we may suggest that it overrides a thema moral/immoral, i.e. the thema that might, conceivably prevail, if other phenomena became thematised, e.g. the achievement of justice or vengeance.

7.4.3   Medical confidentiality is not negotiable but could become negotiable

Dialogues in some focus groups in our data considered that medical confidentiality could be negotiable and they also discussed implications of that possibility. This included problematising the doctor's responsibilities, patient's rights, the guiding rules of confidentiality and the doctor's and patient's duties. The participants considered that both the doctor and patient have rights and responsibilities. However, these are distributed asymmetrically. Doctors are mainly thought to have duties and responsibilities and patients have mainly rights. Yet even in view of this, the participants thought that medical confidentiality might perhaps be restricted to certain classes of people but not to others.

Excerpt (4) 'HIV/AIDS' dilemma: Marková, Moodie and Collins, 2000

```
1    Maria    yeh I think it should be (    ) kind
2             of people (that-) should have the
3             confidentiality (-) which agree to (.) they
4             should (.) sign some (    ) or something that-
5             (.) they: (.) they
6    Tom      mhmm
7    Maria    going to .hhh behave responsibly (    )
8    Tom      (and let people know)
9    Garry    an uh (.) yeh an um
10   Anne     an if they don't (.) (it's up to) the
11            doctor's
12   Maria    if they don't the
13            confidentiality is lost
14   Anne     s:- si-)is lost
```

```
15  Garry   yeh
16  Tom     yeh
17  Maria   (but) I think there should be some: (.)
18          erm (.) what do you call it (.) uh (.) document
19          (confession) or something (-) to sign and uh
20          (-) and this should be confidential but if it's
21          (.) if the person uh
22  Anne    doesn't behave responsibly
23  Tom     ((nod))
24          behave responsibly it should be (-)
25          unconfidential=
26  Anne    yeh
27  Garry   =yeh but how do you find out that this
28          person is not behaving responsibly
```

In this excerpt the participants again construct utterances jointly but here they foreground the patient's responsibility as a precondition for sustaining medical confidentiality. Maria attempts three times to say that the patient should stick to a written contract, i.e. that he or she will behave responsibly (lines 1–4 and 7, 12–13, 17–21). Other participants in the group support this position and they spell out that responsibility is a pre-condition to be fulfilled if medical confidentiality is to be maintained. In fact, this excerpt, constructed of several contributions by different individuals, seems to be expressed as a seamless continuum of a non-ending utterance as if constructed by one person. Only at the end Garry (lines 27–28) raises the problem as to how behaving responsibly could be verified, and this question then changes the direction of dialogue.

In the next excerpt the participants expose openly both cases, negotiability and non-negotiability, and discuss their pros and cons:

Excerpt (5) 'HIV/AIDS' dilemma: Marková, Moodie and Collins, 2000

```
 1  Helen   I think you'd have to (say) if that you
 2          were giving advice to the minister you'd have to
 3          sort've: lay it open and just (.) argue the two
 4          cases (you know) like
 5  Edith   mhm
 6  Helen   you said you know discuss the problems of .hhh
 7          breaking confidentiality but at the same time (
 8          ) there are certain advantages to
 9          retaining that (-)
10  Edith   mhm
11  Helen   confidentiality cos of the sort of: .hh legal
12          (-) position and private rights and
13  Edith   mm
14  Helen   (-) and things and also because of the sort of
15          general prejudice of: people but I
```

```
16  Edith   yeh
17  Helen   think the im- I think one of the things that
18          you might ad- ad- advise is is s-still
19          increasing more sort of awareness programmes of
20          it because all this thing about the whole
21          dilemma of confidentiality: yes- yes or no the-
22          basically the idea of confidentiality is is
23          protecting the person isn't it protecting them
24          from
25  Edith   mhm
26          the prejudices that kind of exist cos if there
27          wasn't such a stigma about it then
28  Peter   yeh
29  ?       mm
30  Edith   yeh
31          there wouldn't be such a need to sort've
32  Helen   keep
33  Ruth    yeh
34  Peter   keep it
35  Ruth    it would always be a sort of neutral
36          public health issue as opposed to a- a- a-
37          massive personal problem (you know     )
38  Peter   yes so I mean that- .hh you- I- I don't
39          know how how either of you feel about it I mean
40          I'd be- I'd be very disinclined to take away
41          that (basic right) of confidentiality (   )
42          me too yeh
43  Helen   me too I'm doing counselling course …
```

The participants are aware that the breaching of medical confidentiality would create problems. They acknowledge the legal importance of medical confidentiality, the safeguarding of the rights of individuals and the protection of people with HIV/AIDS from stigma. The participants imply that, in fact, there would be no need to maintain confidentiality if there was not the problem of stigma and prejudice. This excerpt shows that one topic is interdependent with another one; the medical confidentiality and the specific nature of social representations of HIV/AIDS are associated with the prejudice against the individual concerned. Here again, the excerpt takes a form of one continuing voice although it is expressed by different individuals.

In Excerpts (4) and (5), despite a general agreement concerning pros and cons of medical confidentiality, the dialogue shows a multifaceted flow of ideas. Collaborative utterances, rather than being completions of utterances, seem to be displaying the participants' states of understanding. The participants add their own interpretations and continue building upon what has already been said; they support and expand positions that they have already constructed. Or, this kind of continuation without completion can be viewed as the participants' effort to develop their own understanding and to justify their positions.

Another example that could serve as a case attempting clarification of others' positions and developing one's own understanding is the case of testing boundaries of socially shared knowledge. The following excerpt, showing this case, is not taken from the above AIDS dilemma but from a dilemma that concerns the question as to whether very young children, who murder someone, are or should be made responsible for their act:

Excerpt (6) 'Child criminality' dilemma: Marková, Moodie and Collins, 2000

```
1    Judith   then therefore there should be a jury for
2             little children as well (.) an see well (.) what
3             the circumstances were (.) and (.) how it
4             happened and then: (.) they should decide
5             together with the judge if the sh- if the kid
6             should be taken away and put (at) some sort of
7             institution for young offenders (.) or not
8    Elaine   for life  (('for' starts on a
9             higher pitch than Judith's preceding 'offenders'))
10   Judith   not for life (.) not for life because (.)
11            I agree with Elaine that at that age you can't
12            really know…
```

We can observe that Judith's first contribution (lines 1–7) is syntactically complete in itself. However, Elaine (lines 8–9) extends it by re-completing the utterance. We can suggest that Elaine tests a boundary of the position that Judith is taking: does Judith propose that 'the kid should be taken away' 'for life?' We can further suggest that the contribution – or the continuation of Elaine 'for life' tests the boundaries of Judith's position and perhaps serves as an attempt of Elaine to clarify her own position. This supposition seems to be confirmed by the fact that while this completion 'for life' (line 8) is syntactically continuous with Judith's prior utterance, it is dissimilar in prosody ('for' starts on a higher pitch than Judith's preceding 'offenders'; there is a marked rise in pitch on the beginning of 'life', and 'life' is stretched, with a slight drop in pitch at its end) (Collins and Marková, 2004).

Testing the boundaries of shared knowledge is a frequent strategy in dialogues of any kinds. In a group discussion it may be important when one is not sure about the position of others with respect to one's own and does not wish to step out of the group. Alternatively, one may not wish to reveal one's true thoughts because that might be either embarrassing or it could threaten one's social recognition. Clearly, the individual may use various linguistic and communicative strategies enabling to test the limits of what the individual may say in order to avoid losing one's face.

7.4.4 Medical confidentiality is negotiable: displaying a difference or showing a disagreement

Negotiability of medical confidentiality is usually underlined by the question as to what should be given priority: rights of the individual or benefits to society? And of course there are legal, moral, interpersonal and other implications of these choices. Can the individual be forced by anybody to get tested for HIV? How can the collective or the society be protected from someone who does not behave responsibly? For example, if patients do not inform their partners of their HIV infection and endanger them, is the doctor justified in breaking the contract of medical confidentiality? Our data show that negotiability of medical confidentiality, underlain by such considerations, is largely determined by socio-political contexts in which people live and by the level of personal risk or conflict that the participants may anticipate for themselves and for others (e.g. Marková et al., 1995).

Consider for example the following Excerpts (7) and (8):

Excerpt (7) 'HIV/AIDS' dilemma: Marková, Moodie and Collins, 2000

```
 1   Hazel   I suppose it depends what you think was
 2           (-) at the end of the day more: (.) more
 3           important (.) (you know) the patient's
 4           confidentiality or the health of the public
 5           (-) (Hazel looking at Paul)
 6   Paul    the health of the public
 7   Hazel   you know (.) (you're dealin:) (.) you're
 8           dealing like with (.) everyone:
 9           ((looks to
10           others))
11   Kerry   (or
12           just one)
13   Hazel   or just one person
14   Paul    mhmm= ((nods))
15   Hazel   =but then: (.) you'd be like (.) (you'd
16           be) losing the trust of the medical profession
17           wouldn't you (.) people with HIV wouldn't
18           go (.) HIV
19   Paul    I spose the only way is to get (the)- (.)
20           hhh force them to come back in to the (.)
21           surgery or whatever again .hh an interview them
22           an talk to them an .hh see how they('ll) answer
```

```
23              your questions cos (it's:) bound to be some
24              kind of (set way) (.) they shou- you must be
25              able to tell when a person's not quite (.)
26              telling: (you) what they really are doing an
27              what they aren't
28   Hazel      yeh but then:
29   Paul       but I do- (.) I don't know I mean (.) (u-
30              hh)
31   Hazel      it's not really your right to call them
32              back in an say:
33   Kerry      exactly: it's no-
34              it's none of your business what they do:
35   Hazel      in that sense
36   Paul       sit them down and say right you know
37              what're you doing (.) I mean people just aren't
38              gonna say anything are they (.) you can't force
39              people to come back in (-) an do something like
40              that...
```

Excerpt (8) 'HIV/AIDS' dilemma: Marková, Moodie and Collins, 2000

```
1    Nicki      yeh (.) but I don't think that people who
2               ( ) should be any confidential
3    Kay        you don't
4    Jim        no because it's- it's- it's killing
5               people sin't it
6    Guy        but ho- how do you monitor how do you
7               control that (-) do you say to d- all doctors
8               (-) right-
9               (uh) patient confidentiality .hhh stands for all
10              conditions (.) you know if you've got (.) any
11   Nicki      mm
12   Guy        other condition then: n-nothing's being said
13              but if you've got Aids then (-) ermm (.) it has
14              to
15   Kay        mm
16   Guy        be made public an these people are (.) are like
17              (-) highlighted as lepers or something (-) i-
18              (.)
19              you know i- is that fair on the people who have
20              got Aids u- (-) m- (.) maybe wasn't their fault
```

In Excerpt (7) the participants raise the subject of public health versus the individual's right to be protected by medical confidentiality; the view that considers breaking medical confidentiality is then challenged because trust of the medical profession would be lost. But equally, can you force the individual to come back to the surgery and tell him/her what he/she should do? Excerpt

(8), again, discusses the negotiability of medical confidentiality. Two contrasting ideas, one against and one for maintaining confidentiality are presented, each voice justifying its position. People, who do not behave responsibly, kill others; but how does one cope with that? Medical confidentiality 'stands for all conditions'. The danger of making the individuals' HIV infection public is that such persons would be treated like lepers although having HIV/AIDS may not be their fault.

Both excerpts imply yet another asymmetry between doctor and patient (we have discussed one asymmetry with respect to rights and responsibilities), this time in relation to holding and revealing the medical secret. While both the doctor and patient can hold the secret, only one of them, the doctor, has the duty to keep secret, i.e. maintain the medical confidentiality concerning the patient's illness. The doctor must not disclose the secret even if he/she knows that this could endanger others. In contrast, the patient is at liberty to tell or not to tell his/her secret. While the thema trust/distrust is an a priori reciprocal interpersonal obligation to which focus-group discussions often refer, medical confidentiality as an institutionalised form of confidence in the profession is not viewed as a reciprocal obligation. Instead, dialogue in focus groups is underlined by differences in responsibility between doctor and patient, patient's rights and doctor's obligations, and so on.

One can expect that the jointly constructed utterances would be less common if the dialogue is not based on the expectation that knowledge or opinions are socially shared, but if the participants assume diverse perspectives. Moreover, when in these cases the participants used collaborative utterances with respect to the negotiability of medical confidentiality, syntactically, the diverse perspectives are not expressed in the same way as when the participants test the boundaries of socially shared knowledge. We have seen that in the case of testing the boundaries of socially shared knowledge the collaborative utterance (a question, a suggestion) was a re-completion, in order to ascertain the position of the other speaker. In contrast, collaborative utterances showing disagreements and conflicts are actually independently stated positions. They could be either expressed by different participants in a focus group or they could even be conflicts negotiated within the single individual. In other words, collaborative utterances of the latter kind can offer an opportunity to the proponent of the contested view to point out the contradiction inherent in his/her own argument before someone else does it. We can observe this in the case below.

Excerpt (9) 'HIV/AIDS' dilemma: Marková, Moodie and Collins, 2000

```
1    Tim      as Robert was saying (-) there (h) (.) if
2             he was going out and behaving irresponsibly
3             knowing
4             that he's got this disease (.) that's not a
5             criminal offence (-) so: (-) surely: somebody
6             should know (.) and: (.) if the doctor can't
7             keep an eye on him (.) somebody should at least
8             be: aware
9             of it (.)an:d have him reporting in: (.) a lot
10            more regularly than: just the: (.) regular (.)
11            doctor visits
12   Moderator yeh ( )
13   Mark     if you're making somebody else aw- (.)
14            aware of it then: you're
15   Tim      you're breaching confidentiality
16   Moderator °confidentiality °
17   Tim      tha- (.) yeh that's- that's where I'm
18            gettin (-) that's the difficulty I'm gettin to
```

To be sure, having AIDS is not a criminal offence but if the doctor cannot monitor the irresponsible behaviour of the patient, then, Tim proposes (lines 5–11), somebody should be made aware of it; Tim points out that something more should be done than arranging regular visits to the doctor: AIDS should be reported. However, Mark contests this proposal (lines 13–14) and starts formulating an 'if-then' construction, showing logical implications of that proposal. The 'if' clause, i.e. 'if you're making somebody else … aware of it', points to that aspect of Tim's proposal where lies the contradiction or difficulty. Tim is able to complete the 'if-then' construction before Mark does it himself. He completes the utterance with 'you're breaching confidentiality' because this is the conclusion to which his proposal leads, and effectively, it points to the contradiction inherent in Tim's own line of reasoning. Tim acknowledges this point, whether retrospectively or being aware of it beforehand: 'tha- (.) yeh that's- that's where I'm gettin (-) that's the difficulty I'm gettin to' (lines 15 and 17–18) (Collins and Marková, 2004).

The syntactic, prosodic, interactional (and possibly other) differences with respect to the negotiability or otherwise, of medical confidentiality, that we have shown in the above excerpts cannot of course serve as rigid and/or conclusive claims in these kinds of communication. They are no more than analytical indicators to which the researcher can pay attention and they serve as demonstrations of interdependencies between social psychological phenomena (e.g. interactions, social representations), thinking, and language. For example, we have seen that the degree of socially shared knowledge as well as of the knowledge taken as shared is associated with different levels of implicitness and explicitness, with face work, with linguistic and discursive markers, as well as with specific ways of thematising the content. Hence, something that is recognised as 'testing boundaries of socially shared knowledge' may or may not involve face work, may or may not be characterised by certain syntactic features, e.g. questions, suggestions, by certain contents, and so on. Recognising a discourse or part of it as 'testing boundaries of socially shared knowledge' will partly depend on the involved themata (morality, trust) and the ways in which they are problematised. It is to be expected that other researchers will discover other kinds of syntactic and semantic interdependencies enriching studies of socially shared knowledge in focus groups.

In analysing the excerpts in this chapter we have attempted to find out about two things. First, to see whether, depending on negotiability, possible negotiability and non-negotiability of medical confidentiality, the thema trust/distrust or other themata may play part in focus-group discussions. Second, to see the production of collaborative utterances in cases the participants assume that they share certain kinds of knowledge or test the boundaries of shared knowledge. This enables the researcher to trace the development of an idea starting in the mind of one speaker who articulates it in language and to study how it is brought to the mind of the other speaker who then joins in the formation and transformation of that idea by co-producing it in language.

7.5   Conclusion

In this chapter, discussing relational categories, proto-themata and themata, we have shown that circulation of ideas refers not only to contents that the participants co-construct in dialogue here-and-now, but that they also refer to commonly shared knowledge which is rooted in the past and to ideas that are open towards the future.

While we conceive proto-themata as cultural assumptions 'from' which the participants speak, themata are oppositional relational categories 'about' which the participants speak, which they negotiate and about which they argue. Themata generate, together with other themata, more complex topics, like in our case, medical confidentiality.

Socially shared knowledge, its boundaries and uncertainties surrounding them, can be marked by various linguistic and discursive means, e.g. by incomplete utterances, by jokes, by code switching or by collaborative utterances. We have presented here some examples of the use of collaborative utterances in focus groups, in order to show how they mark boundaries of the assumed aspects of socially shared knowledge. The study of collaborative utterances allows the researcher to understand how participants construct, re-construct or de-construct specific aspects of meaning of their utterances.

Thus we have seen that the way in which the participants in the focus group discuss a dilemma is not determined solely by their stable socially shared knowledge but also by its thematisation, by the framing of the dilemma and positions that they take in communication.

Notes

1   Geoffrey Holton (1975; 1978) coined the term 'thema' to refer to very basic relational categories that help to explain the formation of traditions of schools of thought, and their controversies in physics. These very basic preconceptions in science, usually of dyadic nature, are antithetical couples, like atom/continuum, stability/change or complexity/simplicity that guide the direction of scientific thinking. The analysis of themata in scientific thinking, Holton argues, reveals certain kinds of constancy and continuities in the history and progression of science. For example, a thema, e.g. stability/change, can be found in very different scientific theories (for more details see Moscovici and Vignaux, 1994/2000; Marková, 2003a).

If we turn to human and social sciences, we can find that their theories are also often underlain by very basic relational categories like body/mind, subject/object, stability/change, nature/nurture.

2   Oppositional categories could be of various types, e.g. complementarities, antonyms, reversives (cf. Croft and Cruse, 2004), some could relate to nouns, others to actions, etc. Although these distinctions are important, we shall not go into these.

3   Excerpts used in this chapter were transcribed and analysed by Sarah Collins as part of our ESRC funded project. For the purpose of this chapter I have simplified transcriptions.

8 Focus groups as a dialogical method

8.1 Introduction

Throughout this book we have implied that a method, e.g. focus groups, is not a priori dialogical, but rather, that researcher's epistemological and theoretical assumptions determine whether focus groups are used as a dialogical or a non-dialogical method. We have been repeatedly drawing attention to the fact that there are many ways of analysing discourse in non-dialogical fashions. For example, some of them treat a conversation as if it was a sequence of independent individual speech acts, in each of which the speaker alone realises his/her individual intention; others use conventional content analysis; or they illustrate the content, without much analysis, by presenting some excerpts. Such techniques turn a blind eye on the fact that a discourse, in our case focus groups, is inherently dialogical.

In this final chapter, in order to account for what we have done in terms of dialogical analysis, we shall focus on two issues. First, we shall bring into attention the general question of a research method and its implications for focus groups. Second, using dialogical concepts that we have introduced in Chapter 1, i.e. dialogue, interaction and socially shared knowledge, we shall return to the study of content in focus groups in terms of our analysis, that is, in relation to communicative activity types, heterogeneities of voicing, themes and themata. These two issues, i.e. the research method and the analysis of content, will bring us to the final question: do they help us understand research methods based on dialogism?

8.2   What is a good method?

When social psychologists engage in a conversation about their research, sooner or later they are likely to arrive, in one way or another, on the subject of the method, for example: 'What methods are you using in your study?' or: 'I am really trying hard to find a good method'. The assumption that a method – a good method – holds a secret to the progress in science is widespread in social psychology and to some extent also in other social sciences. We can even say that methodological concerns can be so far-reaching that the field of inquiry may be defined by its method, e.g. experimental social psychology, rather than by phenomena that are to be studied in that field (Moscovici and Marková, 2006).

But what is a good method? In social psychology it is usually presupposed that a good method must be reliable and valid. Statistical concepts of reliability and validity are based on the presupposition that phenomena in objective reality, e.g. psychological traits, social facts, opinions and otherwise, can be measured. Reliable findings must yield the same results when phenomena are re-tested, whether by the same or by a similar technique. And for findings to be valid, they must remain unchanged if tested by different instruments. Thus in both cases the object of measurement must show stability over time and over instrument. Furthermore, high degrees of validity and reliability imply that data are credible when results can be generalised to other cases.

If we turn from social psychology to linguistics, it has been orientated not so much by prescriptions of the method but by conceptual issues. These might have concerned the written language bias (Linell, 2005), the researcher's assumptions about the nature of language (e.g. whether conceived as a static structure or a dynamic discourse) and the kinds of linguistic data that are being gathered. For example, interests in the study of language structure have led to the analysis of noun and verb phrases; the analysis of syntax or of phonological phenomena have called for specific ways of conceiving the data; and so on. In view of this, analysts transcribe texts in ways that are determined by their research concerns and goals.

Generally speaking, we may notice that, on the one hand, transcriptions and analyses of language-based data involve primarily interactions while the content of what is spoken about is more or less neglected. On the other hand, transcriptions that are intended to analyse content, may bracket interactional aspects of the discourse. True, some transcriptions may mark how content is expressed, e.g. hesitation, confidence, a joke, a piece of professional advice and so on, while others may mark the topic and its transformations. Rarely, however, can one find more than that. Interactions and content have usually been analysed as two independent phenomena.

8.3   The method by proof and the method by invention

Analytical assumptions and methodological considerations are mutually interconnected. The former determine to a large extent the latter, and in turn, methodological considerations often put our analytical assumptions to question. If we turn to focus groups, while the kind of transcription is usually determined by the researcher's analytical assumptions and his/her research questions, the transcription, in turn, may determine the kind of the analysis of data that follows, e.g. content analysis, linguistic analysis, conversation analysis, discourse analysis etc. There are at least two different kinds of presupposition about the nature of science and these determine which conception of the scientific method is to be used: either the method by proof or the method by invention (Moscovici, 1992b).

8.3.1   The method by proof and hypothesis testing

Today, a large part of social psychology, and sometimes of other social sciences, is still based on the presupposition that science is only about 'hypothesis testing'. Researchers form predictions and test hypotheses about phenomena of their study and their relations, e.g. about relations between self-judgement and behaviour, or about causes and effects of events, and so on. In this case, research methods serve the purpose of proving or disproving predictions and/or hypotheses.

In order to refute a particular hypothesis, the researcher proposes 'interpretations which provide an alternative to a theory and experiments allowing them to discard it' (Moscovici, 1992b, p. 110). This procedure, however, ignores that 'refuting one particular hypothesis does not dismantle the theoretical construct to which it belongs' (ibid.). The consequence is that instead of discovering new phenomena and broadening the scope of the scientific field, the main effort of the scientist is to refute or jeopardise hypotheses and 'to explain the same facts in a different way' (ibid.). Since this procedure does not address the question as to what may underlie the hypotheses that are being tested, it often goes round in circles. Only getting under the surface of the hypothesis in question might enable an exploration of the underlying theoretical construct. Yet given the procedure of hypothesis testing, this is not a viable option.

The point of view that a method, and more specifically, the method based on hypothesis-testing, holds the clue to scientific progress is not a prerogative of social sciences. The British biologist Peter Medawar (1967), a Fellow of the Royal Society, was concerned with different conceptions of the method. According to Medawar, in one conception of science the researcher looks above all for evidence, believing that 'truth resides in nature and is to be got at only through the evidence of the senses' (ibid. p. 118). In order to find evidence, the scientist's obligation is above all discernment: 'This act of discernment can be carried out according to a Method which, though imagination can help it, does not depend on the imagination: the Scientific Method will see him through' (ibid. p. 118).

Notice that Medawar uses here the word Method with capital M to emphasise that actually method is a defining feature in this conception of science. It builds on critical and evidence-based activity; imagination must be 'under the censorship of a dispassionate and sceptical habit of thought' (ibid.). For this kind of science, the Method is based on hypothesis-testing. In other words, the researcher's mind is involved in the activity of search for proofs. Medawar insists, however, that a one-sided perspective of a single, i.e. of the inductive conception of science, is damaging. He says:

> Unfortunately, we in England have been brought up to believe that scientific discovery turns upon the use of a method ... of Induction – a logically mechanized process of thought which, starting from simple declarations of fact arising out of the evidence of the senses, can lead us to certainty to the truth of general laws...the chief weakness of Millian [John Stuart Mill's methodology] induction was its failure to distinguish between the acts of mind involved in discovery and in proof. (Medawar, 1967, p. 119)

8.3.2   The method by invention

While testing the alternative hypotheses is a relatively new methodological enterprise reinforced by the use of statistics, in contrast to this, the history and philosophy of science shows that doing science has usually been something like the art of discovery and the strife to invent new facts. In analysing problems relating to different ways of science-making, Moscovici (1992, p. 100) has drawn attention to the dynamic theory of physics of relativity, which is not based on the idea that if one hypothesis is 'true', the other must be 'false'. Rather than excluding one another, alternative hypotheses may be in a complementary relation. This position is particularly important in dynamic theories, like the theory of relativity that are concerned with open-ended systems in a continuous change. The method of dynamic theories is heuristics, i.e. the art of discovery. It is the method focusing on the production of thoughts and the invention of new phenomena rather than on testing hypotheses and searching for proofs. Heuristic methods enable the researcher to see how one idea leads to another one; how one thought produces another thought and how it combines with other thoughts; and in the end, how ideas give birth to a faithful portrait of the region of reality to which they aspire (Heisenberg, 1942/2003, p. 20).

Clearly, if the researcher presupposes that a science is dynamic, he/she uses different conceptual tools than in case of holding a presupposition that it is static. This perspective applies to any sciences, whether natural or social and human. Equally, this holds for those theories of social psychology that do not define their arenas of research in terms of making induction, i.e. generalising findings from limited samples to populations. For example, Piaget discovered the child's operational stages while studying very few cases. It was the sense of reality and intuition that guided his work in in-depth clinical observations and interviews; from these he arrived at discoveries of a general nature. Similarly, Kurt Lewin's discovery of group relations pertaining to democratic and non-democratic thinking did not require representative samples from which to generalise to the population. His experiments pursued the question of the dynamics of interaction between individuals in groups and their social environment. For Lewin, interactions modelled realities of daily life. Like for Piaget, so for Lewin it was important that a social psychologist has a sense of reality:

> The 'reality' of that to which the concept refers is established by 'doing something with' rather than 'looking at', and this reality is independent of certain 'subjective' elements of classification. (Lewin, 1947/1951, p. 193)

Equally, Fritz Heider's (e.g. Heider and Simmel, 1944) studies of the personal and impersonal causality, as well as those of Albert Michotte (1946) of phenomenal causality, were all based on theoretically postulated models and demonstrations rather than on sampling. Moscovici's (1980) discovery of conversion, that is, the latent effects of minority influence was, in the first instance, largely a matter of a 'Gedanke experiment' rather than of an empirical hypothesis testing.

This perspective, based on interaction as a dynamic social phenomenon and on socially shared knowledge as dialogically generated, it goes without arguing, is also fundamental in the study of language, dialogue and any kind of symbolic communication. Here, too, we are dealing with open-ended systems in which a relative stability and a continuous change are mutually interdependent, complementing one another.

While, as we have seen above, according to Medawar (1967), in one kind of science, a method carries capital M for a Method by proof, it is not the case for another conception of science in which the method is a tool of discovery. In this conception it is heuristics, and we could say, the Pascalian 'Spirit of Finesse' (Pascal, 1976), i.e. the intuitive feature of the mind, that contributes significantly to the production of thoughts and to moving a science forward. In this conception, science is a great intellectual adventure based not only on 'the Spirit of Geometry' that requires systematic and rigorous thought, but also on creativity and exploration, in which the researcher's accomplishment is having intuition and new ideas.

In discussing these two scientific approaches, i.e. 'the spirit of geometry' and the science based on hypothesis testing on the one hand, and 'the spirit of finesse' and the science as invention on the other hand, neither Pascal nor Medawar, rejected one kind of science in favour of the other. They both viewed them as complementary and as both having something to contribute to the scientific enterprise.

8.3.3   Focus group: what kind of a method?

We can say that a focus group highlights the controversial subject matter concerning the distinction between the two kinds of method as discussed above. But the issue of controversy is not whether a focus group should be used as a method by proof or a method by invention. This issue has hardly ever been considered. Instead, today we find several dominant approaches in social sciences that use focus groups in order to study the contents of beliefs, opinions, ideologies or knowledge. Let us mention two of them. One approach is based on traditional content analysis; another one is represented by some forms of discourse analysis. These two approaches are critical of one another and have very different methodological orientations. Nevertheless, they have in common a very basic characteristic: they both have a strong empirical inclination; their research is guided by data collection and their method of analysis rather than by explicit theoretical positions. One could even say that they view the lack of a theoretical position prior to data collection as a significant and desirable feature of their research. A theoretical position, if at all required, could only be derived from the empirical study.

Let us first turn to the former of these approaches, i.e. traditional content analysis. In social sciences, content analysis in the study of communication has been defined during many decades as an objective, systematic and statistical technique enabling the classification of messages or their parts into units (for numerous definitions see Holsti, 1968). It can be said without exaggeration that in this perspective, content is represented as a bundle of items or messages that fill 'the container of a discourse'. This image of content enables messages and their parts to be taken out of the container, dissected into codes and subsequently treated in quantitative manners. As Holsti (1968, p. 604) explains:

> The investigator may analyze messages to test hypotheses and make inferences about (1) characteristics of the text, (2) causes of antecedents of the message, or (3) effects of the communication.

This characteristic clearly describes content analysis as 'the method by proof and hypothesis testing' based on induction and inferences. Since the main focus is the stable and objective categorisation of units of socially shared knowledge, therefore, content analysis does not do justice to the communicative richness of these data.

Another approach to the study of content is represented by some current forms of discourse analysis, sometimes combined with conversation analysis. These approaches emphasise participants' joint construction of messages and the situated nature of communicative activities and interactions; and they reject dissection of communicative activities into stable units of content. They argue that expressions of socially shared knowledge, e.g. opinions, are talk (e.g. 'Opinions as talk', Myers, 2004, p. 223) and that they should be analysed 'as situated acts, not reduced to given categories'. These approaches study situated interactions, emphasise participants' similarities and differences of perspectives in relation to forms of socially shared knowledge, in rhetoric and in general, in talking together. However, since these approaches start and finish with talk-in-interaction, they treat the forms of socially shared knowledge, attitudes and opinions, largely in talk here-and-now. Their concept of content, therefore, is rather narrow. In fact, they do not use the word 'content', presumably because it implies a static and objectivistic position which both the discourse and conversation analysis resolutely reject. Neither do they make any contribution to theorizing language or institutional macro-social structures.

So we are faced with two empirical orientations in studying content in communication, i.e. content analysis on the one hand and the talk-in-interaction on the other, mutually rejecting one another. All this necessarily begs the question: to what extent can sheer data-gathering and their treatment, without an explicit theoretical position and a clear question: 'what problem do I want to solve?', expand inquiries into communication and the socially shared knowledge?

8.4   Towards a dialogical analysis of content

Let us recapitulate. A focus group, being inherently dialogical, gives the participants a scope for a relatively free communication of ideas. Therefore, there would be no point in carrying out focus group studies if the researcher treated focus groups in the manner that is commonly used in the analysis of questionnaires or attitude scales. Since focus groups are dialogues, they appear to be a particularly suitable means of exploring contents and forms of socially shared knowledge, attitudes, opinions and beliefs in their dynamics. At the same time, because dialogue is not a transmission of neutral information or of facts from speaker to listener, the contents of what participants say and the forms, in which these contents circulate, cannot be meaningfully separated from participants' interactions and relationships in which they are involved. Rather, actively engaged interlocutors jointly co-construct messages and meanings, and they change their positions, once as speakers, once as listeners. One can pose a number of questions about these intertwined dynamics. For example, why do interlocutors say what they say? Why do they express contents in a particular way? Do they convey their own or someone else's opinion? Answers to such questions given by interlocutors always involve judgements and evaluations not only of messages that are being communicated but also of interlocutors themselves. As a result, interlocutors may be embarrassed, could have feelings of disapproval and even of rejection; criticism from others could be experienced as undesirable and it can even engender a conflict.

Just like interaction, socially shared knowledge and dialogue, so the concept of content has been used in social sciences and humanities for a long time but, we have seen, traditional content analysis has given this concept a very static and mechanistic meaning. While we do not claim any originality in bringing concepts of interaction, socially shared knowledge and dialogue into the discussion of focus group research, we have re-conceptualised them and provided them with novel meanings in terms of dialogism.

In our attempt to re-conceptualise content in terms of dialogism, the theory of social representations (Moscovici, 1961) has proved important. The theory of social representations has paid from the beginning a great deal of attention to content of what people talk and think about and one of its main goals has been the study of movement and progression of contents of ideas and thoughts in talk. The theory of social representations presupposes that contents of talk have dynamic structures and that the themes of talk show progression and changes. Some themes are being developed during talk while others are reformulated or may even disappear. Moreover, contents of talk reflect themselves not only in word meanings but also in grammatical structures, in the use of ellipsis, referential expressions, intonation, and so on. Therefore, in this book we have had good grounds for transforming the meaning of a static content into a dialogical concept.

In Chapter 3 we have postulated four analytic assumptions guiding our dialogical approach. Let us see how and in what ways these analytic assumptions have featured in our analysis of content.

8.4.1   Focus-group discussions as group discussions

Our analyses have shown that one cannot separate the content of discourse from the interactions in which that content is being made manifest. That is, what people say is interdependent with how and why they say it. Participants in a focus group are engaged in diverse forms of the Ego-Alter interdependencies, e.g. an interlocutor in relation to other participants, the Ego in relation to inner dialogism or the Ego in relation to absent participants.

In an attempt to bring out these dialogical diversities more clearly, let us start with 'handling the content'. While the traditional content analysis would be based on categorisation of selected items, our dialogical analysis has been concerned with the quality of reasoning 'in which topics glide ... and the talk slips rather seamlessly into new topics' (Chapter 4, p. 96). The analysis of the topical trajectory in concrete examples in Chapter 4 has shown that participants talk about contents as not something external or neutral to them but in terms of activities that they intimately know and in which they are involved with others, whether it is self-irony, black humour, contradictions or other familiar features.

We argued in Chapters 3 and 4 that one cannot think of a focus group simply as an assembly of individuals who are nothing but members of that group. Rather, participants in each focus group jointly enact some kind of communicative activity type. In Chapter 4 we have provided evidence that participants in different groups orientate to divergent activity types, such as group interviews, seminars, fairly unconstrained free-floating conversations, or, for that matter, mixtures (hybrid forms) of several activities. A certain communicative activity type implies that participants relate themselves towards topics and the others in particular ways. In this dynamic process the participation framework may shift from moment to moment, or at least from episode to episode (Chapter 3). In several senses, the group discussion involves multiple parties. Participants draw upon knowledge and social roles that they differentially 'import' into their discussion. For example, we have seen how employees in a military garrison facing a potential closing-down of their workplace may discuss reorganisations in general from their own particular circumstances, or they may draw analogies to other categories of employees (e.g. in banks) who have been forced into unemployment (Chapter 4, Excerpt (6)). When participants in focus groups discuss issues-in-focus, they draw upon knowledge of the world, whether biographical knowledge, explicit social representations or more implicit cultural assumptions. Thus, we can say that the external and internal framings of the communicative activities are necessarily dialogically interdependent.

8.4.2   Subjects' heterogeneity

The analysis in Chapter 5 has shown that focus group participants do not construct the 'same' content in the 'same' manner. They necessarily adopt different positions and change them. However, these positions may not correspond to the researchers' predetermined framing nor do they remain static or homogeneous during the discussion. On the contrary, our observations have shown the importance of dynamic positioning. Moreover, we could see that the participants' positions reveal different forms of socially shared knowledge. Thus it is important not only to identify positions from which participants speak, but 'to identify dialogical characteristics at the heart of the construction of social representations and being truthful to their density and dynamism' (Chapter 5, p. 127).

The position, from which the participants speak also affect, in various ways, their relations with other participants. It may call to the question the speakers' trustworthiness; it may raise questions about social recognition, bring out implicit conflicts and so on. In addition, through modalisations and through quoting or referring to others, speakers make a distance between themselves and their own discourse. They mitigate the polemic positions and exhibit non-politically correct opinions. And so speakers present themselves in heterogeneous ways; they bring forward aspects of a variety of the Ego-Alter relations, like fear of non-recognition, as well as struggles and desires to gain social recognition.

The content, therefore, can be communicated in very different ways. As we have argued, content could be something to be taken at face value; or it might be doubted; it can emerge from internal dialogue or from other discourses; and from agreement or conflict. These different kinds of heterogeneity in terms of content also raise the question as to how participants commit themselves to interaction. For example, we have seen that themes and topics do not peacefully reside in the discourse but are interactively engaged. They result from clashes of different voices, some of them arising from internal dialogues, others from the external dynamics of arguments and oppositions.

8.4.3   The circulation of ideas

We have posed a number of questions as to how ideas circulate, are constructed and transformed in the dialogical process of discussion. Circulation of contents is intertwined with the management of relationships, negotiating of identities and emotions. Our analyses have also shown that the participants do not just plainly declare their beliefs or opinions. When discussing sensitive topics they may try out their views in order to see responses of others and they test how far they can go in exposing their ideas. Moreover, contents are dynamically topicalised as the participants construct and deconstruct their opinions and quote absent 'third parties', either to support their positions or to present them as non-committal quotes of outside authorities. We have seen in Chapter 6 that topics are not arranged in a linear progression but emerge from past themes and project themselves into future ones.

8.4.4   Knowledge taken-as-shared and themata

Our analyses have brought out the perspective that dialogue cannot be restricted to talk-in-interaction but that it is deeply rooted in history and culture. It has its past, present and future. Our analysis of themata in Chapter 7 has shown that some relational categories can be implicit parts of dialogue (and to that extent of common sense) for many generations until, due to changes in societal circumstances, they become explicitly problematised and thematised. When this happens, contents of such relational categories are being transformed and generate new forms of socially shared knowledge.

The dialogical analysis of content, because it is engendered from the theoretical position, enables the researcher to go beyond empirical demonstrations towards elaboration of concepts. However, the clarification of concepts is not the end in itself. Rather, it enables asking further meaningful questions about the content and so expanding the field of inquiry. Examples of such questions could be the following: Can we identify conditions under which certain issues are being topicalised and become subject of linguistic modalisations? What can we find about the nature of phenomena that are taken as socially shared knowledge? In what manners are social representations thematised in different historical periods?

8.5   Conclusion

Our examination in this book of four analytic assumptions in focus groups opens up a number of issues for further consideration.

Since dialogism is by definition an approach to the study of change, this also implies that the key concepts of statistics, i.e. validity and reliability, that presuppose the stability of data, cannot be easily applicable to focus groups. This further means that focus groups do not abide by the criteria of hypothesis testing based on such concepts. The question arises whether the focus group could ever be conceived as either an inductive or a deductive method of proof based on hypothesis testing. It appears that such criteria of hypothesis testing would require researchers to ignore the dynamic exchanges in spoken discourse, e.g. the development and sequential nature of topics, positions taken by speakers, the quality of arguments and so on.

Epistemologies and theories are based on habits of thinking and communication that are often implicit and not likely to be amenable to explicit reflection. This also means that we, as researchers, rarely pay them enough attention. Therefore, we may not be aware of the effects of these habits of thinking and communication on our research activities. This implies that meanings of terms that are often routinely used in theory expositions require careful analysis. For example, terms like 'information-processing', 'independent variable', 'dependent variable', 'the mind/brain', 'mechanism', and so on, rarely have any parallel in the dialogical approach. Likewise, terms like 'tension', the 'Ego-Alter', the 'Ego-Alter-Object', 'positioning', 'communicative heterogeneity', and so on, are not usually used in non-dialogical approaches. Yet some other terms could be used in both, dialogical and non-dialogical approaches, e.g. 'the self', 'Other(s)', 'interaction', 'attitude', 'function' and so on. But although these terms are used in both kinds of approach their contents and meanings are not identical because they are parts of different epistemological systems. This also means that we cannot 'compare', one by one, meanings of terms and attributes of concepts in these different epistemologies.

The capacity of the participants in focus groups to collaborate, jointly produce new knowledge and invent ways of thinking in communication is often implicit and non-transparent. While, for example, psychoanalysis deals directly with unconscious phenomena, in social sciences and specifically in psychology, forms of unconscious, latent and implicitly shared social knowledge will require considerably more attention than it has been given so far.

Our emphasis on heterogeneity and a multifaceted nature of thinking and dialogue does not imply that all this richness can be captured dialogically at the same time and in the same study. Very often the researcher, in order to explore a particular problem, must temporarily fix or freeze his/her perspective with respect to a specific issue in order to see details of interactions and relations in question. This does not mean that he/she abandons dialogism as epistemology. Temporary fixation and freezing the details of interactions and relations must be followed by the return to conceptual de-freezing of perspectives so that the meaning of these details can be comprehended in the problem as a whole.

As we have proposed in this book, one needs an explicit theoretical position and research question at the beginning of research, rather than starting with empirical observations and trying to build a theory from these. We have attempted to discover dynamic and heterogeneous characteristics of the content of socially shared knowledge (or of knowledge taken as shared). It is these features and their multifaceted characteristics in and through their change that epitomise the focus group both as 'a method of invention' and as a miniature society.

References

Adelswärd, V., Holsánová, J. and Wibeck, V. (2002) Virtual talk as a communicative resource. Explorations in the field of gene technology. *Sprachtheorie und Germanistische Linguistik* 12: 3–26.

Åkerblom, M. (2003) Arbetslivets förändringar i fokus: fokusgruppssamtal om förändrade arbetssätt vid ett svenskt industriföretag. (Working life changes in focus: focus group discussions about changes in workplace organisation at a Swedish industrial company) Master's thesis from tema K, 2003, 3. Linköping University: Department of Communication Studies.

Albrecht, T. L., Johnson, G. M. and Walther, J. B. (1993) Understanding communication processes in focus groups. In D. L. Morgan (ed.) *Successful Focus Groups: advancing the state of the art* 51–64. Newbury Park: Sage.

Allport, F. H. (1924) *Social Psychology*. Boston: Houghton Mifflin.

Amossy, R. (ed.) (1999) *Images de soi dans le discours. La construction de l'ethos*. Neuchâtel: Delachaux et Niestlé.

Ancelin-Schützenberger, A. (1972) *L'observation dans les groupes de formation et de thérapie*. Paris: EPI.

Antaki, C. and Wetherell, M. (1999) Showing concession. *Discourse Studies* 1: 7–27.

Anward, J. (1997) Parameters of institutional discourse In B.-L. Gunnarsson, P. Linell and B. Nordberg (eds) *The Construction of Professional Discourse* 127–150. London: Longman.

Anzieu, D. (1971) L'illusion groupale. *Nouvelle Revue de Psychanalyse* 4: 73–93.

Anzieu, D. (1984) *The Group and the Unconscious*. London: Routledge and Kegan Paul.

Asbury, J.-E. (1995) Overview of focus group research. *Qualitative Health Research* 5: 414–420.

Bakhtin, M. M. (1981a) Discourse in the novel. In M. Holquist (ed.) *The Dialogical Imagination: four essays by M. M. Bakhtin* 259–422. Austin: University of Texas Press.

Bakhtin, M. M. (1981b) *The Dialogical Imagination: four essays by M. M. Bakhtin*. Edited by M. Holquist. Austin: University of Texas Press.

Bakhtin, M. M. (1984) *Problems of Dostoyevsky's Poetics*. Edited and translated by C. Emerson. Minneapolis: University of Minnesota Press.

Bakhtin, M. M. (1986) *Speech Genres and Other Late Essays*. Translated by V. W. McGee, edited by C. Emerson and M. Holquist. Austin: University of Texas.

Bakshi, A.-S., Wibeck, V., Linell, P. and Adelswärd, V. (2000) Att dra gränser mot det onaturliga och det otillåtna: Fokusgrupper om genteknik och fosterdiagnostik. (Drawing boundaries against the unnatural and the impermissible: focus groups on gene technology and fetal diagnosis) *Working Paper from tema K*, 2000, 1. Linköping University: Department of Communication Studies.

Baldwin, J. M. (1895) *Mental Development in the Child and the Race: methods and processes*. New York and London: Macmillan.

Baldwin, J. M. (1897) *Social and Ethical Interpretations in Mental Development*. London: Macmillan.

Bales, R. F. (1950) A set of categories for the analysis of small group interaction. *American Sociological Review* 15: 257–263.

Bales, R. F. (1951) *Interaction Process Analysis. A Method for the Study of Small Groups*. Cambridge, MA: Addison-Wesley Press.

Bales, R. F. and Strodtbeck, F. (1951) Phases in group problem-solving. *Journal of Abnormal and Social Psychology* 46: 485–495.

Bartlett, F. C. (1932) *Remembering: an experimental and social study*. Cambridge: Cambridge University Press.

Bateson, G. (1972) *Steps to an Ecology of Mind*. New York: Ballantine Books.

Bauer, M. and Gaskell, G. (1999) Towards a paradigm for research on social representations. *Journal for the Theory of Social Behaviour* 29: 163–188.

Benne, K. D. (1964) History of the T-group in the laboratory setting. In L. P. Bradford, J. R. Gibb and K. B. Benne (eds) *T-Group Theory and Laboratory Method* 80–135. New York: Wiley.

Benveniste, E. (1977) Subjectivity in language. In M. Nystrand (ed.) *Language as a Way of Knowing. A Book of Readings*. Toronto: The Ontario Institute for Studies in Education.

Bierwisch, M. (1970) Semantics. In J. Lyons (ed.) *New Horizons in Linguistics* 166–184. Harmondsworth: Penguin.

Billig, M. (1987) *Arguing and Thinking: a rhetorical approach to social psychology*. Cambridge: Cambridge University Press.

Billig, M. (1993) Studying the thinking society: social representations, rhetoric, and attitudes. In G. Breakwell and D. Canter (eds) *Empirical Approaches to Social Representations* 39–62. Oxford: Clarendon Press.

Billington, J. (1966) *The Icon and the Axe: the interpretative history of Russian culture*. Weidenfeld and Niolson.

Bion, W. R. (1961) *Experiences in Groups and Other Papers*. London: Tavistock Publications.

Bloor, M., Frankland, J., Thomas, M. and Robson, K. (2001) *Focus Groups in Social Research*. London: Sage.

Boudon, R. and Bourricaut, F. (1982) *Dictionnaire critique de la sociologie*. Paris: Presses Universitaires de France.

Brandt, A. M. (1988) AIDS in historical perspective: four lessons from the history of sexually transmitted diseases. *American Journal of Public Health* 78: 367–371.

Bres, J. (1998) Entendre des voix: de quelques marqueurs dialogiques en français. In J. Bres, R. Delamotte-Legrand, F. Madray-Lesigne and P. Siblot (eds) *L'autre en discours* 191–212. Montpellier et Rouen: Praxiling et Dyalang.

Bres, J. (1999) Vous les entendez? Analyse du discours et dialogisme. *Modèles linguistiques* 20: 71–86.

Bres, J. and Vérine, B. (2002) Le bruissement des voix dans le discours: dialogisme et discours rapporté. *Faits de langues* 19: 159–169.

Buber, M. (1923/1962) *I and Thou*. Edinburgh: T. and T. Clark.

Carey, M. A. and Smith, M. W. (1994) Capturing the group effect in focus groups. *Qualitative Health Research* 4: 123–127.

Clark, H. H. (1994) *Using Language*. Cambridge: Cambridge University Press.

Clark, H. H. and Gerrig, R. (1990) Quotations as demonstrations. *Language* 66: 764–805.

Collins, S. and Marková, I. (2004) Les énoncés collaboratifs: une nouvelle méthode dans l'étude des focus groups. *Bulletin de Psychologie* 57: 291–298.

Croft, W. and Cruse, D. A. (2004) *Cognitive Linguistics*. Cambridge: Cambridge University Press.

Cruse, D. A. (1986) *Lexical Semantics*. Cambridge: Cambridge University Press.

Drew, P. (1998) An exercise in the comparative analysis of talk-in-interaction in different (institutional) settings: the case of 'formulations'. In H. Lehti-Eklund (ed) *Samtalsstudier* (Conversation Studies) 29–42. Helsinki: Department of Scandinavian Languages and Literature.

Ducrot, O. (1984) *Le dire et le dit*. Paris: Minuit.

Duranti, A. (1997) *Linguistic Anthropology*. Cambridge: Cambridge University Press.

Durkheim, E. (1938) *The Rules of Sociological Method*. Translated by S. A. Solovay and J. H. Mueller. New York: Free Press.

Eemeren, F. van, Grootendorst, R., Blair, A. and Willard, C. (eds) (1987) *Argumentation: perspectives and approaches*. Dordrecht: Foris Publications.

Eemeren, F. van, Grootendorst, R., Blair, A. and Willard, C. (eds) (1992) *Argumentation Illuminated*. (SICSAT, ISSA) Amsterdam.

Egbert, M. (1997) Schisming: the collaborative transformation from a single conversation to multiple conversations. *Research on Language and Social Interaction* 30: 1–51.

Elster, J. (ed.) (1985) *The Multiple Self*. Cambridge, Cambridge University Press. Emerson, Manchester: Manchester University Press.

Engeström, Y. and Middleton, D. (1996) *Cognition and Communication at Work*. Cambridge: Cambridge University Press

Erickson, F. (1982) Money tree, lasagna bush, salt and pepper: social construction of topical cohesion in a conversation among Italian-Americans. In D. Tannen (ed.) *Analyzing Discourse: text and talk* 43–70. (Georgetown University Round Table on Language and Linguistics, 1981) Washington, DC: Georgetown University Press.

Fairclough, N. (1992) *Discourse and Social Change*. Cambridge: Polity Press.

Farr, R. M. (personal communication)

Fleck, L. (1935) *Zustehung und Entwicklung einer Wissenschaften Tatsache*. Suhrkamp: Frankfurt n.Main.

François, F. (1982) Ebauches d'une dialogique. *Connexions* 38: 61–87.

François, F. (1990) Introduction. In F. François (ed.) *La communication inégale. Heurs et malheurs de l'interaction verbale* 7–12. Neuchâtel, Delachaux et Niestlé.

François, F. (1993) *Pratiques de l'oral. Dialogue, jeu et variations des figures du sens*. Paris: Nathan pédagogie.

François, F. (1994) *Morale et mise en mots*. Paris: L'Harmattan.

Gellner, E. (1992) *Reason and Culture*. Oxford: Blackwell.

Gellner, E. (1998) *Language and Solitude*. Cambridge: Cambridge University Press.

Gergen, K. J. (1972) Multiple identity: the healthy, happy, human being wears many masks. *Psychology Today* 5: 64–66.

Gille, J. (2001) Pautas argumenttaivas en el diálogo espontáneo. Un estudio de conversaciones intra e interculturales. (Doctoral dissertation) Stockholm University: Department of Spanish, Portuguese and Latin American Studies.

Goffman, E. (1961) *Encounters: two studies in the sociology of interaction*. Indianapolis: The Bobbs-Merrill.

Goffman, E. (1974) *Frame Analysis*. Cambridge, MA: Harvard University Press.

Goffman, E. (1981) *Forms of Talk*. Philadelphia: University of Pennsylvania Press.

Goodwin, C. and Duranti, A. (1992) Rethinking context: an introduction. In A. Duranti and C. Goodwin (eds) *Rethinking Context* 1–42. Cambridge: Cambridge University Press.

Graumann, C. F. (1988) Introduction to a history of social psychology. In M. Hewstone, W. Stroebe, J.-P. Codol and G. Stephenson (eds) *Introduction to Social Psychology* 21–37. Cambridge: Cambridge University Press.

Grize, J.-B. (1990) *Logique et langage*. Paris: Ophrys.

Grize, J.-B. (1996) *Logique naturelle et communications*. Paris: Presses Universitaires de France.

Grosjean, M. and Traverso, V. (2002) Les polylogues: typologie, problèmes méthodologiques et théoriques. *Psychologie de l'Interaction* 15–16: 283–303.

Grossen, M. (1998) Where is the dilemma? The definition of the task in the joint problem solving situation. Paper presented at workshop on 'Language and Conversation II', Paris, May 1998.

Grossen, M. (in press) Interaction analysis and psychology: a dialogical perspective. In C. Prevignano and P. Thibault (eds) *Interaction Analysis and Language: discussing the state-of-the-art*. Amsterdam: John Benjamins.

Grossen, M. and Salazar Orvig, A. (2000) Discourse and social representations: framing cognition in focus groups. Paper presented at the workshop 'Language and Social Representations', Paris, EHESS.

Grossen, M. and Salazar Orvig, A. (2002) *Heterogeneity and social representations through the lenses of focus-groups*. Paper presented at the Sixth International Conference on Social Representations, University of Stirling, UK.

Gumperz, J. (1982) *Discourse Strategies*. Cambridge: Cambridge University Press.

Habermas, J. (1991) *The Theory of Communicative Action: reason and the rationalization of society*. Cambridge: Polity Press.

Heider, F. (1958) *The Psychology of Interpersonal Relations*. New York and London: Wiley.

Heider, F. and Simmel, M. (1944) An experimental study of apparent behaviour. *American Journal of Psychology* 57: 243–259.

Heisenberg, W. (2003) *Le Manuscrit de 1942*. Paris: Allia.

Holšanová, J. (2006) Quotations as a vehicle for social positioning. In H. Hausendorf and A. Bora (eds) *Analyzing Citizenship Talk* 251–275. Amsterdam: John Benjamins.

Holsti, O. R. (1968) Content analysis. In G. Lindzey and E. Aronson (eds) *The Handbook of Social Psychology* Vol. II 596–692. Reading, MA: Addison-Wesley.

Holton, G. (1975) On the role of themata in scientific thought. *Science* 188: 324–334.

Holton, G. (1978) *The Scientific Imagination: case studies*. Cambridge, New York.

Hosking, G. (2004) Forms of social solidarity in Russia and the Soviet Union. In I. Marková (ed.) *Trust and Democratic Transition in Post-Communist Europe* 47–62. Oxford: Oxford University Press for The British Academy

Hudelot, C. (1994) La circulation interactive du sens dans le dialogue. In A. Trognon, U. Dausendschön-Gay, U. Krafft and C. Riboni. (eds) *La construction interactive du quotidien*. Nancy: Presses Universitaires de Nancy.

Hydén, L.-C. and Bülow, P. (2003) Who's talking: drawing conclusions from focus groups – some methodological considerations. *International Journal of Social Research Methodology* 6: 305–321.

Jackson, S. (1992) 'Virtual standpoints' and the pragmatics of conversational argument. In F. van Eemeren, R. Grootendorst, A. Blair and C. Willard (eds) *Argumentation Illuminated* (SICSAT, ISSA) 260–269. Amsterdam.

Jahoda, A. (1995) Quality of life: hope for the future or an echo from the distant past? In I. Marková and R. Farr (eds) *Representations of Health, Illness and Handicap* 205–224. Amsterdam: Harwood.

James, W. (1975) *Pragmatism*. Cambridge, MA: Harvard University Press.

Josephs, I. E. (1998) Do you know Ragnar Rommetveit? On dialogue and silence, poetry and pedantry, and cleverness and wisdom in psychology (an interview with Ragnar Rommetveit) *Culture and Psychology* 4: 189–212.

Jovchelovitch, S. (1995) Social representations in and of the public sphere: towards a theoretical articulation. *Journal for the Theory of Social Behaviour* 25: 81–102.

Jovchelovitch, S. (2000) *Representações Sociais e Espaço Público: a construção simbólica dos espaços públicos no Brasil.* (Social Representations and Public Life: the symbolic construction of public spaces in Brazil) Petrópolis: Vozes.

Jovchelovitch, S. (2004) Contextualiser les *focus groups* comme espace de pensée et l'argumentation à propos des aliments génétiquement modifiés. *Bulletin de Psychologie* 57: 245–252.

Jovchelovitch, S. (2007) *Knowledge in Context. Representations, Community and Culture.* London: Routledge.

Kaës, R. (1976) *L'appareil psychique groupal. Constructions du groupe.* Paris: Dunod.

Kaës, R. (1993) *Le groupe et le sujet du groupe.* Paris: Dunod.

Keppler, A. and Luckmann, T. (1991) 'Teaching': conversational transmission of knowledge. In I. Marková and K. Foppa (eds) *Asymmetries in Dialogue* 143–165. Hemel Hempstead: Harvester Wheatsheaf.

Kerbrat-Orecchioni, C. (1980) *L'énonciation. De la subjectivité dans le langage.* Paris: Armand Colin.

Kerbrat-Orecchioni, C. (1995) *Le trilogue.* Lyon: Presses Universitaires de Lyon.

Kerbrat-Orecchioni, C. (1997) A multilevel approach in the study of talk-in-interaction. *Pragmatics* 7: 1–10.

Kidd, P. S. and Parshall, M. B. (2000) Getting the focus and the group: enhancing analytical rigor in focus group research. *Qualitative Health Research* 10: 293–308.

Kitzinger, J. (1994) The methodology of focus group: the importance of interaction between research participants. *Sociology of Health and Illness* 16: 103–121.

Kitzinger, J. (2004) Le sable dans l'huitre: analyser des discussions de focus group. *Bulletin de psychologie* 57: 299–307.

Kitzinger, J. and Barbour, R. S. (1999) Introduction: the challenge and promise of focus groups. In R. S. Barbour and J. Kitzinger (eds) (1999) *Developing Focus Group Research* 1–20. London: Sage.

Kitzinger, J. and Farquhar, C. (1999) The analytical potential of 'sensitive moments' in focus group discussions. In R. S. Barbour and J. Kitzinger (eds) *Developing Focus Group Research* 156–172. London: Sage.

Kitzinger, J., Marková, I. and Kalampalikis, N. (2004) Qu'est-ce que les focus groups? *Bulletin de Psychologie* 57: 237–243.

Korén, R. and Amossy, R. (eds) (2002) *Après Perelman: quelles politiques pour les nouvelles rhétoriques? L'argumentation dans les sciences du langage*. Paris: L'Harmattan.

Korolija, N. (1998) *Episodes in Talk*. Linköping Studies in Arts and Science, 171. Linköping: The Tema Institute.

Krueger, R. A. (1994) *Focus Groups: a practical guide for applied research*. Thousand Oaks, CA: Sage.

Lakoff, G. and Johnson, M. (1980) *Metaphors We Live By*. Chicago: University of Chicago Press.

Lazarsfeld, P. and Stanton, F. N. (1944) *Radio Research 1942–43*. New York: Duell, Sloan and Pearce.

Levin, L. (2003) Massmedial gestaltning och vardagsförståelse: versioner av en arbetsplatsomvandling. (Mediated renditions and everyday understandings: versions of a work-site change) (Diss.) Linköping Studies in Arts and Science, 279 Linköping: The Tema Institute.

Levinson, S. (1979/1992) Activity types and language. *Linguistics* 17: 365–399. Reprinted in P. Drew and J. Heritage (eds) *Talk at Work* 66–100. Cambridge: Cambridge University Press.

Levinson, S. (1983) *Pragmatics*. Cambridge: Cambridge University Press.

Levinson, S. (1988) Putting linguistics on a proper footing: explorations in Goffman's concepts of participation. In P. Drew and A. Wootton (eds) *Erving Goffman: exploring the interaction order* 161–227. Cambridge: Polity Press.

Lewin, K. (1939/1951) Field theory and experiment in social psychology. In D. Cartwright (ed.) *Field Theory in Social Science. Selected Theoretical Papers. Kurt Lewin* 130–169. New York: Harper and Row.

Lewin, K. (1943/1951) Defining the 'field at a given time'. In D. Cartwright (ed.) *Field Theory in Social Science. Selected Theoretical Papers. Kurt Lewin* 43–58. New York: Harper and Row.

Lewin, K. (1946/1951) Behavior and development as a function of the total situation. In D. Cartwright (ed.) *Field Theory in Social Science. Selected Theoretical Papers. Kurt Lewin* 238–303. New York: Harper and Row.

Lewin, K. (1947/1951) Frontiers in group dynamics. In D. Cartwright (ed.) *Field Theory in Social Science. Selected Theoretical Papers. Kurt Lewin* 188–237. New York: Harper and Row.

Lewin, K. (1948) *Resolving Social Conflicts. Selected Papers on Group Dynamics*. Edited by G. W. Lewin. New York: Harper and Row.

Linell, P. (1998a) *Approaching Dialogue: talk, interaction and contexts in dialogical perspectives*. Amsterdam: John Benjamins.

Linell, P. (1998b) Discourse across boundaries: On recontextualizations and the blending of voices in professional discourse. *Text* 18: 143–157.

Linell, P. (1998c) Leken och avgörandet: försök till en elementär samtalstypologi. (Playing and decision-making: trying out an elementary typology of conversations) In *Samtalsstudier* (Studies of conversations) 155–164. Helsinki: Department of Nordic Languages and Literature.

Linell, P. (2001) A dialogical conception of focus groups and social representations. In U. Sätterlund Larsson (ed.) *Socio-Cultural Theory and Methods*: *an anthology* 163–206. Uddevalla/Trollhättan: University of Trollhättan.

Linell, P. (2005) *The Written Language Bias in Linguistics: its nature, origin and transformations*. London: Routledge.

Linell, P. and Korolija, N. (1995) On the division of communicative labour within episodes in aphasic discourse. *International Journal of Psycholinguistics* 11: 143–165.

Linell, P. and Marková, I. (1993) Acts in discourse: from monological speech acts to dialogical interacts. *Journal for the Theory of Social Behaviour* 23: 173–195.

Linell, P., Wibeck, V., Adelswärd, V. and Bakshi, A-S. (2001) Arguing in conversation as a case of distributed cognition: Discussing biotechnology in focus groups. In E. Németh (ed.) *Cognition in Language Use*: *selected papers from the 7th international pragmatics conference* Vol. I 243–255. Amsterdam: International Pragmatics Association.

Lotman, Yu. (1990) *Universe of the Mind. A Semiotic Theory of Culture.* Translated by A. Shukman. London and New York: Tausis.

Luckmann, T. (1990) Social communication, dialogue and conversation. In I. Marková and K. Foppa (eds) *The Dynamics of Dialogue* 45–61. New York and London: Harvester Wheatsheaf.

Luckmann, T. (1992) On the communicative adjustment of perspectives, dialogue and communicative genres. In A. H. Wold (ed.) *The Dialogical Alternative*: *towards a theory of language and mind* 219–234. Oslo: Scandinavian University Press.

Luckmann, T. (1995) Interaction planning and intersubjective adjustment of perspectives by communicative genres. In E. Goody (ed.) *Social Intelligence and Interaction* 175–186. Cambridge: Cambridge University Press.

Luckmann, T. (2002) On the methodology of (oral) genres. In P. Linell and K. Aronsson (eds) *Selves and Voices*: *Goffman, Viveka and dialogue* (Jagen och rösterna: Goffman, Viveka och samtalet) SIC, 42: 319–337. Linköping: Department of Communication Studies.

MacLachlan, G. and Reid, I. (1994) *Framing and Interpretation*. Carlton, Victoria: Melbourne University Press.

Marková, I. (1997) On two concepts of interaction. In M. Grossen and B. Py (eds) *Pratiques sociales et médiations symboliques* 23–44. Bern: Peter Lang.

Marková, I. (2000) Amédée or how to get rid of it: social representations from a dialogical perspective. *Culture and Psychology* 6: 419–460.

Marková, I. (2003a) *Dialogicality and Social Representations. The Dynamics of Mind.* Cambridge: Cambridge University Press.

Marková, I. (2003b) *Les focus groups*. In S. Moscovici and F. Buschini (eds) *Méthodes des sciences humaines* 221–22. Paris: Presses Universitaires de France.

Marková, I. (2004) Langage et communication en psychologie sociale: dialoguer dans les *focus groups*. *Bulletin de Psychologie* 57: 231–236.

Marková, I. (2006) On the 'inner Alter' in dialogue. *International Journal for Dialogical Science* 1: 125–148.

Marková, I., Wilkie, P. A., Naji, S. and Forbes, C. (1990) Self- and other awareness of the risk of HIV/AIDS in people with haemophilia and implications for behavioural change. *Social Science and Medicine* 31: 73–79.

Marková, I. and Wilkie, P. (1987) Representations, concepts and social change: The phenomenon of AIDS. *Journal for the Theory of Social Behaviour* 17: 389–401.

Marková, I. and Foppa, K. (eds) (1990) *The Dynamics of Dialogue*. New York and London: Harvester Wheatsheaf.

Marková, I., Graumann, C. and Foppa, K. (eds) (1995) *Mutualities in Dialogue*. Cambridge: Cambridge University Press.

Marková, I. and Linell, P. (1996) Coding elementary contributions to dialogue: Individual acts versus dialogical interactions. *Journal for the Theory of Social Behaviour* 26: 353–373.

Marková, I., McKee, K., Power, K. and Moodie, E. (1995) The self, the other and perceived risk: lay representations of HIV/AIDS in Scottish prisons. In I. Marková and R. M. Farr (eds) *Representations of Health, Illness and Handicap* 111–129. New York: Harwood.

Marková, I., Moodie, E. and Collins, S. (2000) Final report on the ESRC funded project. *Responsibilities/entitlements: a study in language and social representations in Central and Western Europe* R000237206.

Marková, I., Moodie, I., Farr, R., Drozda-Senkowska, E., Erös, F., Plichtová, J., Gervais, M-C., Hoffmannová, J. and Mullerová, O. (1998) Social representations of the individual: a post-communist perspective. *European Journal of Social Psychology* 28: 797–829.

Marková, I., Moodie, E., Plichtová, J., Mullerová, O., Hoffmannová, J. (2001) Démocratie: Réalité, espoir et déception. *Bulletin de Psychologie* 54: 611–621.

Marková, I. and Wilkie, P. (1987) Representations, concepts and social change: the phenomenon of AIDS. *Journal for the Theory of Social Behaviour* 17: 389–401.

Mead, G. H. (1927) The objective reality of perspectives. *Proceedings of the Sixth International Congress of Philosophy* 75–85. Edited by E. S. Brightmann. New York: Longmans.

Mead, G. (1934/1967) *Mind, Self and Society*. Chicago: The Chicago University Press.

Medawar, P. B. (1967) *The Art of the Soluble*. London: Methuen.

Merton, R. K. (1987) The focused interview and focus groups: continuities and discontinuities. *Public Opinion Quarterly* 51: 550–556.

Merton, R. K., Fiske, M. and Kendall, P. L. (1956) *The Focused Interview*. Glencoe, IL: Free Press.

Michotte, A. (1946) *La Perception de la Causalité*. Louvain: Editions de l'Institut Supérieur de Philosophie.

Minsky, M. (1975) Frame-system theory. In R. C. Schank and B. Nash-Webber (eds) *Theoretical Issues in Natural Language Processing*. Cambridge, MA: The M. I. T. Press.

Moghaddam, F. M. and Harré, R. (1996) Psychological limits to political revolutions: an application of social reducton theory. In E. H. Hasselberg, L. Martienssen and F. Radtke (eds) *Der Dialogbegriff am Ende des 20. Jahrhunderts* 230–240. Berlin: Hegel Institute.

Moodie, E., Marková, I. and Plichtová, J. (1995) Lay representations of democracy: a study in two cultures. *Culture and Psychology* 1: 423–453.

Morgan, D. L. (1993) Future directions for focus groups. In D. L. Morgan (ed.) *Successful Focus Groups. Advancing the State of the Art* 225–244. London: Sage.

Morgan, D. and Krueger, R. (1998) *The Focus Group Kit*. Thousand Oaks, CA: Sage.

Morgan, H. and Thomas, K. (1996) A psychodynamic perspective on group processes. In M. Wetherell (ed.) *Identities, Groups and Social Issues* 63–117. London: Sage, The Open University.

Moscovici, S. (1961) *La psychanalyse: son image et son public*. (Second edition 1976b) Paris: Presses Universitaires de France.

Moscovici, S. (1976a) *La psychanalyse: son image et son public*. (Second edition) Paris: Presses Universitaires de France.

Moscovici, S. (1979) *Psychologie des minorités actives*. Paris: Presses Universitaires de France.

Moscovici, S. (1980) Towards a theory of conversion behavior. In L. Berkowitz (ed.) *Advances in Experimental Social Psychology*. Vol. XIII 209–239. New York and London: Academic Press.

Moscovici, S. (1984) The phenomenon of social representations. In R. M. Farr and S. Moscovici (eds) *Social Representations* 3–69. Cambridge: Cambridge University Press.

Moscovici, S. (1992) The discovery of group polarization. In D. Granberg and G. Sarup (eds) *Social Judgement and Intergroup Relations* 107–127. New York: Springer.

Moscovici, S. (2000) *Social Representations: explorations in social psychology*. Edited by G. Duveen. Cambridge: Polity Press.

Moscovici, S. (2001) Why a theory of social representations? In K. Deaux and G. Philogène (eds) *Representations of the Social* 8–35. Oxford: Blackwell.

Moscovici, S. (2005a) Le regard psychosocial. Entretien avec Birgitta Orfali. *Hermès* 41: 17–24.

Moscovici, S. (2005b) *Memória, imaginário e representações sociais*. Rio de Janeiro: Museu de República.

Moscovici, S. and Hewstone, M. (1983) Social representations and social explanations: from the 'naïve' to the 'amateur' scientist. In M. Hewstone (ed.) *Attribution Theory* 98–125. Oxford: Basil Blackwell.

Moscovici, S. and Vignaux, G. (1994) Le Concept de Thêmata. In Ch. Guimelli (ed.) *Structures et transformations des représentations sociales* 25–72. Neuchatel: Delachaux et Niestlé. Reprinted in S. Moscovici (2000) *Social Representations* 156–183. Edited by G. Duveen. London: Polity Press.

Moscovici, S. and Marková, I. (2000) Ideas and their development: a dialogue between Serge Moscovici and Ivana Marková. In S. Moscovici *Social Representations. Explorations in Social Psychology* 224–286. Edited by G. Duveen. Cambridge: Polity Press.

Moscovici, S. and Marková, I. (2006) *The Making of Modern Social Psychology: the hidden story of how an international social science was created.* Cambridge: Polity Press.

Musolff, A. (2004) *Metaphor and Political Discourse: analogical reasoning in debates about Europe*. Basingstoke: Palgrave.

Myers, G. (1998) Displaying opinions: disagreement and topic shift in focus groups. *Language in Society* 27: 85–111.

Myers, G. (1999) Unspoken speech: hypothetical reported discourse and the rhetoric of everyday talk. *Text* 19: 571–590.

Myers, G. (2000) Becoming a group: face and sociability in moderated discussions. In S. Sarangi and M. Coulthard (eds) *Discourse and Social Life* 121–137. Harlow: Longman.

Myers, G. (2004) *Matters of Opinion. Talking About Public Issues.* Cambridge: Cambridge University Press.

Myers, G. and Macnaghten, P. (1999) Can focus groups be analysed as talk? In R. S. Barbour and J. Kitzinger (eds) *Developing Focus Group Research* 173–185. London: Sage.

Naess, A. (1953) *Preciseness and Interpretation*. Oslo: Universitetsforlaget.

Newson, J. (1979) The growth of shared understandings between infant and caregiver. In M. Bullowa (ed.) *Before Speech: the beginning of interpersonal communication* 207–222. Cambridge and New York: Cambridge University Press.

Norén, K. and Linell, P. (2007) Meaning potentials and the interaction between lexis and contexts: some empirical substantiations. Submitted to *Pragmatics*.

Orfali. B. (2004) Typologie des focus groups à partir d'un dilemme sur le SIDA: le rôle du « compère spontané ». *Bulletin de Psychologie* 57: 273–279.

Orfali, B. and Marková. I. (2002) Analogies in focus groups: from the victim to the murderer and from the murderer to the victim. *European Review of Applied Psychology* 52: 263–271.

Pascal, B. (1941) *Pensées and Provincial Letters*. Translated by W. F. Trotter and T. McCrie. New York: The Modern Library.

Perelman, C. (1997) *L'empire rhétorique*. Paris: Vrin.

Pomerantz, A. (1984) Agreeing and disagreeing with assessments: some features of preferred/dispreferred turn shapes. In M. Atkinson and J. Heritage (eds) *Structures of Social Action: studies in conversation analysis* 57–101. Cambridge: Cambridge University Press.

Pomerantz, A. (1986) Extreme case formulations: a way of legitimising claims. *Human Studies* 9: 219–230.

Puchta, C. and Potter, J. (1999) Asking elaborate questions: focus groups and the management of spontaneity. *Journal of Sociolinguistics* 3: 314–335.

Rogers, C. (1961) *On Becoming a Person: a therapist's view of psychotherapy*. Boston: Houghton Mifflin.

Rommetveit, R. (1974) *On Message Structure*. Chichester and New York: Wiley.

Rommetveit, R. (1990) On axiomatic features of a dialogical approach to language and mind. In I. Marková and K. Foppa (eds) *The Dynamics of Dialogue* 83–104. Hemel Hempstead: Harvester Wheatsheaf.

Rommetveit, R. (1991) On epistemic responsibility in human communication. In H. Ronning and K. Lundby (eds) *Media and Communication* 13–27. Oslo: Norwegian University Press.

Rommetveit, R. (1992) Outlines of dialogically based social-cognitive approach to human cognition and communication. In A. H. Wold (ed.) *The Dialogical Alternative. Towards Theories of Language and Minds* 19–44. Oslo: Scandinavian University Press.

Rommetveit, R. (1998) On human beings, computers and representational-computational vs. hermeneutic-dialogical approaches to human cognition and communication. *Culture and Psychology* 4: 213–233.

Rosenberg, S. (1968) Mathematical models of social behavior. In G. Lindzey and E. Aronson (eds) *The Handbook of Social Psychology*. Vol. I 179–244. Reading, MA: Addison-Wesley.

Sacks, H., Schegloff, E. A. and Jefferson, G. (1974) A simplest systematics for the organization of turn-taking for conversation. *Language* 50: 696–735.

Salazar Orvig, A. and Grossen, M. (2004) Représentations sociales et analyse de discours produit dans des *focus groups*: un point de vue dialogique. *Bulletin de Psychologie* 57: 263–272.

Sarangi, S. (2000) Activity types, discourse types and interactional hybridity: the case of genetic counselling. In S. Sarangi and M. Coulthard (eds) *Discourse and Social Life* 1–27. Harlow: Longman.

Sarangi, S. and Slembrouck, S. (1996) *Language, Bureaucracy and Social Control*. London: Longman.

Sarfati, G.-E. (2002) Aspects épistémologiques et conceptuels d'une théorie linguistique de la doxa. In R. Koren and R. Amossy (eds) *Après Perelman: Quelles politiques pour les nouvelles rhétoriques? L'argumentation dans les sciences du langage* 57–90. Paris: L'Harmattan.

Schank, R. C. and Abelson, R. P. (1975) *Scripts, Plans, Goals, and Understanding*. Hillsdale, NJ: Erlbaum.

Schegloff, E. A. (1991) Reflections on talk and social structure. In D. Boden and D. Zimmerman (eds) *Talk and Social Structure: studies in ethnomethodology and conversation analysis* 44–70. Cambridge: Polity Press.

Schütz, A. (1962) *Collected Papers. I. The Problem of Social Reality*. Edited by M. Natanson. The Hague: Martinus Nijhoff.

Schütz, A. (1975) *Collected Papers. III. Studies in Phenomenological Philosophy*. Introd. A. Gurwitsch. Edited by I. Schütz. Hague: Martinus Nijhoff.

Seca, J. (2001) *Les représentations sociales*. Paris: Armand Colin.

Shannon, C. E. and Weaver, W. (1949) *The Mathematical Theory of Communication*. Urbana: University of Illinois.

Silverman, D. (1998) *Harvey Sacks: social science and conversation analysis*. Cambridge: Polity Press.

Simmel, G. (1910/1949) The sociology of sociability. *American Journal of Sociology* 55: 3.

Simmel, G. (1950) *The Sociology of Georg Simmel*. Translated, edited and with an introduction by K. H. Wolff. New York: The Free Press.

Simmel, G. (1955) *Conflict and the Web of Group Affiliations*. Translated by R. Bendix and K. H. Wolff. New York: Free Press of Glencoe.

Sperber, D. (1985) Anthropology and psychology. Towards an epidemiology of representations. *Man* 20: 73–89.

Stern, D. (1985) *The Interpersonal World of the Infant*. New York: Basic Books.

Svennevig, J. (1999) *Getting Acquainted in Conversation: a study of initial interactions*. Amsterdam: John Benjamins.

Tannen, D. (1989) *Talking Voices*. Cambridge: Cambridge University Press.

Tannen, D. (1993) What's in a frame? Surface evidence for underlying expectations. In D. Tannen (ed.) *Framing in Discourse*. New York: Oxford University Press.

Thomas, J. (1986) *The Dynamics of Discourse: a pragmatic analysis of confrontational interaction*. Unpublished PhD thesis. Lancaster University.

Thomas, W. and Znaniecki, F. (1928/1981) The Polish peasant in Europe and America. In A. Furnham and M. Argyle (eds) *The Psychology of Social Situations*. Oxford: Pergamon Press.

Todorov, T. (1986) *Mikhail Bakhtin: the dialogical principle*. Translated by W. Godzich. Manchester: Manchester University Press.

Trevarthen, C. (1979) Communication and cooperation in early infancy: a description of primary intersubjectivity. In M. Bullowa (ed.) *Before Speech: the beginning of interpersonal communication* 321–347. Cambridge: Cambridge University Press.

Trevarthen, C. (1992) An infant's motives for speaking and thinking in the culture. In A. Heen Wold (ed.) *The Dialogical Alternative* 99–137. Oslo: Scandinavian University Press.

Tuckman, B. W. (1965) Developmental sequence in small groups. *Psychological Bulletin* 63: 384–399.

Vion, R. (1998a) De l'instabilité des positionnement énonciatifs dans le discours. In J. Verschueren (ed.) *Pragmatics in 1998: selected papers from the 6th international conference* 2: 577–589. Anvers: International Pragmatics Association.

Vion, R. (1998b) Le sujet en linguistique. In R. Vion (ed.) *Les sujets et leurs discours* 189–202. Aix en Provence: Publications de l'Université de Provence.

Voloshinov, V. N. (1929/1973) *Marxism and the Philosophy of Language*. Translated by L. Matejka and I. R. Titunik. New York and London: Seminar Press.

Vygotsky, L. S. (1979) Consciousness as a problem in the psychology of behaviour. *Soviet Psychology* 17: 3–35.

Wästerfors, D. and Holšanová, J. (2005) Examples as crucial arguments in discourse on 'others'. *Text* 25: 519–554.

Watzlawick, P., Helmick Beavin, J. and Jackson, D. D. (1967) *Pragmatics of Human Communication. A Study of Interactional Patterns, Pathologies and Paradoxes*. New York: W. W. Norton.

Weber, R. (1990) *Basic Content Analysis*. (Second edition) London: Sage.

Wibeck, V. (2002) *Genmat i fokus: Analyser av fokusgruppssamtal om genförändrade livsmedel*. (Genetically Modified Food in Focus: analyses of focus group discussions) Linköping Studies in Arts and Science, 260. Linköping: Department of Theme Research.

Wibeck, V., Adelswärd, V. and Linell, P. (2004) Comprendre la complexité: les *focus groups* comme espace de pensée et d'argumentation à propos les aliments génétiquement modifiés. *Bulletin de Psychologie* 57 (3): 253–261.

Wilkinson, S. (1998) Focus groups in health research: exploring the meanings of health and illness. *Journal of Health Psychology* 3: 329–348.

Wilkinson, S. (1999) Focus groups. A feminist method. *Psychology of Women Quarterly* 23 (2): 221–244.

Wilson, J. (1989) *On the Boundaries of Conversation*. Oxford: Pergamon Press.

Wittgenstein, L. (1968/1958) *Philosophical Investigations*. Translated by G. E. M. Anscombe. Oxford: Blackwell.

Zimmerman, D. (1998) Identity, context and interaction. In C. Antaki and S. Widdicombe (eds) *Identities in Talk* 87–106. London: Sage.

Appendix 1
Basic bibliography on tool kits and methodological guidelines

Albrecht, T. L., Johnson, G. M. and Walther, J. B. (1993) Understanding communication processes in focus groups. In D. L. Morgan (ed.) *Successful Focus Groups: advancing the state of the art* 51–64. Newbury Park: Sage.

Asbury, J.-E. (1995) Overview of focus group research. *Qualitative Health Research* 5 (4): 414–420.

Bader, G. E. and Rossi, C. A. (2002) *Focus Groups: a step-by-step guide.* San Diego: The Bader Group.

Bloor, M., Frankland, J., Thomas, M. and Robson, K. (2001) *Focus Groups in Social Research.* London: Sage.

Fern, E. F. (2001) *Advanced Focus Group Research.* Thousand Oaks and London: Sage.

Greenbaum, T. L. (1998) *The Handbook for Focus Group Research.* (Second edition) Thousand Oaks and London: Sage.

Holly, E. (2000) *The Focus Group Research Handbook.* New York: McGraw-Hill.

Kitzinger, J. (1994) The methodology of focus group: the importance of interaction between research participants. *Sociology of Health and Illness* 16: 103–121.

Kitzinger, J. and Farquhar, C. (1999) The analytical potential of 'sensitive moments' in focus group discussions. In R. S. Barbour and J. Kitzinger (eds) *Developing Focus Group Research* 156–172. London: Sage.

Kitzinger, J., Marková, I. and Kalampalikis, N. (2004) Qu'est-ce que les focus groups? *Bulletin de Psychologie* 57 (3): 237–243.

Krueger, R. A. (1994) *Focus Groups: a practical guide for applied research.* Thousand Oaks, CA: Sage.

Krueger, R. A. (1998a) *Developing Questions for Focus Groups. Focus Group Kit 3.* Thousand Oaks and London: Sage.

Krueger, R. A. (1998b) *Moderating Focus Groups. Focus Group Kit 4.* Thousand Oaks and London: Sage.

Langford, J. and McDonagh (2002) *Focus Groups.* London: Taylor and Francis.

Litosseliti, L. (2003) *Using Focus Groups in Research.* London and New York: Continuum.

Morgan, D. L. (1993) Future directions for focus groups. In D. L. Morgan (ed.) *Successful Focus Groups. Advancing the State of the Art* 225–244. London: Sage.

Morgan, D. L. (1998a) *Focus Group Guidebook. Focus Group Kit 1*. Thousand Oaks and London: Sage.
Morgan, D. L. (1998b) *Planning Focus Groups. Focus Group Kit 2*. Thousand Oaks and London: Sage.
Morgan, D. and Krueger, R. (1998) *The Focus Group Kit*. Thousand Oaks, CA: Sage.
Morgan, H. and Thomas, K. (1996) A psychodynamic perspective on group processes. In M. Wetherell (ed.) *Identities, Groups and Social Issues* 63–117. London: Sage, The Open University.
Puchta, C. and Potter, J. (2004) *Focus Group Practice*. London: Sage.

Appendix 2
Focus group data corpuses

The following provides some reference information about the focus group studies used in this book.

Dilemma focus-groups

1. Six groups conducted in 2000 and 2003 in the University of Lausanne (Switzerland), the University of Neuchâtel (Switzerland) and the University Paris 5 (LEAPLE). Original language in French. Reference: Salazar Orvig and Grossen (2004).

> LAU1B Students in psychology, University of Lausanne (Switzerland): 1 man and 2 women.
>
> LAU2B Students in psychology, University of Lausanne (Switzerland): 2 men and 3 women.
>
> LAU3B. Students in psychology, University of Lausanne (Switzerland): 4 women.
>
> PAR1A Students in linguistics, University Paris 5: 2 men and 3 women.
>
> PAR2B Students in linguistics, University Paris 5: 2 men and 3 women.
>
> NEU1A Students in law, University of Neuchâtel (Switzerland): 1 man and 2 women.

2. University of Stirling (Scotland, UK). ESRC funded research project on 'Responsibilities and entitlements: a study in language and social representations in Central and Western Europe', R000237206, 1.10. 1997–29.6.2000. Reference: Marková, I., Moodie, E. and Collins, S. (2000) Final report on the ESRC funded project *Responsibilities/entitlements: a study in language and social representations in Central and Western Europe* R000237206.

Eight focus groups were carried out in each of the following countries: the UK, France, the Czech Republic, the Slovak Republic and Russia. Each of the 5 centres ran 8 discussion groups of 4–5 people. There were 4 groups in the 16–18 age group and 4 in the 19–21 age groups. Six dilemmas on entitlements and responsibilities were presented to each group, ranging from personal and societal responsibilities to legal and moral responsibilities. In this book only two dilemmas the one on HIV/AIDS, and child criminality dilemmas are analysed in Chapter 7.

GEF: Genetically engineered food

Linköping University, Department of Communication Studies. Eleven groups conducted in 1997–1998 (GEF1) and 2000–2001 (GEF2). Bank of Sweden Tercentenary Foundation Award no. 1995–5123 and K-LIV Award 1997–1998. References: Wibeck (2002), Adelswärd et al. (2002), Linell et al. (2001), Wibeck et al. (2004).

a) GEF1   'Lay people'.
GEF1:1. Christian students, 3 women, 2 men, age range: 21–25.
GEF1:3. Dieticians, 6 women, 29–47.
GEF1:4. Farmers, 2 women, 3 men, 33–49.
GEF1:5. Biology students, 2 women, 2 men, 21–24.
GEF1:6. Restaurant staff, 1 woman, 2 men, 35–59.
GEF1:7. Managers of local grocery stores, 1 woman, 3 men, 27–40.
GEF1:8. Recent mothers, 6 women (5 mothers, 28–31, 1 leader of the talk group, 54).
GEF1:9. Members of a Greenpeace group, 3 women, 2 men, 18–26.

b) GEF2   'Decision-makers'.
GEF2:1. Wholesale traders, 5 men.
GEF2:2. Retail trade representatives, 6 men.
GEF2:3. Representatives of a producer firm, 3 men.
GTD: Gene therapy and diagnostics.

Linköping University, Department of Communication Studies. Four groups focused on gene technology as applied to therapy and diagnostics on humans. Groups conducted in 1996–1997. Bank of Sweden Tercentenary Foundation Award no. 1995–5123. References: Bakshi et al. (2000), Linell et al. (2001).

GTD1. University undergraduates (Master's students in communication studies), 3 women, 1 man, 23–30.
GTD2. Nurses at neonatal wards, 4 women, 37–45.
GTD3. Members of an organisation for people with disabilities,

2 women, 3 men, 26–67. (2 men had disabilities, 2 women and 1 man (one married couple) were parents of children with disabilities).

GTD4. Parents of children at a secondary school, 3 women, 2 men, 35–52.

ROM: Reorganising the military

Linköping University, Department of Communication Studies. Groups focused on the regional consequences at an army garrison of a national reorganisation of the military. Seven groups conducted in 2000–2001. Reference: Levin (2003).

ROM1. Civilian administrators at the garrison, 4 women, 1 man, 30–50 (approximate ages).

ROM2. Army officers at company level (military degree: army captain), 4 men, 25–35.

ROM3. Civilian service personnel (technology, stores, restaurants), 2 women, 3 men, 30–50.

ROM4. Officers holding leading positions (military degrees: colonels, lieutenant-colonels), 6 men, 40–60.

ROM5. Union members (civilian and military staff), 3 women, 1 man, 40–60.

ROM6. Senior employees (officers, technicians, educators, administrators, bound to take early pension), 4 men, 54–55.

ROM7. Local community politicians, 5 women, 6 men.

WPC: Workplace changes in an industrial company

Linköping University, Department of Communication Studies. Groups focused on workplace changes (actual, planned, imaginary) within one large high-tech industrial company. All participants worked within company. Five groups conducted in 2002–2003. Reference: Åkerblom (2003).

WPC1. Production workers, 6 men, 30–53.

WPC2. Civil engineers, 5 men, 31–61.

WPC3. Product testers, 5 men, 34–43.

WPC4. Members of development unit, 4 men, 36–42.

WPC5. Project leaders, 3 men, 34–54.

Appendix 3
The 'moral dilemma' focus groups: excerpts in original language

The excerpts are presented with the norms of transcriptions that have been used for this corpus.

Chapter 3

(1)   'The Couple' dilemma; LAU1A
MOD: moderator; ANA: Anabelle; JOE: Joël; MON: Monique

```
MOD            (…) le médecin devrait-il dire à Jean que sa femme est
               séropositive? <7s.> <rire étouffé d'un ou plusieurs
               participants>
               Plusieurs personnes: mmh
ANA 30         et ben moi je pense que: oui, <petit rire>
MON 28         moi je pense aussi <rire>
ANA 31         parce que il y a déjà- la confiance déjà entre le couple elle
               n'y est plus. parce que bon ben si depuis des années elle a
               des relations extraconjugales, alors je pense que c'est un
               tiers qui doit intervenir, dans ce cas
JOE 48         moi c'est OUI MAIS, + <rire général> OUI MAIS <rires des
               autres>,
JOE            parce que déjà quand tu dis la relation de confiance est
               rompue, oui et non, + dans le sens que c'est toi qui porte un
               jugement sur le fait que la relation de confiance est rompue
               §mais je pense§
ANA 32         §mais si elle le dit§ pas parce que §{xxx}§
JOE 49         §mais oui§ mais c'est c'est c'est je pense que c'est aussi
               c'est aussi à 'elle d'être amenée à le à un certain moment à
               le dire, je crois pas que c'est au-, je crois pas que tu peux
               dire # simplement comme ça
ANA 33         # oui mais
```

JOE   je pense que le médecin il doit il a il a une possibilité,
           c'est de nouveau 1- comme déjà de rediscuter avec Pauline, de
           ça, et de l'amener à lui faire réaliser les risques qu'elle
           fait encourir à son mari et je pense que dans un certain
           nombre de cas, il y a la possibilité de faire admettre à
           la personne que bon il faut 'quand même le dire, même si
           c'est dur. et deuxièmement si y a quand même résistance à ce
           moment-là il y a une autre possibilité, c'est de faire une
           réunion entre Pauline, son mari et euh §de de§

MOD 56   §avec le médecin?§

JOE 50   avec le médecin, et de simplement dire 'voilà euh euh j'ai:
           eu récemment Pauline euh::: comme comme euh patiente + et
           euh: j'ai découvert quelque chose d'assez délicat' et de
           voir quelle est la réaction de Pauline. et à ce moment-là
           de petit à petit peut-être simplement présenter que le test
           est 'positif, sans forcément dire que: voilà <soufflement>,
           révéler la vie privée, parce qu'il y a plusieurs manières,
           y a transfusion sanguine, y a # y a y a y a je veux dire
           peut-être que elle euh bon ça me paraît difficile parce que
           {il faudrait se cacher} des piqûres mais disons y a y a la
           drogue, il y a plusieurs possibilités. donc 'oui, je suis
           d'accord avec toi mais il faut y aller doucement,

MOD 57   #mhmh

ANA 34   bon moi je je suis peut-être un peu un peu dure parce
           que- <rires en arrière fond> mais bon je pars du fait qu'un
           couple-, et pis bon moi je pense qu'il doit avoir confiance
           entre le couple, et pis moi il me semble que c'est déjà par
           les les remarques ici, c'est déjà une femme qu'a déjà pas
           pris ses responsabilités, parce que pour moi bon si elle a
           déjà fait des aventures extraconjugales, après elle s'est pas
           protégée, euh + elle a besoin peut-être d'un soutien oui de
           quelqu'un d'autre, peut-être c'est 'vrai qu'il faut peut-être
           au début l'amener à à le dire à son mari elle-même, mais je
           veux dire entre temps, s'il y a deux mois qui s'écoulent
           et tout ça, et pis le mari il en sait rien pis qu'y a des
           relations qui continuent, et pis que 'avant il l'avait pas et
           pis qu'entre ces deux mois qui se sont écoulés, il il peut le
           il peut l'attraper c'est aussi c'est aussi grave, je me dis,
           + alors que le médecin aurait pu euh aurait pu sauver cette
           vie-là, parce que bon ben elle elle l'a déjà mais +

Chapter 4

(1)   'Day Nursery' dilemma; LAU2B
       FLO : Florian; PAU : Paul; LIL : Liliane

```
LIL 23      c'est encore plus compliqué qu'avant
            <rires> <4 sec>
FLO 23      je pense je pense que non quoi {ce truc là} ça me paraît
            moins compliqué quoi,
PAU 23      hm
LIL 24      non?
FLO 24      non je pense que non ouais, parce que je trouve que: + enfin
            ma mère est enseignante, moi elle me parle souvent que les
            parents sont plus difficiles que les...
```

(2)   'The Couple' dilemma; LAU2B
       FLO : Florian; PAU : Paul; LIL : Liliane

```
FLO 11      §mais justement c'est la§ c'est là c'est c'est de nouveau un
            combat, c'est de nouveau un sujet enfin un débat idéologique,
            mais mis à la faveur d'une bonne cause, je sais pas je je
            trouve qu'il n'y a pas forcément du mal quoi,§
LIL 11      §quand tu dis euh le changement de comportement il serait
            plutôt global ce serait pas que sur une chose, donc ça serait
            carrément un changement d'esprit intérieur §ou {xxxxxx}§
FLO 12      §non parce qu'elle se- enfin on peut§ pas ce serait pas ce
            serait pas une autre personne un changement de caractère§
LIL 12      §non je veux dire pas un changement d'état d'esprit, mais par
            exemple changement d'idée en tout cas à ce sujet-là,
FLO 13      euh peut-être ouais§
LIL 13      §au niveau des relations de confiance etc §de cachotterie§
FLO 14      §peut-être ouais§ mais après je sais pas du tout comment
            mettre en œuvre et tout c'est :§
```

(3)   'Day Nursery' dilemma; LAU1A
       MOD: moderator; ANA: Anabelle; JOE: Joël; MON: Monique

```
MOD 21      donc là 'vous vous êtes pour le- effectivement le maintien
            du s(e)cret médical dans ce cas, et puis plutôt euh c'est
            c'est c'est les parents eux-mêmes au fond si je résume un peu
            vos vos différentes positions, c'est c'est les PArents qui
            qui doivent aussi être amenés à 'réfléchir un peu euh aux
            relations que: que §leur fille doit avoir§
```

ANA 12   §pis je dis là si§ si les responsables savent, parce que
          c'est quand même une situation gérable vingt enfants je
          pense, s'il y a plusieurs euh, donc on peut très bien
          contrôler si justement cette enfant a une blessure, je dis
          vingt enfants c'est encore une situation gérable #, c'est
          clair qu'après s'il y a moins de responsable là bon
MOD 22   hmhm
MOD 23   hmhm et puis les euh ce ce donc le-, vous avez dit que le
          personnel de la crèche doit être euh informé ça, par le
          médecin?, par les parents? euh +
JOE 13   je crois ensemble
MON 9   §ouais§
ANA 13   §ouais§
JOE 14   faut faire une réunion faut faire une réunion de l'ensemble
          sûrement euh et ++++ et surtout bien rappeler au personnel
          que eux-mêmes sont justement soumis à une forme de secret
          professionnel # qu'ils ont pas le droit d'aller divulguer ça
          à tort et à travers,
MOD 24   hmm
MOD 25   hmmm
ANA 14   tout à fait, pour qu'ils aient les les deux avis un peu plus
          personnel des parents et puis # vraiment l'avis médical +
MOD 26   ouais
MOD 27   d'accord§

(1)   'Sport' dilemma; PAR2B
       NOE: Noël; MAR: Marine; CAR: Carine; SYL: Sylvie; SER: Serge; MOD: Moderator

NOE 129   mais à # partir du moment où i(l) y a pas d(e) risque + si tu
          veux le médecin lui
SYL 37   # ouais!
NOE   est plus[1] obligé d(e) le dire. +++ à partir du moment où i(l)
          y a risque, il est obligé d(e) prévenir le patient POUR, +
          justement l'empêcher d(e) tomber malade.
CAR 106   ouais mais l(e) patient!, mais pas les autres!.
NOE 130   b(i)en si le:: § - le patient § potentiel!.
MAR 111   § le patient!§ ++ b(i)en voilà! ++ donc le patient DONC pas les
          autres!. + c'est c(e) que tu dis! + § donc i(l) n(e) prévient
          pas §
NOE 131   § SI! + puisque ≠a priori § #1 a priori tous #2 les gens sont
          patients, + mais + il y a -, §
MAR 112   #1< appuyé > NON:!
CAR 107   #2< appuyé aussi. > OUI:! °
CAR   < s'adressant aors à Marine > § en fait il est- il est- il
          est su(r) l(e) même point- point d(e) vue que: l(e) premier
          cas en fait!.
MAR 113   b(i)en oui donc justement!.

CAR 108   §1 i(l) dit que § b(i)en: i(l) faudrait prévenir les aut(res)
           joueurs
syl 38   §2 il faut qu'il le dise §
NOE 132   §1 mais c'est- c'est- c'est c(e) § que j(e) veux dire ++ §2
           tous les joueurs- § tous les joueurs sont des pa- sont- tous
           les joueurs sont des patients du::- du médecin < très rapide
           > t(u) es d'accord avec moi? §
MAR 114   § donc là les aut(res) gens n'ont pas à l(e) savoir que l(e)
           premier §
CAR 109   § voilà!
NOE 133   i(l) y a + a priori pas d(e) risque euh: + majeur!
MAR 115   ouais! + alors que # dans l(e) premier cas i(l) disait
           qu'i(l) fallait que le mari
CAR 110   # voilà!
MAR   sache. §
NOE 134   § oui! § pa(r)ce qu'i(l) y avait § un RISQUE MAJEUR!.
SYL 39   § i(l) y avait plus de risque! §+++ qu'i(l) soit contaminé
           alors que les joueurs non!, ++ enfin moins!. §
NOE 135   § < enchaînement très rapide > i(l) y a j(e) chais pas mes
           parents sont mariés d(e)puis 21 ans, si tu veux à mon avis
           ça fait longtemps qu'i(l)s ont laissé tomber la capote tu
           vois!°, < petits rires en réponse > < 2 s. > a priori tu t(e)
           protèges plus quoi!.
MAR 116   b(i)en oui! mais euh:: < 3 s. > j(e) sais pas!.
NOE 136   alors qu(e) là, bon à la limite on met une capote su(r) l(e)
           ballon d(e) rugby là!.
           < rires >
CAR 111   < en riant > on met une capote sur toi comme ça t(u) as pas
           d(e) risque¿
NOE 137   ouais! mais c'est vachement moins facile pour courir
CAR 112   < riant et faisant le geste de se mettre quelque chose sur la
           tête > ouais faut- + { c'est quand i(l) y a un risque } < 3
           s. > bon b(i)en voilà!
NOE 138   voilà bon voilà!
SYL 40   non!
CAR 117   non.
MOD 13   non?
ser 28   non.
MOD 14   { ah c'est marrant! } vous arrivez à des concensus là! ++ bon
           très bien + mais pourquoi pas?

Chapter 5

(1)   'Work' dilemma; LAU1A
        MOD: moderator; ANA: Anabelle; JOE: Joël; MON: Monique

```
MOD 30      (…) pis on va passer au deuxième euh deuxième situation
            <10s.> alors c'est une situation je vous la lis. vous avez
            une formation de base en médecine et vous êtes chef du
            département de la santé et de l'action sociale du canton
            de Vaud. vous trouvez sur votre bureau une lettre signée
            de plusieurs directeurs d'hôpitaux qui vous demandent de
            les autoriser à exiger des tests HIV lors de l'engagement
            de personnel. en tant que responsable du département de la
            santé, devriez-vous leur accorder cette autorisation ?
            <3s.>
ANA 17      bon moi j'ai déjà une question euh #, vous avez une formation
            de base en médecine et vous êtes chef du département, ça veut
            dire qu'elle qu'elle fait seulement de l'administratif ? ou
            bien elle a un contact avec le§
MOD 31      oui
JOE 19      §non, c'est le c'est le: responsable 'politique si tu veux
            c'est§
ANA 18      §ouais donc à la fin§
JOE 20      § {le plus haut} qui va qui prendre la décision politique,
            alors, + là justement <rire> c'est un peu <rire général>
            un peu le juriste qui va qui va qui va qui va alimenter,
            qui va dire que + de toute façon il se- euh, parce qu'il
            va faire appel à des juristes qui lui diront que ce serait
            possible d'imaginer de telles choses mais il y a déjà une
            loi au niveau fédéral sur la protection des données, donc
            ça veut dire que toute donnée récoltée devra se faire euh
            euh sans que l'identité de la personne puisse être forcément
            identifiable en dehors des- de ces professionnels de la
            santé hein, # donc + il faut- ça me paraît ça me par- ça me
            paraît déjà très compliqué à imaginer dans le sens où on
            est- il y a le principe de protection de la personnalité et
            des données # qui qui est assez proche du principe du secret
            médical # qui est # déjà préexistant, donc euh <3s.> ouais
            quant au principe, faudrait aussi voir dans quel so- c'est
            très vague la la la donnée, faudrait voir dans quel domaine
            professionnel §parce que§
???         voilà
MOD 32      hmm
MOD 33      d'accord
MOD 34      hmm
MOD 35      §oui ben pour des§
JOE 21      il y a des domaines à risque aussi donc§
```

ANA 19	§voilà c'est ce qui # parce que si: si c'est vraiment médecin médecin de terrain euh, c'est quand mêmee le sida au niveau de la contagion, je ne sais pas comment +, je sais pas comment ça se passe, si en fait les médecins sont séropositifs, si les gants, j'ai vraiment aucune idée
MOD 36	voilà
MOD 37	hmhm moi j'ai j'ai pas plus d'information là que§
ANA 20	je poserais plus de question déjà dans cette situation < je sais pas/je suis pas>
MON 11	moi je trouve trivial de de de ouais tout de suite faire passer un test comme ça au # personnel pour dire 'alors on vous fait pas confiance dès le départ et puis on va vérifier', d'un autre côté c'est clair que: ben voilà # c'est vrai que certaines personnes peuvent être amenées à ca'cher leur séropositivité parce que justement elles savent que elles ont encore un risque de 'pas être engagées, donc c'est: vrai, mais d'un autre côté je trouve que c'est c'est un peu trivial quoi de s'y prendre comme ça§
ANA 21	oui tout à fait
JOE 22	mais mais
JOE 23	§oui mais il y a le fameux petit groupe des gens qui le 'sont sans le savoir,
MON 12	aussi <petit rire étouffé>
JOE 24	donc euh mais effectivement, c'est vrai qu'il y a ce fameux problème de protection de la personnalité, si j'ai pas envie de forcément dire euh: que je suis séropositif et donc j'imagine qu'on pourrait imaginer à la limite une autorisation dans des métiers qui sont rarissimes à très hauts 'risques parce que §des§

(2)   'Work' dilemma; LAU1
        MON: Monique

MON 15	ouais moi je pense qu'il y a un grand problème du secret professionnel alors, parce qu'il est plus du tout maintenu, parce que si si tu tu dis oui si t'es patiente tu aimerais le savoir, les patients doivent le savoir,

(3)   'Day Nursery' dilemma; PAR1A
        CLA: Claire

CLA 2	(…)j j'ai travaillé dans l(e) médical, c'est pas une d-, ++ et::: ++ je pense que c'est plus dans le: dans le secteur humain, et moi je dis que-, + j(e) donne carrément mon avis, + +

(4)   'Day Nursery' dilemma; PAR1A
        NAT: Natacha

NAT 4   i(l) y a un point qui me gênee, on me demande mon avis,
            enfin, mon avis + personnel sur ce que devrait fairee + un
            médecin. ++ bon je:: je considère que je ne suis pas médecin,
            +++ et que: il me paraît difficile, ++ j- j'ai bien sûr un
            avis mais je ne peux pas me substituer + euh au médecin,
            + dans la mesure où j(e) n'ai pas une formation médicale
            euh::, je- je connais bien ce: ce problème, + bon je suis
            enseignante et:, je sais: je connais le décalage qu'il peut y
            avoir, ++ entre des points de vue euh + bon tout à fait euh
            ++ pertinents de certains parents mais qui n'ont pas toutes
            les données + euh:: de:: les données de:: du: +++ du métier
            de l'activité d'enseignement + les données de terrain, <2
            s.> et qui ne sont pas véritablement en mesure de pouvoire +
            traiter d'un problème. ++ je-je vais euh + toutefois donner
            mon avis, mais: je- il me paraît difficile de pouvoir me
            substituere +++ à- à l'avis d'un médecin.

(5)   'Day Nursery' dilemma; LAU2B
        FLO : Florian; PAU : Paul; LIL : Liliane; MOD : moderator

LIL 31   mais alors vous vous laisseriez vos enfants si vous le
            saviez? {vous avez xxx enfant}<rire général et brouhaha>
MOD 20   {vous} ou pas?
LIL 32   non je §sais pas moi§
MOD 21   : §ça vous fait réfléchir?§
LIL 33   bon j'ai pas d'enfant§ mais je veux dire je sais pas, je: si
            ça me faisait réfléchir ça quand même ouais # §si le risque
            est moindre§
            (…)
MAU 32   bon moi je me demande à quel point, bon j'ai un §enfant # +
            euh : + §
LIL 39   §voilà ouais je me demandais ce que t'en pensais§ <rire>
MAU   je j'ai l'impression qu'en terme de 'risque, moi ce qui
            me terrorise ces temps, c'est qu'il se fasse écraser en
            traversant la route, # j'ai l'impression + que: si à la
            garderie où il va il y avait une situation comme ça et que
            j'étais mise au courant + alors, bon c'est pas le cas je suis
            pas mise au courant j'en sais rien, mais si ça se présentait
            je pourrais imaginer que je continuerais de penser qu'il
            court plus de risques de se faire écraser en traversant la
            route + # que §d'attraper le sida comme ça§

(6)   Beginning the meeting; LAU1A
       MOD: moderator; ANA: Anabelle; JOE: Joël; MON: Monique

Au début de la séance l'animatrice demande à chacun de se présenter. A la suite du
tour de table Joël ajoute:

```
JOE 2      alors j'aimerais p(eu)t-être juste apporter une précision, #
           qui me semble a une
MOD 3      oui
JOE        légère importance, j'ai fait des études de droit précédemment
           j'ai pas de licence mais j'ai fait des études # de droit qui
           peuvent peut-être affecter le raisonnement, mon
MOD 4      oui
JOE -      raisonnement je trouvais important de le # préciser avant
           d'entrer dans la discussion
MOD 5      oui !
MOD 6      ouais
MOD 7      d'accord ben c'est c'est c'est bien de le savoir
           effectivement de savoir que vous avez suivi ces cours en
           droit # et puis que: vous vous # basez je pense aussi en
JOE 3      voilà
MOD        partie sur ce
JOE 4      sur ce
MOD        sur ces connaissances là hmhm
ANA 2      juste une question #, vous avez choisi que des personnes
           venant de psychologie
MOD 8      oui
MOD 9      oui
ANA 3      oui
MOD 10     ouais
ANA 4      <-fort> pourquoi
MOD 11     oh ya pas il y a pas de raison c'est une- des raisons
           pratiques de recrutement en fait mais c'est vrai comme je
           vous ai dit, on en est au début et puis ce serait peut-être
           intéressant de de effectivement de discuter de ces cas avec
           des gens qui qui qui font autre chose que de la psychologie§
ANA 5      §ouais parce que je veux dire on est peut-être plus préparé #
           à des situations comme ça
MOD 12     hmhm
```

(7)   'The Couple' dilemma; LAU1A
        JOE: Joël

JOE 51   (…) puis deuxièmement il y a une chose très importante
            qu'il faut pas oublier, en TANT que médecin ou en tant que
            psychologue ou n'importe quoi, on a pas le droit de porter un
            jugement sur le comportement des gens,

(8)   'Work' dilemma; LAU1A
        ANA: Anabelle

ANA 23   ouais tout à fait, bon moi je dirais vraiment euh dans les
            cas où on sait exactement dans les situations où il y a des
            hauts risques, je pense que c'est quand même bon de le savoir
            enfin je sais pas, il me semblee: par honnêteté vis-à-vis
            de la patiente aussi # parce que je veux dire si on va se
            faire soigner on a confiance # et pis mais c'est vrai qu'il
            faut faire la distinction entre les différents- différents
            domaines, parce que je pense qu'il y a des domaines où on je
            veux dire médecin généraliste on risque rien, mais des des
            cas + oui opération chirurgie: euh je sais pas je me poserais
            déjà plus de questions, MOI par exemple si j'étais patiente
            je voudrais le savoir #<très doucement> je sais pas °

(9)   'The Couple' dilemma; PAR2B
        NOE : Noël

NOE 21 -   § mais ima- imagi- § imagines qu'i(l) t'a- qu'i(l) t'arrive
            ça et que:- et que tu saches que ton médecin était au courant
            d(e)puis longtemps.

(10)   'The Couple' dilemma; LAU1A
         JOE: Joël

JOE 51   §je peux porter deux petites précisions <rires>peut-être,
           déjà j'imagine mal le médecin se laisser couler deux mois.
           quand il a un tel cas, il va tout faire pour dire et à Jean
           et à Pauline que c'est important qu'il faut qu'il les voie,
           et que si vraiment euh il est il est opposé à un refus de
           Pauline, alors voilà il doit peut-être dire à Jean 'j'ai
           quelque chose d'urgent à vous dire faut qu'on se voie
           immédiatement'. puis deuxièmement il y a une chose très
           importante qu'il faut pas oublier, en TANT que médecin ou en
           tant que psychologue ou n'importe quoi, on a pas le droit
           de porter un jugement sur le comportement des gens, parce
           que c'est ce qui m'a beaucoup étonné dans ce que tu as dit,
           c'est que t'as porté un jugement de valeur. or le médecin
           n'a- ou qui- ou le psychologue ou quelque personne dans ce
           genre de cadre professionnel, on n'a pas le droit de porter
           de jugement de valeur, on doit juste éviter que + mon autre
           patient avec lequel j'ai une relation de confiance attrape
           cette maladie. donc je dois tout faire pour le révéler mais
           SANS porter de jugement de valeur et sans justement euh pouf,
           je dois aussi tenir compte, plus ou moins, {que} Pauline a le
           droit d'amener la chose à un certain à un certain rythme et
           avec une certaine manière j'entends.

(11)   'Work' dilemma; LAU1A
         ANA: Anabelle; JOE: Joël; MON: Monique

MON 11   moi je trouve trivial de de de ouais tout de suite faire
           passer un test comme ça au # personnel pour dire 'alors
           on vous fait pas confiance dès le départ et puis on va
           vérifier', d'un autre côté c'est clair que: ben voilà # c'est
           vrai que certaines personnes peuvent être amenées à ca'cher
           leur séropositivité parce que justement elles savent que
           elles ont encore un risque de 'pas être engagées, donc c'est:
           vrai, mais d'un autre côté je trouve que c'est c'est un peu
           trivial quoi de s'y prendre comme ça§
ANA 21   oui tout à fait
JOE 22   mais mais
JOE 23   §oui mais il y a le fameux petit groupe des gens qui le 'sont
           sans le savoir,
MON 12   aussi <petit rire étouffé>

JOE 24   donc euh mais effectivement, c'est vrai qu'il y a ce fameux
           problème de protection de la personnalité, si j'ai pas
           envie de forcément dire euh: que je suis séropositif et
           donc j'imagine qu'on pourrait imaginer à la limite une
           autorisation dans des métiers qui sont rarissimes à très
           hauts 'risques parce que §des§

(12)   'Work' dilemma; LAU1A
        ANA: Anabelle; MON: Monique

ANA 23   ouais tout à fait, bon moi je dirais vraiment euh dans les
           cas où on sait exactement dans les situations où il y a des
           hauts risques, je pense que c'est quand même bon de le savoir
           enfin je sais pas, il me semblee: par honnêteté vis-à-vis
           de la patiente aussi # parce que je veux dire si on va se
           faire soigner on a confiance # et pis mais c'est vrai qu'il
           faut faire la distinction entre les différents- différents
           domaines, parce que je pense qu'il y a des domaines où on je
           veux dire médecin généraliste on risque rien, mais des des
           cas + oui opération chirurgie: euh je sais pas je me poserais
           déjà plus de questions, MOI par exemple si j'étais patiente
           je voudrais le savoir #<très doucement> je sais pas °
MON 15   ouais moi je pense qu'il y a un grand problème du secret
           professionnel alors, parce qu'il est plus du tout maintenu,
           parce que si si tu tu dis oui si t'es patiente tu aimerais
           le savoir, les patients doivent le savoir, mais alors en
           fait si on on fait ce test mais qui est habilité à avoir le
           résultat après? # les gens qui engagent? les collègues? # ou
           bien le personnel? on va pas l'afficher §sur elle qu'elle
           est séropositive§, alors qu'est-ce qu'on va faire de ces
           résultats après?

(13)   'Work' dilemma; PAR2B
        NOE: Noël; MAR: Marine

NOE 89   i(ls) traitent tous les patients en:: § en tant § qu(e)
           séropositifs potentiels.
MAR 80   § i(ls) m- §
MAR 81   i(ls) m'ont dit 'vous coagulez bien?' j'ai dit 'oui', i(l)
           m'a dit 'bon b(i)en merci! et: + et à l'opération!' < rire de
           Carine > i(ls) m'ont rien d(e)mandé! § i(ls) vont rien m(e)
           faire! et c'est tout quoi! §

(14)   'Work' dilemma; LAU1A
        MON: Monique

MON 11   moi je trouve trivial de de de ouais tout de suite faire
            passer un test comme ça au # personnel pour dire 'alors on
            vous fait pas confiance dès le départ et puis on va vérifier'

(15)   'The Couple' dilemma; LAU2B
        PAU : Paul

PAU 9   §{bon c'est clair} l'objectif final c'est quand mêmee de #
            {d'arriver à le dire}, mais je pense que la rupture de de du
            secret est:: un acte je veux pas dire encore plus dramatique
            mais + au niveau 'macro euh personnele c'est c'est clair
            que s'il y a quelques cas comme ça euh c'est fini de tout
            ce qui est confiance thérapeutique, # on peut plus avoir
            confiance en son avocat si on lui dit 'j'ai effectivement tué
            la personne' mais l'avocat il va pas aller répéter + donc on
            peut plus du tout avoir euh de de: confiance, de sincérité #
            dans tous ces domaines assez euh pénibles, là c'est vrai que
            ben je vais pas chez un thérapeute et dire 'voilà d'habitude
            tous les vendredi je tue quelqu'un', c'est vraiment un cas
            encore plus §euh§

(16)   'The Couple' dilemma; LAU3B
        MAR: Marcelle

MAR 3   bon c'est pas euh: je crois qu'il y a- quelque part il faut
            voir- le le secret professionnel de ce médecin indique qu'il
            n'a pas le droit de dire quoi que ce soit au mari concernant
            sa femme, point. c'est c'est le code déontologique éthique
            médical.

(17)   'Work' dilemma; LAU1A
        JOE: Joël

JOE 26   moi je pense je pense pas vraiment, parce que je pense c'est
            plutôt- le risque du médecin c'est plutôt de l'avoir que de
            le 'donner <en riant> si je puis dire# de §l'attraper§

(18)   'The Couple' dilemma; PAR1A
          INE: Inès

INE 34   < très rapide > est-ce que là ce n(e) s(e)rait pas un cas de
               non-assistance à personne en danger?§°

(19)   'The Couple' dilemma; LAU1A
          MOD: moderator; ANA: Anabelle; JOE: Joël; MON: Monique

MOD 59   et puis 'vous vous êtiez 1§aussi§
MON 29   1§alors moi§ dans le cas 2§présent§
MOD 60   2§eh ouais§ <rire étouffé>
MON   bon je trouve que c'est c'est sûr quoi les bémols il faut
               en mettre hein, mais euh dans le cas présent dans la mesure
               où le médecin euh, comme c'est dit là, a établi une relation
               de confiance avec Jean autant qu'avec Pauline, je pense que:
               ouais les risques sont trop grands, comme tu dis aussi deux
               mois peuvent s'écouler, voire plus, # pour euh pour euh
               cacher cette ce diagnostic à à Jean

Index

A
Act-activity interdependence 69, 134
activity role 72f, 78, 96
activity type 69
AIDS 174ff
alliance 96
analogy 95, 140
analogy-distinction cycle 95, 146
anchoring 151, 157
a-priori trust 177
associative cline 149
author 109, 129,n.1

B
Backchannelling 59, 165,n.6
Bakhtin, M.M. 26, 27, 109, 126, 133, 157
Baldwin, J.M. 11
big theme 135, 139, 164
bringing (categories) into language 171

C
Categories
    relational 23
category-bound activity 158
characters as alter-egos 119
circulation of ideas 133, 205
cognitive frame 72
collaborative utterance/s 181, 186, 193
common-sense 124, 127, 171
communicative activity type 59, 69ff,
    165,n.2, 203
communicative dilemma 75
communicative genre 69
communicative project 136, 165,n.2,n.4
competition 96
consensus-orientation 77, 79, 97
constructed collectivity 157
content analysis 134
    dialogical 133
    traditional 134, 200
context 40
counter-argumentation 77, 97, 150
counter-story 150
cultural assumptions/presuppositions 164,
    166,n.12, 171
    about which we think 169, 192
    from which we think 169, 192
cultural sphere, dialogue with 109, 124
culture 2, 205

D
Decision-making 77, 86, 100
dialogue 1, 24
    as concrete and empirical 24
    as historically and culturally situated 24
    as interaction between thoughts and
        ideas 3, 24, 132
    as situated interpersonal interaction 133
    between cultural traditions 25, 133
    efficiency of 107
    normative sense of 24
    with common sense 127
    with oneself 104, 110, 126f
dialogical 1
dialogical discourse analysis 165,n.1, 201
dialogical method 38
dialogism 1, 7
    double 26, 49, 126
    internal 27, 104, 126
disagreement 97, 110
discourse type 72, 78, 84
    subordinated 101
discursive figure 134
discursive role 73
distinction 95, 141
distributed cognition 131

E
Ego-Alter 10-11, 203, 204
Ego-Alter-Object 22
enunciator 109, 126, 129,n.1
episode 136, 165,n.2
equilibrium 40
example (as a rhetorical device) 155
exchange 8
extreme case formulation 99

F
Face work 192
figure – ground 169
focused interaction 70, 77
focus group/s 32ff
    analyzed as juxtaposed individual con-
        tributions 35
    and dialogism 45, 195
    as challenge to individual psychology 41
    as circulation of ideas 64
    as communicative activity types 74ff
    as research method 32, 195ff
    as thinking societies in miniature 46,
        100

as group discussions 48, 59ff
as informal conversations 90ff
composition of 76
footing 79, 93
frame 71
framing 71
  external 48, 73, 103, 115
  hybridity of 88
  internal 48, 73, 77, 103
  on-line 72
  pre-interactional 72

G
Generic 'I' 119
genetic model of social change 12
goal-directedness 100
Goffman, E. 79, 129,n.1
groupality 44
group as a bias 36, 44
group dynamics studies
  interaction-based 42
  interpretation-based 42
group illusion 43
group interview 88f

H
Heterogeneities 25, 61, 103, 108, 122, 126,
  204
heteroglossia 126
hidden polemic 26, 104
HIV 174ff
hybridity of activity 84, 89, 93
hypothesis testing 197
hypothetical quote 99, 108, 157

I
Identification/s with activity or character
  roles 116
  explicit mode of 118
  implicit mode of 118
identities 104
implicitness 25
information-processing model 45
interaction
  as external 8
  as internal 8
interactional order 76
interpretation of dilemma 116
institutional order 76
irony 100

J
James, W. 14

K
Knowledge
  based on individual rationality 16
  common-sense 19
  scientific 14
  taken as shared 65, 169, 205

L
Lewin, K. 12, 38
life space 38
listener support item 59, 165,n.6
locutor 109, 126, 129,n.1

M
Male/female 172
Mead, G.M. 11
medical confidentiality 178
  negotiability of 180, 188
  non-negotiability of 184
metaphor 154
method
  by invention 198
  by proof 197
  not a priori dialogical
metonymy 155
minor genre 70
minorities 13
modalisation 128
moral/immoral 172
moral dilemma focus groups 52, 79ff
  participants' engagements as witnesses
    or arbiters 116
Moscovici, S. 13, 168, 197
multi-party talk 48, 60, 90

O
Objectification 155
open discussion focus group 54, 85ff
opinion-making 86
ordinary conversation 72, 101, 102,n.9
others' discourse 119
  world of 7

P
Participation framework 59, 77, 78
participation status 59
personal pronoun/s 117, 124
phase structure 78, 84, 86
play 100
point of view 110, 118
positioning 74, 105ff, 111, 129,n.1
principal 129,n.1
proto-thema/ta 170ff

psychoanalytical theory 43
purpose/s 76

Q
Quote 157

R
Recipient design 60
reciprocity of perspectives 21
recurrent topic 135, 138, 175
relations as primary 23, 168ff
remote audience 179
responsibilit/y(ies) 184
rhetorical analysis 133
rhetorical devices 134
right/s 184
role/s 107
    dynamically conceived 74
Rommetveit, R. 25, 40

S
Schisming 95, 96
Schütz, A. 21
self-dialogism 126
self/other(s)
    interdependence between 1
    sense-making 2
    in interaction 3
setting 77
Simmel, Georg 10, 100, 177
situation definition 40, 71
sociability 100
social change 13
social framing 72
socially shared knowledge 1, 14, 17, 104,
    128, 159, 167, 201
social psychology 37
social representation(s) 21, 151, 155, 159,
    164, 167, 202
    formation of 175
    socially shared 21
    taken as (socially) shared 19, 169, 205
social role 73, 77, 79
social science 14
    speaker
    heterogeneity of 108ff
    positionings of 103ff
speech event 102, n.1
stimulus materials 77
subject/s
    heterogeneity of 49, 61, 108
    homogeneity of 104

T
Task/s 76, 80
Tavistock Institute of Human Relations 43
teacher-led group discussion 88
team meeting 88
tension in communication/talk/dialogue 7
testing boundaries (of socially shared
    knowledge) 185, 192
thema/ta 135, 164, 166,n.12, 172ff,
    193,n.1, 205
    trust/distrust as 178ff
theme 135, 174
thesis – elaboration – reprise 151
thinking in oppositions 168
third party 79, 84, 205
topic 78, 134
topic analysis 135
topical boundary 136
topical derailment 99
topical episode 135
topical glide 99
topic control 97
trust 11, 177
turn-taking 78

U
University seminar 88

V
Value judgment 176
virtual participant 79, 99, 157
virtual speaker 122
virtual voice 124
voice/s 110, 122, 124
Vygotsky, L. 11

W
'We-they' dichotomy 99
work group 88

CPSIA information can be obtained
at www.ICGtesting.com
Printed in the USA
BVHW041408160222
629163BV00003B/7